Richard Baxter

Imputative Righteousness Truly Stated

According to the Tenour of the Gospel

Richard Baxter

Imputative Righteousness Truly Stated
According to the Tenour of the Gospel

ISBN/EAN: 9783337404918

Printed in Europe, USA, Canada, Australia, Japan

Cover: Foto ©Lupo / pixelio.de

More available books at **www.hansebooks.com**

IMPUTATIVE RIGHTEOUSNES Truly Stated,

According to the TENOUR of the GOSPEL:

Manifesting,

In what Sence sound PROTE-STANTS hold it:

And in what Sence LIBER-TINES pervert it.

By RICHARD BAXTER, a compassionat Lamenter of the Churches Wounds.

LONDON,

Printed by *J. D.* and are to be sold by *Jonathan Robinson*, at the Golden Lion in St. *Paul's* Church-Yard, and *William Abington*, at the black-spread Eagle at the West End of St. *Paul's*. 1679.

The Preface.

Reader,

IF thou blame me for writing again, on a Subject which I have written on so oft, and so lately (specially in my *Life of Faith,* and Disputations of Justification) I shall not blame thee for so doing; but I shall excuse my self by telling thee my reasons. 1. The occasion is many loud accusations of my self, of which I have before given an account. I publish it, because I see the Contention still so hot in the Church of Christ, and mens Charity destroyed against each other; one side calling the other *Socinians,* and the other *Libertines,* (who are neither of them *Christians*) and if I mistake not, for the most part in the dark about *one Phrase,* and that of mens devising, rather than about the sence: But if indeed it be the sence that they differ about, it's time to do our best to rectifie such Fundamental Errours.

I find that all of us agree in all the Phrases of Scripture. And a Mans Sence is no way known but by his expressions: The que-

question is then, Which is the *necessary Phrase* which we must express our sence by? We all say that to Believers, *Christ is made our Righteousness; We are made the Righteousness of God in him*; *He hath ransomed, redeemed us, as a Sacrifice for our sins, a price*; *He hath merited and obtained eternal Redemption for us, that Sin is remitted, covered, not imputed; that Righteousness is Reckoned or Imputed to us; that Faith is Imputed to us for Righteousness,* and any thing else that is in the Scripture. But all this will not serve to make us Christians! What is wanting? Why, we must say that *Christs Righteousness is Imputed to us as ours, and that Christ satisfied for our sins!* Well; The thing signified seemeth to us true and good and needful, (though the Scripture hath as good words for it as any of us can invent.) We consent therefore to use these Phrases, so be it you put no false and wicked sence on them by *other words* of your own: Though we will not allow them to be *necessary*, because not in Scripture, (And we are more against adding new Fundamental Articles of Faith to the Scripture, than against adding new Orders, Forms or Ceremonies). But yet it will not serve: what is yet wanting? why, we must hold these words in a right sense! What? yet are not your own devised

words

The PREFACE.

words a sufficient expression of the matter! When we have opened *those words* by *other words*, how will you know that we use those *other words* in a right sence, and *so in infinitum*. Our sence is, that *Righteousness is Imputed to us; that is, we are accounted Righteous, because for the Merits of Christs total fulfilling the Conditions of his Mediatorial Covenant with the Father, by his Habitual Holiness, his Actual Perfect Obedience, and his Sacrifice, or satisfactory Suffering for our sins in our stead, freely without any merit or Conditional act of mans.* God hath made an *Act of Oblivion* and *Deed of Gift*, *pardoning all sin, justifying and adopting and giving Right to the Spirit and Life eternally to every one that believingly accepteth Christ and the Gifts with and by and from him. And when we accept them, they are all ours by virtue of this purchased Covenant-Gift.* This is our short and plain explication. But yet this will not serve: Christianity is yet another thing. What is wanting? Why, we must say, that *Christ was habitually and actually perfectly Holy and Obedient, Imputatively in our particular Persons, and that each one of us did perfectly fulfil that Law which requireth perfect Habits and Acts in and by Christ imputatively, and yet did also in and by him suffer our selves Imputatively for not fulfilling it, and*

Impu-

Imputatively did our selves both satisfy God's Justice and merit Heaven; and that we have our selves Imputatively a Righteousness of perfect Holiness and Obedience as sinless, and must be justified by the Law of Innocency, or Works, as having our selves imputatively fulfilled it in Christ; And that this is our sole Righteousness; and that Faith it self is not imputed to us for Righteousness; no not a meer particular subordinate Righteousness, answering the Conditional part of the new Justifying Covenant, as necessary to our participation of Christ, and his freely given Righteousness. And must all this go into our Christianity! But where is it written? who devised it? was it in the ancient Creeds and Baptism? Or known in the Church for five thousand years from the Creation? I profess I take the Pope to be no more to be blamed for making a new Church-Government, than for making us so many new Articles of Faith: And I will not justifie those that Symbolize with him, or imitate him in either.

But yet many of the men that do this, are good men in other respects: and I love their *zeal* that doth all this evil, *as it is for God* and the *honour of Jesus Christ*, though I love it not as blind, nor their Errour or their Evil. But how hard is it to know what Spirit we are of! But it is the doleful mis-

mischief which their blind zeal doth, that maketh me speak; That three or four of them have made it their practice to back-bite my self, and tell People, *He holdeth dangerous opinions; He is erroneous in the point of Justification. And his Books are unsound and have dangerous Doctrines; He leaveth the old way of Justification, he favoureth Socinianism,* and such-like: this is a small matter comparatively. Back-biting and *false reports,* are the ordinary fruits of *bitter contentious Zeal,* and the Spirit of a *Sect* as such doth usually so work (yea to confusion and every evil work,) when it hath banished the *Zeal* of Love and of Good Works. *Jam.* 3. 14, 15, 16. *Tit.* 2. 14. And I never counted it any great loss to their followers, that they disswade them from the reading of my writings (as the Papists do their Proselytes) as long as God hath blest our Land with so many better.

But there are other effects that command me once again to speak to them. 1. One is, that I have good proof of the lamentable Scandal of some very hopeful Persons of quality, who by hearing such language from these men, have bin ready to turn away from Religion, and say, If they thus set against and condemn one another, away with them all.

A 4   2. Be-

bitterly revile it as a most Libertine Irreligious Doctrine.

3. But above all, that they do so exceedingly confirm the Papists, I must profess that *besides carnal Interest and the snare of ill Education*, I do not think that there is any thing in the World that *maketh or hardneth* and *confirmeth* Papists more, and *hindreth* their reception of the Truth, than these same wellmeaning people that are most zealous against them, by two means: 1. One by *Divisions* and *unruliness* in Church-respects, by which they perswade men, especially Rulers, that without such a Center as the Papacy, there will be no Union, and without such *Violence* as theirs, there will be no Rule and Order. Thus one extreme doth breed and feed another. 2. The other is by this unsound sence of the Doctrine of *Imputation of Christs Righteousness*, (*with an unsound Description of Faith*) saying that every man is to believe it as Gods word (or *fide divinâ*) that his own sins are pardoned; which when the Papists read (that, these men make it one of the chief Points of our difference from *Rome*,)

resolve me to neglect them at least, or suspect them in the rest which seem more dubious. And when the Papists find men most *grosly erring* in the very point where they lay the main stress of the difference, who can expect otherwise, but that this should make them despise and cast away our Books, and take us as men self-condemned and already vanquished, and dispute with us with the prejudice as we do with an *Arrian* or *Socinian*? They themselves that cast away *our Books* because *they dissent from us*, may feel in themselves what the *Papists* are like to do on this temptation.

4. And it is not to be disregarded, that many private persons not studied in these points, are led away by the Authority of these men (for more than *Papists* believe as the Church believeth) to speak evil of the Truth, and sinfully to Backbite and Slander those Teachers, whom they hear others slander: and to speak evil of the things which they know not. And to see Gods own Servants seduced into *Disaffection* and *abuse* and *false Speeches* against those Ministers

mong Christians, and of the *Truth* and their *Brethrens Souls*, and that are displeased with that which the Devil is most pleased and God displeased with. These are my Reasons, submitted to every Readers Censure; which may be as various as their Capacities, Interests or Prejudices.

My Arguments in the third Chapter I have but briefly and hastily mentioned, as dealing with the lovers of naked Truth, who will not refuse it when they see it in its self-evidence. But they that desire larger proof, may find enough in Mr. *Gataker* and Mr. *Wotton de Reconcil.* and in *John Goodwin* of *Justification*, (If they can read him without prejudice). From whom yet I differ in the Meritorious Cause of our Justification, and take in the habitual and actual Holiness of Christ as well as his Sufferings, and equal in Merits; and think that *pardon it self* is *merited* by his *Obedience* as well as by his *Satisfaction*: To say nothing of some of his too harsh expressions, about the Imputation of Faith, and non-imputation of Christs Obedience, which yet in some explications he mollifyeth, and sheweth that his sence is the same with theirs that place all our Righteousness

in

Faith is *taken* properly, and another that it is taken Relatively in Imputation, they seem to mean the same thing : For Faith properly taken is essentiated by its *Object* ; And what *Christ's* Office is, and what *Faith's* Office is, I find almost all Protestants are agreed in sence, while they differ in the manner of expression, except there be a real difference in this point *of simple Personating us in his perfect Holiness*, and making the *Person of a Mediator* to contain *essentially in sensu Civili the very Person of every elect sinner, and every such one to have verily been and done, in sensu civili, what Christ was and did.*

I much marvel to find that with most the Imputation of *Satisfaction* is said to be for *Remission of the penalty*, and Imputation of *perfect Holiness* for the obtaining of the *Reward Eternal Life* ; and yet that the far greater part of them that go that way say, that *Imputation of all Christs Righteousness goeth first as the Cause, and Remission of Sin followeth as the Effect* : So even Mr. Roborough pag. 55. and others. Which seemeth to me to have this Sence, as f God said to a Believer, [*I do repute thee to have perfectly fulfilled the Law in Christ, and so to be no sinner, if he had been a sinner, in the Person of a Sponsor, by his own Consent, and that in the very place, and stead of sinners* ; and by this to have satisfyed my Justice, and by both to have merited free *Justification* and *Life*, to be given by the new Covenant to all Believers: *And thou being a Believer, I do repute thee justified and adopted by this satisfactory and meritorious Righteousness of Christ, and by this free Covenant-Gift, as verily and surely as if thou hadst done it and suffered thy self.*

For my own part I find by experience, that almost all Christians that I talk with of it, have just this very notion of our Justification which I have expressed, till some particular Disputer by way of Controversie hath thrust the other notion into their mind. And for peace-sake I will say again, what I have elsewhere said, that I cannot think but that almost all Protestants agree in the substance of this point of Justification (though some having not Acuteness enough to form their *Notions* of it rightly, nor Humility enough to suspect their Understandings, wrangle about *Words*, supposing it to be about

The PREFACE.

bout the *Matter*); Becaufe I find that all are agreed, 1. That no Elect Perfon is Juftified or Righteous by Imputation while he is an Infidel or Ungodly (except three or four that fpeak confufedly, and fupport the *Antinomians*) 2. That God doth not repute us to have done what Chrift did in our *individual natural Perfons Phyfically:* The Controverfie is about a *Civil perfonating.* 3. That God judgeth not falfly. 4. That Chrift was not our Delegate and Inftrument fent by us to do this in our ftead, as a man payeth his debt by a Servant whom he fendeth with the money. 5. That therefore Chrifts Righteoufnefs is not Imputed to us, as if we had done it by him as our Inftrument. 6. That all the fruits of Chrifts Merits and Satisfaction are not ours upon our firft believing (much lefs before). But we receive them by degrees: we have new pardon daily of new fins: We bear caftigatory punifhments, even Death and Denials, or lofs of the greater affiftance of the Spirit: Our Grace is all imperfect, &c. 7. That we are under a Law (and not left ungoverned and lawlefs) and that Chrift is our King and Judge: And this Law is the Law or Covenant of Grace, containing, befides the Precepts of perfect Obedience to the Law natural and fuperadded, a *Gift of Chrift with Pardon and Life*; but

The PREFACE.

but only on Condition that we thankfully and believingly *accept the Gift*; And threatning non-liberation, and a far sorer punishment, to all that unbelievingly and unthankfully reject it. 8. That therefore this Testament or Covenant-Gift is God's Instrument, by which he giveth us our Right to Christ and Pardon and Life: And no man hath such Right but by this Testament-Gift. 9. That this, (called a Testament, *Covenant, Promise, and Law* in several respects) doth, besides the Conditions of our first Right, impose on us Continuance in the Faith, with sincere Holiness, as the necessary Condition of our continued Justification, and our actual Glorification. And that Heaven is the Reward of this keeping of the new Covenant, as to the *order of Gods Collation*, though as to the *value* of the Benefit, it is a *Free Gift*, purchased, merited and given by Christ. 10. That we shall all be judged by this Law of Christ. 11. That we shall all be judged according to our deeds; and those that have done good (not according to the Law of Innocency or Works, but according to the Law of Grace) shall go into everlasting life, and those that have done evil (not by meer sin as sin against the Law of Innocency) but by not keeping the Conditions
of

The PREFACE.

of the Law of Grace, shall go into everlasting punishment. The sober reading of these following texts may end all our Controversie with men that dare not grosly make void the Word of God. *Rev.* 20. 12, 13. 22. 12. & 2. 23.) 12. That to be Justified at the day of Judgment, is, to be *adjudged to Life Eternal, and not condemned to Hell.* And therefore to be the cause or condition that we are *Judged to Glory,* and the Cause or Condition that we are *Justified* then, will be all one. 13. That to be *Judged* according to our deeds, is to be *Justified* or *Condemned* according to them. 14. That the great tryal of that day (as I have after said) will not be, whether Christ hath done his part, but whether we have part in him, and so whether we have believed, and performed the Condition of that Covenant which giveth Christ and Life. 15. That the whole scope of Christ's Sermons, and all the Gospel, calleth us from sin, on the motive of avoiding Hell, (after we are reputed Righteous) and calleth us to Holiness, Perseverance and overcoming, on the motive of laying up a good Foundation, and having a Treasure in Heaven, and getting the Crown of Righteousness. 16. That the after-sins of men imputed Righteous deserve Hell, or at least temporal punish-

The PREFACE.

punishments, and abatements of Grace and Glory. 17. That after such sins, especially hainous, we must pray for Pardon, and repent that we may be pardoned, (and not say I fulfilled the Law in Christ as from my birth to my death, and therefore have no more need of Pardon.) 18. That he that saith he hath no sin, deceiveth himself, and is a lyar. 19. That Magistrates must punish sin as God's Officers; and Pastors by Censure in Christs name; and Parents also in their Children. 20. That if Chrifts *Holiness* and *perfect Obedience,* and Satisfaction and Merit, had bin *Ours* in *Right* and *Imputation,* as *simply* and *absolutely* and *fully* as it was his own, we could have no *Guilt,* no need of *Pardon,* no suspension or detention of the proper fruits of it, no punishment for sin, (specially not so great as the with-holding of degrees of Grace and Glory); And many of the consequents aforesaid could not have followed.

All this I think we are all agreed on ; and none of it can with any face be denied by a Christian. And if so; 1. Then whether Chrifts *perfect Holiness* and *Obedience,* and *Sufferings,* *Merit* and *Satisfaction,* be all given us, and imputed unto us at our first believing as *Our own* in the very thing it self, by a full and proper *Title* to the thing;

Or

Or only so *imputed to us,* as to be *judged a just cause of giving us all the effects in the degrees and time forementioned as God pleaseth,* let all judge as evidence shall convince them. 2. And then, whether they do well that thrust their devised sence on the Churches as an Article of Faith, let the more impartial judge.

I conclude with this confession to the Reader, that though the matter of these Papers hath been thought on these thirty years, yet the Script is *hasty,* and defective in order and fulness; I could not have leisure so much as to affix in the margin all the texts which say what I assert: And several things, especially the state of the Case, are oft repeated. But that is, left once reading suffice not to make them observed and understood; which if many times will do, I have my end. If any say, that I should take time to do things more accurately, I tell him that I know my straights of time, and quantity of business better than he doth; and I will rather be defective in the mode of one work, than leave undone the substance of another as great.

July, 20. 1672.   *Richard Baxter.*

B   The

The Contents.

Chap. 1. *The History of the Controversie. In the Apostles days: In the following Ages.* Augustine *and his followers Opinion. The Schoolmen.* Luther: Islebius: *The Lutherans*: Andr. Osiander: *The latter German Divines who were against the Imputation of Christ's Active Righteousness: Our English Divines:* Davenant's *sense of Imputation.* Wotton. de Reconcil. Bradshaw, Gataker, Dr. Crisp, Jo. Simpson, Randal, Towne, &c. *And the Army*-Antinomians *checkt by the rising of* Arminianism *there against it.* Jo. Goodwin, Mr. Walker, *and Mr.* Roborough; Mr. Ant. Burges; *My Own endeavours*; Mr. Cranden, Mr. Eyres, &c. Mr. Woodbridge, Mr. Tho. Warren, Mr. Hotchkis, Mr. Hopkins, Mr. Gibbon, Mr. Warton, Mr. Grailes, Mr. Jessop: *What I then asserted:* Corn. a Lapide, Vasquez, Suarez, Grotius de Satisf. *Of the Savoy Declaration; Of the Faith of the Congregational-Divines: Their saying that Christ's Active and Passive Obedience is imputed for our sole Righteousness, confuted by Scripture.* Gataker, Usher, *and* Vines *read and approved my Confession of Faith.* Placeus *his Writings and trouble about the Imputation of* Adam's *Sin.* Dr. Gell, Mr. Thorndike, &c. *vehemently accusing the doctrine of Imputed Righteousness. The Consent of all Christians, especially Protestants, about the sense of Imputed Righteousness* 1. *The form of Baptism.* 2. *The Apostles Creed.* 3. *The* Nicene *and* Constantinopolitan *Creed.* 4. Athanasius's *Creed.* 5. *The Fathers sense:* Laurentius *his Collections:* Damasus *his Creed.* 6. *The* Augustan

The Contents.

stan *Confession.* 7. *The* English *Articles, Homilies and Confession.* 8. *The* Saxon *Confession.* 9. *The* Wittenberg *Confession.* 10. *The* Bohemian *Confession.* 11. *The* Palatinate *Confession.* 12. *The* Polonian *Confessions.* 13. *The* Helvetian *Confession.* 14. *The* Basil *Confession.* 15. *The* Argentine *Confession of the four Cities.* 16. *The* Synod *of* Dort, *and the* Belgick *Confession.* 17. *The* Scottish *Confession.* 18. *The* French *Confession. Whether Imputation of Passion and Satisfaction, or of meritorious Perfection go first: How Christ's Righteousness is called the formal Cause, &c. That it is confessed that Christ's Righteousness is imputed to us, as our sin was to him.* Molinæus: Marelius, Vasseur, Bellarmine *is constrained to agree with us. A recommendation of some brief, most clear, and sufficient Treatises on this subject;* viz. 1. *Mr.* Bradshaw; 2. *Mr.* Gibbon's *Sermon;* 3. *Mr.* Truman's *Great Propitiation.* 4. Placeus *his Disput. in Thes. Salmur.* 5. Le Blank's *Theses: And those that will read larger, Mr.* Watton, John Goodwin, *and Dr.* Stillingfleet.

Chap. 2. *The opening of the Case, by some Distinctions, and many Propositions:* Joh. Crocius *Concessions premised: Mr.* Lawson's *Judgment.*

Chap. 3. *A further Explication of the Controversie.*

Chap. 4. *My Reasons against the denied sense of Imputation and personating. The denied sense repeated plainly. Forty three Reasons briefly named.*

Chap. 5. *Some Objections answered.*

Chap. 6, 7, 8. *Replies to Dr.* Tully; *and a Defence of the Concord of* Protestants *against his Military Alarm, and false pretence of greater discord than there is.*

Of the Imputation of Christs Righteousness (Material or Formal) to Believers:

Whether we are Reputed personally to have suffered on the Cross, and to have satisfied God's Justice for our own sins, and to have been habitually perfectly Holy, and Actually perfectly Obedient, in Christ, or by Christ, and so to have merited our own Justification and Salvation. And whether Christ's Righteousness Habitual Active and Passive, be strictly made our own Righteousness, in the very thing it self simply Imputed to us, or only be made ours in the effects, and Righteousness Imputed to us when we believe, because Christ hath satisfied and fulfilled the Law, and thereby merited it for us. The last is affirmed, and the two first Questions denied.

I Have said so much of this subject already in my Confession, but especially in my Disputations of Justification, and in my Life of Faith that I thought not to have meddled with it any more; But some occasions tell me that it is not yet needless, though those that have most need will not read it. But while some of them held, that nothing which they account a Truth about the *Form* and *Manner* of *Worship* is to be silenced for the Churches peace, they should grant to me that *Real Truth*

Truth so near the Foundation (in their own account) is not to be silenced when it *tendeth unto Peace.*

In opening my thoughts on this subject I shall reduce all to these Heads. 1. I shall give the brief *History* of this Controversie. 2. I shall open the true state of it, and assert what is to be asserted, and deny what is to be denied. 3. I shall give you the Reasons of my Denials. 4. I shall answer some Objections.

CHAP. I.

The History of the Controversie.

§ 1. IN the Gospel it self we have first *Christ's Doctrine delivered by his own mouth.* And in that there is so little said of this Subject that I find few that will pretend thence to resolve the Controversie, for Imputation in the rigorous sence. The same I say of the Acts of the Apostles, and all the rest of the New Testament, except *Pauls* Epistles.

The Apostle *Paul*, having to do with the *Jews*, who could not digest the equalizing of the *Gentiles* with them, and specially with the factious Jewish Christians, who thought the *Gentiles* must become *Proselytes* to *Moses* as well as to Christ, if they would be Justified and Saved, at large confuteth this opinion, and freeth the Consciences of the Gentile Christians from the Imposition of this yoke (as also did all the Apostles, *Act.* 15.) And in his ar-

guing

h that the Mosaical Law is so far from
y to the Justification of the *Gentiles*,
and the Godly *Jews* themselves were
y it, but by *Faith*; And that by the
nd consequently not by the works of
ovenant of Innocency, which no man
man could ever be justified: And
they were to look for Justification by
and by Faith in him, or by meer
which the *Gentiles* might have as
Jews, the Partition-wall being taken
riefly is the true scope of *Paul* in these

Paul's own days, there were some-
pistles which the unlearned and un-
st, as they did the other Scriptures, to
truction, as *Peter* tells us, 2 *Pet.* 2.
by the Epistle of *James*, that this
For he is fain there earnestly to dis-
me, who thought that Faith without
ks themselves, would justifie, and
, that we are *Justified by Works, and*
ly; that is, as it is a *Practical Faith*,
tained a *Consent* or *Covenant* to *obey*,
:eth us into a justified state; so it is
Faith *actually working by Love*, and
rmance of our *Covenant*, which by
m is *necessary* to our *Justification*, as
is *Consummate by the Sentence of Judg-*
t which sentence of *James* there is
o be found in *Paul*. But all the Scrip-
lat *all men shall be Judged*, that is,
ndemned, *according to their works*.
is Controversie (between Faith and
Works)

Works) which I am now to speak to, having done it enough heretofore.

§ 3. From the days of the Apostles till *Pelagius* and *Augustine*, this Controversie was little meddled with: For the truth is, the Pastors and Doctors took not Christianity in those days for a matter of Shcolastick subtilty, but of plain *Faith* and *Piety*. And contented themselves to say that Christ dyed for our sins, and that we are Justified by Faith; and that Christ was made unto us Righteousness, as he was made to us Wisdom, Sanctification and Redemption.

§ 4. But withal those three first Ages were so intent upon Holiness of Life, as that they addicted their Doctrine, their Zeal, and their constant endeavours to it: And particularly to great austerities to their Bodies, in great Fastings, and great contempt of the World, and exercises of Mortification, to kill their fleshly Lusts, and deny their Wills, and Worldly Interests; to which end at last they got into Wildernesses, and Monasteries, where, in Fasting and Prayer, and a single life, they might live as it were out of the World, while they were in it; (Though indeed *persecution* first drove them thither to save themselves.) Into these Deserts and Monasteries those went that had most Zeal, but not usually most *Knowledg*: And they turned much of their Doctrine and discourses about these Austerities, and about the practices of a Godly Life, and about all the Miracles which were (some really) done, and (some feigned) by credulous soft people said to be done among them. So that in all these ages most of their writings are taken up, 1. In defending Christianity against the Heathens, which was the work

work of the Learned Doctors. 2. And in confuting swarms of Heresies that sprung up. 3. And in matters of Church-order, and Ecclesiastical and Monastical discipline. 4. And in the precepts of a Godly Life: But the point of Imputation was not only not meddled with distinctly, but almost all the Writers of those times, seem to give very much to *Mans free-will*, and to *works of Holiness*, and *sufferings*, making too rare and obscure mention of the distinct Interests of Christs Merits in our Justification, at least, with any touch upon this Controversie: Yet generally holding *Pardon*, and *Grace* and *Salvation* only by Christs Sacrifice and Merits; though they *spake* most of *Mans Holiness*, when they called men to seek to make sure of Salvation.

§ 5. And indeed at the day of Judgment, the Question to be decided, will not be, Whether Christ dyed and did his part, but, Whether we believed and obeyed him and did our part: Not, Whether Christ performed his Covenant with the Father; but, Whether we performed our Covenant with him: For it is not Christ that is to be judged, *but we by Christ*.

§ 6. But *Pelagius* and *Augustine* disputing about the Power of Nature and Freewill and the Grace of Christ, began to make it a matter of great Ingenuity (as *Erasmus* speaketh) to be a Christian. *Pelagius* (a *Brittain*, of great wit, and continence, and a good and sober life, as *Austin* saith, *Epist*. 120.) stifly defended the Power of Nature and Freewill, and made Grace to consist only in the free Pardon of all sin through Christ, and in the *Doctrine* and *Perswasions* only to a holy life for the time to come, with Gods common ordinary help. *Augustine* copiously

Salvation, did fall away and perish, yet he held that none of the *Elect* did fall *away and perish*; And he maintained that even the Justified that fell away, had their Faith by a special Grace above nature.) *Vid. August. de bono Persever. Cap.* 8, *&* 9. *& de Cor. & Grat. Cap.* 8, *&* 9. *& alibi passim.*

§ 7. In this their Controversie, the point of Justification fell into frequent debate: But no Controversie ever arose between them, *Whether Christ's personal Righteousness considered Materially or Formally,* was by Imputation made ours as Proprietors of the thing it self, distinct from its effects; or, Whether God reputed us to have satisfied and also perfectly obeyed in Christ. For *Augustine* himself, while he vehemently defendeth free Grace, speaketh too little even of the Pardon of sin: And though he say, that *Free Pardon* of sins is part of Grace, yet he maketh *Justification* to be that which we call Sanctification, that makes us inherently Righteous or new-Creatures, by the operation of the Holy Ghost: And he thinketh that this is the Justification which *Paul* pleadeth to be of Grace and not of works; yet including *Pardon of sin*; and confessing that *sometimes* to Justifie, signifieth in Scripture, not to make just, but to *judg just.* And though in it self this be but *de nomine,* and not *de re*; yet, 1. no doubt but as to many texts of Scripture *Austin* was mistaken, though some few texts *Beza* and others confess to be taken in his sence: 2. And the exposition of

many

§ 8. But becaufe, as fome that, it feems, never read *Auguſtine*, or underſtood not plain words, have neverthelefs ventured confidently to deny what I have ſaid of his Judgment in the points of Perſeverance (in my Tract of Perſeverance) ſo, it's like ſuch men will have no more warineſs what they ſay in the point of Juſtification ; I will cite a few of *Auguſtin's* words among many, to ſhow what he took Juſtification to be, though I differ from him *de nomine*.

Nec quia recti ſunt corde, ſed etiam ut recti ſint corde, pretendit Juſtitiam ſuam, quâ juſtificat impium —— Quo motu receditur ab illo fonte vitæ, cujus ſolius hauſtu juſtitiæ bibitur, bona ſcil. vita. Aug. de Spir. & Lit. Cap. 7.

Deus eſt enim qui operatur in eis & velle & operari, pro bona voluntate. Hæc eſt Juſtitia Dei, hoc eſt, quam Deus donat homini quum juſtificat impium. Hanc Dei juſtitiam ignorantes ſuperbi Judæi, & ſuam volentes conſtituere, juſtitiæ Dei non ſunt ſubjecti.—— Dei quippe dixit Juſtitiam, quæ homini ex Deo eſt, ſuam vero, quam putant ſibi ſufficere ad facienda mandata ſine adjutorio & dono ejus qui legem dedit. His autem ſimiles ſunt qui cum profiteantur ſe eſſe Chriſtianos, ipſi gratiæ Chriſti ſic adverſantur ut ſe humanis viribus divina exiſtiment implere mandata. Epiſt. 120. cap. 21. & 22. & Epiſt. 200.

Et de Spir. & lit. c. 26. *Factores juſtificabuntur: —— Non tanquam per opera, nam per Gratiam juſtificentur:*

sciamus eos non esse factores legis nisi justificentur; ut non justificatio factoribus accedat, sed factores legis justificatio precedat: Quid est enim aliud Justificati, quam Justi facti, ab illo scilicet qui justificat Impium, ut ex impio fiat justus? —— Aut certe ita dictum est, Justificabuntur, ac si diceretur Justi habebuntur, justi deputabuntur.

Et ibid. cap. 29. *Gentes quæ non sectabantur justitiam apprehenderunt justitiam; Justitiam autem quæ ex fide est, impretrando eam ex Deo, non ex seipsis presumendo; Israel vero persequens legem justitiæ, in legem justitiæ, non pervenit: Quare? Quia non ex fide, sed tanquam ex operibus: id est tanquam eam per seipsos operantes; non in se credentes operari Deum. Deus est enim qui operatur in nobis —— Finis enim legis Christus est omni credenti. Et adhuc dubitamus quæ sint opera legis, quibus homo non justificatur; si ea tanquam sua crediderit sine adjutorio & dono Dei, quod est ex fide Jesu Christi —— Ut possit homo facere bona & Sancta, Deus operatur in homine per fidem Jesu Christi, qui finis ad Justitiam omni credenti: id est, per Spiritum incorporatus factusque membrum ejus, potest quisque illo incrementum intrinsecus dante, operari justitiam. —— Justificatio autem ex fide impetratur —— In tantum justus, in quantum salvus. Per hanc enim fidem credemus, quod etiam nos Deus a mortuis excitet; interim Spiritu, ut in novitate ejus gratiæ temperanter & juste & pie viva-*

vivamus in hoc seculo —— *qui in Resurrectione sibi congrua, hoc est, in Justificatione precedit:* —— c. 30. *Fides impetrat gratiam qua Lex impleatur.* ——

Cap. 28. pag. 315. *Ibi Lex Dei, non ex omni parte deleta per injustitiam, profecto scribitur, renovata, per gratiam: Nec istam inscriptionem, quæ Justificatio est, poterat efficere in Judæis Lex in tabulis scripta.*

Ibid. Cap. 9. pag. 307, 308. *Justitia Dei manifestata est: non dixit, Justitia hominis vel justitia propriæ voluntatis. sed justitia Dei; Non qua Deus justus est; sed qua induit, hominem cum justificat impium. Hac testificatur per Legem & Prophetas. Huic quippe testimonium perhibent Lex & Prophetæ. Lex quidem hoc ipso, quod jubendo, & minando, & neminem justificando, satis indicat dono Dei justificari hominem per* Adjutorium Spiritus —— *Justitia autem Dei per fidem Jesu Christi, hoc est, per fidem qua Creditur in Christum: sicut autem ista fides Christi dicta non est, qua Credit Christus, sic & illa Justitia Dei non qua Justus est Deus. Utrumque enim Nostrum est sed ideo Dei & Christi dicitur quod ejus nobis largitate donatur.*

—— *Justitia Dei sine lege est quam Deus per* Spiritum Gratiæ Credenti *confert sine adjutorio legis.* —— *Justificati gratis per gratiam ipsius: non quod sine voluntate nostra fiat, sed voluntas nostra ostenditur infirma per legem, ut sanet Gratia Voluntatem, & sanata voluntas impleat Legem.* —— Et cap. 10. *Confugiant per fidem ad Justificantem Gratiam, & per donum Spiritus suavitate justitiæ delectati, pœnam literæ minantis evadant.* Vid. Ep. 89. q. 2. Et lib. 3. ad Bonifac. c. 7.

Et Tract. 3. in Joan. when he saith that, *Omnes qui per Christum Justificati justi, non in se, sed in illo;* he expoundeth it of Regeneration by Christ.

Et

Et Serm. 15. de verb. Apoſt. *Sine voluntate tua non erit in te Juſtitia Dei.* *Voluntas non eſt niſi tua; Juſtitia non eſt niſi Dei:* he expounds it of Holineſs. —— *Traditus eſt propter delicta noſtra, & reſurrexit, propter juſtificationem noſtram. Quid eſt, Propter Juſtificationem noſtram? Ut juſtificet nos, & juſtos faciat nos. Eris opus Dei non ſolum quia homo es, ſed quia Juſtus es: Qui fecit te ſine te, non te juſtificat ſine te: Tamen ipſe juſtificat, ne ſit juſtitia tua.* —— *Dei juſtitiam dat non litera occidens, ſed* vivificans Spiritus. —— Vid. *de* Grat. Chriſti Cap. 13, 14.

Abundance ſuch paſſages in *Auguſtine* fully ſhew that he took Juſtification to ſignifie Sanctification, or the Spirits renovation of us; and thinks it is called the Righteouſneſs of God and Chriſt, and not ours, becauſe by the Spirit he worketh it in us. And when he ſaith that *bona opera ſequuntur Juſtificatum, non precedunt Juſtificandum* (as in ſence he often doth) he meaneth that we are *freely ſanctified,* before we do good. I would cite abundance, but for ſwelling the writing, and tiring the Reader. And his followers *Proſper,* and *Fulgentius* go the ſame way, as you may eaſily find in their writings.

Johan. Crocius in his copious Treatiſe of Juſtification, *Diſp. 9. p.* 442. ſaith, *Auguſtinum Juſtificationis nomine utramque partem complecti, id eſt, tum Remiſſionem peccatorum quæ proprie Juſtificatio dicitur, tum Sanctificationem* —— *Cum quo nos ſentimus quoad rem ipſam, tantum diſſidemus in loquendi formâ.*

§ 9. The Schoolmen being led by the Scholaſtick wit of *Auguſtine,* fell into the ſame phraſe of ſpeech and opinions, *Lombard* making *Auguſtine*
his

his Master, and the rest making him theirs, till some began to look more towards the Semipelagian way.

§ 10. And when Church-Tyranny and Ignorance, had obscured the Christian Light, the true sence of Justification by the Righteousness of Christ, was much obscured with the rest, and a world of humane inventions under the name of Good works, were brought in to take up the peoples minds; And the merits of man, and of the Virgin *Mary*, sounded louder than the merits of Christ, in too many places: And the people that were ignorant of the true Justification, were filled with the noise of Pardons, Indulgences, Satisfactions, Penances, Pilgrimages, and such like.

§ 11. *Luther* finding the Church in this dangerous and woful state, where he lived, did labour to reduce mens minds and trust, from humane fopperies and merits, and indulgences, to Christ, and to help them to the Knowledg of true Righteousness: But according to his temper in the heat of his Spirit, he sometimes let fall some words which seemed plainly to make Christs own personal Righteousness in it self to be every Believers own by Imputation, and our sins to be verily Christs own sins in themselves by Imputation: Though by many other words he sheweth that he meant only, that our sins were Christs in *the effects* and not in themselves, and Christs personal Righteousness ours in the effects and not in it self.

§ 12. But his Book on the *Galatians*, and some other words, gave occasion to the errours of some then called *Antinomians*, and afterward *Libertines* (when some additions were made to their errours.) Of these *Islebius Agricola* was the chief: Whom

Luther

Luther confuted and reduced, better expounding his own words: But *Iflebius* ere long turned back to the Contrary extreme of Popery, and with *Sidonius* and *Julius Pflug*, (three Popish Bishops made for that purpose) promoted the Emperours *Interim* to the persecution of the Protestants.

§ 13. The Protestant Reformers themselves spake variously of this subject. Most of them rightly asserted that Christ's Righteousness was ours by the way of Meriting our Righteousness, which was therefore said to be Imputed to us. Some of them follow'd *Luthers* first words, and said that Christs sufferings and all his personal Righteousness was Imputed to us, so as to be ours in it self, and when judged as if we had personally done what he did, and were righteous with the same Righteousness that he was.

§ 14. *Ambsdorfius, Gallus*, and some other hot *Lutherans* were so jealous of the *name* of works, that they maintained that good works were not necessary to Salvation. (Yea as to Salvation some called them hurtful:) And *Georgius Major* a Learned sober Divine was numbered by them among the *Hereticks*, for maintaining that Good works were necessary to Salvation; as you may see in the perverse writings of *Chlufseburgius* and many others.

§ 15. *Andreas Ofiander* (otherwise a Learned Protestant) took up the opinion, that we are Justified by the very essential Righteousness of God himself. But he had few followers.

§ 16. The Papists fastening upon those Divines who held Imputation of Christs personal Righteousness in it self in the rigid sence, did hereupon greatly insult against the Protestants, as if it had been

been their common doctrine, and it greatly stopt the Reformation: For many seeing that some made that a Fundamental in our difference, and *articulus stantis & cadentis Ecclesiæ*, and seeing how easily it was disproved, how fully it was against the Doctrine of all the ancient Church, and what intolerable Consequences followed, did judge by that of the rest of our Doctrine, and were settledly hardened against all.

§ 17. The Learned Divines of *Germany* perceiving this, fell to a fresh review of the Controversie, and after a while abundance of very Learned Godly Doctors fell to distinguish between the Active and Passive Righteousness of Christ; and not accurately distinguishing of Imputation, because they perceived that Christ suffered in our stead, in a fuller sense than he could be said to be *Holy* in our stead, or fulfil the Law in our stead. Hereupon they principally managed the Controversie, as about the sort of Righteousness Imputed to us: And a great number of the most Learned famous Godly Divines of the Reformed Churches, maintained that Christ's Passive Righteousness was Imputed to us, even his whole Humiliation or Suffering, by which the pardon of all sins of Commission and Omission was procured for us; but that his *Active Righteousness* was not Imputed to us, though it profited us; but was *Justitia Personæ* to make Christ a fit Sacrifice for our sins, having none of his own, but the Suffering was his *Justitia Meriti*. His Obedience they said was performed *nostro bono, non nostro loco,* for our good but not in our stead; but his *Sufferings*, both *nostro bono & loco,* both *for our good* and in *our stead*: but neither of them so strictly *in nostrâ Personâ* in our Person, as if we did it by and in Christ. The Writers that defended

fended this were *Cargius*, and that holy man *Olevian* and *Ursine*, and *Paræus*, and *Scultetus*, and *Piscator*, *Alstedius*, *Wendeline*, *Beckman*, and many more. He that will see the sum of their arguings may read it in *Wendeline's Theolog. lib. 1. cap. 25.* and in *Paræus* his *Miscellanies* after *Ursine's Corpus Theolog.* After them *Camero* with his Learned followers took it up in France. *Leg. Cameron. p. 364. 390. Thes. Sal. vol. 1. Placæi Disp. de Just. § 29. & Part. 2 de Satisf. § 42.* So that at that time (as *Paræus* tells you) there were four opinions: some thought Christ's Passive Righteousness only was Imputed to us; some also his *Active* instead of our Actual Obedience; some also his *Habitual* instead of our Habitual perfection; And some thought also his Divine Righteousness was Imputed to us, because of our Union with Christ, God and Man. (Imputed I say; for I now speak not of *Osiander's* opinion of Inhesion.) And *Lubbertus* wrote a Conciliatory Tractate favouring those that were for the Passive part. And *Forbes* hath written for the Passive only imputed. *Molinæus* casteth away the distinction, *Thes. Sedan. v. 1. p. 625. § 18.*

§ 18. In England most Divines used the phrase, that we were Justified by the forgiveness of sin and the Imputation of Christs Righteousness, and being accepted as Righteous unto life thereon: But the sense of Imputation few pretended accurately to discuss. *Davenant* who dealt most elaborately in it, and maintaineth Imputation stiffly, in terms; yet when he telleth you what Protestants mean by it, saith, that [*Possunt nobis imputari, non solum nostræ passiones, actiones, qualitates, sed etiam extrinseca quædam, quæ nec a nobis fluunt, nec in nobis hærent*

rent : De facto autem Imputantur, quando illorum intuitus & respectus valent nobis ad aliquem effectum, æque ac si a nobis aut in nobis essent. (Note, that he saith, but *ad aliquem effectum, non ad omnem.*) And he instanceth in one that is a *slothful fellow himself, but is advanced to the Kings Favour and Nobility for some great Service done by his Progenitors to the Common-wealth.* And in *one that deserving death is pardoned through the Intercession of a friend, or upon some suffering in his stead which the King imposeth on his Friend.* This is the Imputation which *Davenant* and other such Protestants plead for; which I think is not to be denied. Were it not for lengthening the discourse and wearying the Reader, I would cite many other of our greatest Divines, who plead for the Imputation of Christ's Righteousness, that *Davenant* here expoundeth himself.

But some less judicious grating upon a harsh and unsound sence, Mr. *Anthony Wotton* a very Learned and Godly Divine of *London,* wrote a *Latine* Treatise *de Reconciliatione,* one of the Learnedst that hath ever been written of that subject, in which he laboureth to disprove the rigid Imputation of Chrifts Holiness and Obedience to man; and sheweth that he is Righteous to whom all sin of Omission and Commission is forgiven; and confuteth these three Assertions. 1. That *A Sinner is Reputed to have fulfilled the Law in and by Christ.* 2. *And being reputed to have fulfilled the Law, is taken for formally just as a fulfiller of it.* 3. *And being formally just as a fullfiller of the Law, Life eternal is due to him by that Covenant,* that saith, *do this and live.* Vid. Part. 2. li. 1. Cap. 11. pag. 152. *Cum sequentibus.* Thus and much further Mr. *Wotton* went to the very quick of the Controversie, and irrefragably overthrew the rigid Imputation.

But Mr. *William Bradshaw*, a Learned Godly Nonconformist, being grieved at the differences about the Active and Passive Righteousness, and thinking that Mr. *Wotton* denied all Imputation of the Active Righteousness (which he did not, but owneth it to be Imputed as a meritorious Cause :) Part. 2. li. 1. Cap. 13. pag. 165. *Ne illud quidem negaverim, imputari nobis illius justitiam & obedientiam, ut ad nostrum fructum redundet: Id unum non concedo, Legem nos in Christo & per Christum servâsse, ut propter eam a nobis præstitam vita æterna ex fœdere, Hoc fac et vives, debeatur.* Mr. *Bradshaw* I say attempted a Conciliatory middle way, which indeed is the same in the main with Mr. *Wotton's*: He honoureth the Learned Godly persons on each side, but maintaineth that the Active and Passive Righteousness are both Imputed, but not in the rigid sence of Imputation denying both these Propositions.
1. *That Christ by the Merits of his Passive Obedience only, hath freed us from the guilt of all sin, both Actual and Original, of Omission and Commission.*
2. *That in the Imputation of Christs Obedience both Active and Passive, God doth so behold and consider a sinner in Christ, as if the sinner himself had done and suffered those very particulars which Christ did and suffered for him.* And he wrote a small book with great accurateness in *English* first, and *Latin* after, opening the nature of Justification, which hath been deservedly applauded ever since. His bosom-Friend Mr. *Tho. Gataker*, (a man of rare Learning and Humility) next set in to defend Mr. *Bradshaw's* way, and wrote in *Latin* Animadversions on *Lucius* (who opposed *Piscator*,

Piscator, and erred on one side for rigid Imputation) and on *Piscator* who on the other side was for Justification by the Passive Righteousness only; and other things he wrote with great Learning and Judgment in that cause.

About that time the Doctrine of personal Imputation in the rigid sence began to be fully improved in *England*, by the Sect of the *Antinomians* (trulyer called *Libertines*) of whom Dr. *Crispe* was the most eminent Ring-leader, whose books took wonderfully with ignorant Professors under the pretence of extolling Christ and free-Grace. After him rose Mr. *Randal*, and Mr. *John Simpson*, and then Mr. *Town*, and at last in the Armies of the Parliament, *Saltmarsh*, and so many more, as that it seemed to be likely to have carried most of the Professors in the Army, and abundance in the City and Country that way: But that suddenly (one Novelty being set up against another) the opinions called *Arminianism* rose up against it, and gave it a check and carryed many in the Army and City the clean contrary way: And these two Parties divided a great part of the raw injudicious sort of the professors between them, which usually are the greatest part: but especially in the Army which was like to become a Law and example to others.

Before this *John Goodwin* (not yet turned *Arminian*) preached and wrote with great diligence about Justification against the rigid sence of Imputation, who being answered by Mr. *Walker*, and Mr. *Robourough*, with far inferiour strength, his book had the greater success for such answerers.

The *Antinomians* then swarming in *London*, Mr. *Anthony Burges*, a very worthy Divine was employed

ployed to Preach and Print againſt them; which he did in ſeveral books: but had he been acquainted with the men as I was, he would have found more need to have vindicated the Goſpel againſt them than the Law.

Being daily converſant my ſelf with the *Antinomian* and *Arminian* Souldiers, and hearing their daily conteſts, I thought it pitty that nothing but one extreme ſhould be uſed to beat down that other; and I found the *Antinomian* party far the ſtronger, higher, and more fierce, and working towards greater changes and ſubverſions; And I found that they were juſt falling in with *Saltmarſh*, that *Chriſt hath repented and believed for us, and that we muſt no more queſtion our Faith and Repentance, than Chriſt*. This awakened me better to ſtudy theſe points; And being young, and not furniſhed with ſufficient reading of the Controverſie, and alſo being where were no libraries, I was put to ſtudy only the *naked matter in it ſelf*. Whereupon I ſhortly wrote a ſmall book called *Aphoriſms* of Juſtification, &c. Which contained that Doctrine in ſubſtance which I judg found; but being the firſt that I wrote, it had ſeveral expreſſions in it which needed correction; which made me ſuſpend or retract it till I had time to reform them. Mens judgments of it were various, ſome for it and ſome againſt it: I had before been a great eſteemer of two books of one name, *Vindiciæ Gratiæ*, Mr. *Pembles* and Dr. *Twiſſes*, above moſt other books. And from them I had taken in the opinion of a double Juſtification, one *in foro Dei* as an Immanent eternal Act of God, and another *in foro Conſcientiæ*, the Knowledg of that; and I knew no other: But now I ſaw, that neither of
those

those was the Justification which the Scripture spake of. But some half-*Antinomians* which were for the Justification before Faith, which I wrote against, were most angry with my book. And Mr. *Crandon* wrote against it, which I answered in an *Apologie*, and fullyer wrote my judgment in my *Confession*; and yet more fully in some Disputations of Justification against Mr. *Burges*, who had in a book of Justification made some exceptions; and pag. 346.had defended that [*As in Christ's suffering we were looked upon by God as suffering in him; so by Christs obeying of the Law, we were beheld as fulfilling the Law in him.*] To those Disputations I never had any answer. And since then in my *Life of Faith*, I have opened the *Libertine* errours about Justification, and stated the sence of Imputation.

Divers writers were then employed on these subjects: Mr. *Eyers* for Justification before Faith(that is, of elect Infidels) and Mr. *Benjamin Woodbridg*, Mr. *Tho. Warren* against it. Mr. *Hotchkis* wrote a considerable Book of Forgiveness of sin, defending the sounder way: Mr. *George Hopkins*, wrote to prove that Justification and Sanctification are equally carryed on together: Mr. *Warton*, Mr. *Graile*, Mr. *Jessop*, (clearing the sence of Dr. *Twisse*,) and many others wrote against *Antinomianism*. But no man more clearly opened the whole doctrine of Justification, than Learned and Pious Mr. *Gibbons* Minister at *Black-Fryers*, in a Sermon Printed in the *Lectures* at *St. Giles* in the *Fields*. By such endeavours the before-prevailing *Antinomianism* was suddenly and somewhat marveloufly suppressed, so that there was no great noise made by it.

About Imputation that which I asserted was against

gainst the two fore-described extremes; in short, "That *we are Justified by Christ's whole Righteous-* "*ness,* *Passive,* *Active,* and *Habitual,* yea the *Di-* "*vine* so far included as by *Union* advancing the rest "to a valuable sufficiency : That the Passive, that is, "Christ's whole Humiliation is *satisfactory* first, and "so meritorious, and the Active and Habitual meri- "torious primarily. That as God the Father did "appoint to Christ as Mediator his Duty for our "Redemption by a Law or Covenant, so Christ's "whole fulfilling that Law, or performance of his "Covenant-Conditions as such (by Habitual and "Actual perfection, and by Suffering) made up "one Meritorious Cause of our Justification, not "distinguishing with Mr. *Gataker* of the pure mo- "ral, and the servile part of Christ's Obedience, save "only as one is more a part of Humiliation than the "other, but in point of Merit taking in all : That "as Christ suffered in our stead that we might not "suffer, and obeyed in our nature, that perfection "of Obedience might not be necessary to our *Ju-* "*stification,* and this in the person of a Mediator "and Sponsor for us sinners, but not so in our *Per-* "*sons,* as that we truely in a moral or civil sence, "did all this in and by him ; Even so God repu- "teth the thing to be as it is, and so far Imputeth "Christ's Righteousness and Merits and Satisfaction "to us, as that it is Reputed by him the true Me- "ritorious Cause of our Justification ; and that for "it God maketh a Covenant of Grace, in which he "freely giveth Christ, Pardon and Life to all that "accept the Gift as it is ; so that the Accepters "are by this Covenant or Gift as surely justified "and saved by Christ's Righteousness as if they had
"Obeyed

"Obeyed and Satisfied themselves. Not that Christ
"meriteth that we shall have Grace to fulfil the
"Law our selves and stand before God in a Righ-
"teousness of our own, which will answer the Law
"of works and justifie us: But that the Conditi-
"ons of the Gift in the Covenant of Grace being
"performed by every penitent Believer, that *Cove-*
"*nant* doth *pardon* all *their sins* (as Gods Instru-
"ment) and giveth them a *Right* to *Life eternal*,
"*for Christs Merits.*

This is the sense of Imputation which I and o-
thers asserted as the true healing middle way. And
as bad as they are, among the most Learned Papists,
Cornelius a *Lapide* is cited by Mr. *Wotton*, *Vasquez*
by *Davenant*, *Suarez* by Mr. *Burges*, as speaking
for some such Imputation, and Merit: *Grotius de
Satisf.* is clear for it.

But the Brethren called Congregational or Inde-
pendant in their Meeting at the *Savoy*, *Oct.* 12.
1658. publishing a Declaration of their Faith, *Cap.*
11. have these words [*Those whom God effectually
calleth, he also freely justifieth; not by infusing Righteousness into them, but by pardoning their Sins, and
by accounting and accepting their persons as Righteous,
not for any thing wrought in them, or done by them,
but for Christs sake alone: not by imputing Faith it
self, the act of believing, or any other evangelical Obedience to them, as their Righteousness; but by Imputing Christs Active Obedience to the whole Law, and
Passive Obedience in his death, for their whole and sole
Righteousness; they receiving and resting on him and his
Righteousness by Faith.*]

Upon the publication of this it was variously
spoken of: some thought that it gave the *Papists*

so great a scandal, and advantage to reproach the *Protestants* as denying all inherent Righteousness, that it was necessary that we should disclaim it: Others said that it was not their meaning to deny Inherent Righteousness, though their words so spake, but only that we are not justified by it: Many said that it was not the work of all of that party, but of some few that had an inclination to some of the *Antinomian* principles, out of a mistaken zeal of free Grace; and that it is well known that they differ from us, and therefore it cannot be imputed to us, and that it is best make no stir about it, left it irritate them to make the matter worse by a Defence, & give the Papists too soon notice of it. And I spake with one Godly Minister that was of their Assembly, who told me, that they did not subscribe it, and that they meant but to deny Justification by inherent Righteousness. And though such men in the Articles of their declared Faith, no doubt can speak intelligibly and aptly, and are to be understood as they speak according to the common use of the words; yet even able-men sometimes may be in this excepted, when eager engagement in an opinion and parties, carryeth them too precipitantly, and maketh them forget something, that should be remembred. The Sentences here which we excepted against are these two. But the first was not much offensive because their meaning was right; *And the same words are in the Assemblies Confession, though they might better have been left out.*

Scrip-

Scriptures.	Declaration.
Rom. 4.3. What faith the Scripture? *Abraham believed God, and it was counted to him for Righteousness.*	[1 Not by imputing Faith it self, ☞ of Believing, or any other Evangelical Obedience to them as their Righteousness]

Ver. 5. *To him that worketh not, but believeth on him that Justifyeth the Ungodly, his* Faith *is counted for Righteousness.*

Ver. 9. *For we say that* Faith *was reckoned to Abraham for Righteousness: How was it then reckoned?*

Ver. 11. *And he received the sign of Circumcision, a seal of the righteousness of the Faith, which he had yet being uncircumcised, that he might be the Father of all them that believe, —— that Righteousness might be imputed to them also.* —— Ver 13. *Through the Righteousness of Faith.* —— Ver. 16. *Therefore it is of Faith that it might be by Grace.* —— vid. Ver. 17, 18, 19, 20, 21, 22, 23, 24. *He was strong in Faith, fully perswaded that what he had promised, he was able also to perform; and therefore it was Imputed to him for Righteousness. Now it was not written for his sake alone that it was imputed to him, but for us also, to whom it shall be imputed, if we (*or, who*) believe on him that raised up* Jesus *our Lord from the dead.*

Gen. 15. 5,6. *Tell the Stars —— so shall thy seed be: And he believed in the Lord, and he counted it to him for Righteousness,* Jam. 2. 21, 22, 23, 24. *Was not Abraham our Father justified, by* Works? —— *And the Scripture was fulfilled which saith, Abraham believed God, and it was imputed to him for Righteousness.* Luk.

Luk. 19. 17. *Well done thou good Servant, Because thou hast been Faithful in a very little, have thou authority over ten Cities.*

Mat. 25. 34, 35, 40, *Come ye blessed.* ——— *For I was hungry and ye gave me Meat:*.

Gen. 22. 16, 17, *By my self I have sworn.* ——— *Because thou hast done this thing.* ———

Joh. 16. 27. *For the Father himself loveth you, because you have loved me and have believed that I came out from God.* Many such passages are in Scripture.

Our opinion is, 1. That it is better to justifie and expound the Scripture, than flatly to deny it : If Scripture so oft say, that *Faith is reckoned* or *Imputed* for *Righteousness*, it becometh not Christians, to say, *It is not* : But to shew in what sence it is, and in what it is not. For if it be so Imputed in *no sence*, the Scripture is made false : If in any sence, it should not be universally denied but with distinction.

2. We hold, that in Justification there is considerable, 1. The Purchasing and Meritorious Cause of Justification freely given in the new Covenant. This is only Christ's Sufferings and Righteousness, and so it is Reputed of God, and Imputed to us. 2. The *Order of Donation*, which is, On *Condition of Acceptance*; And so 3. The Condition of our *Title* to the free Gift by this Covenant; And that is, Our Faith, or Acceptance of the Gift according to its nature and use. And thus God Reputeth Faith, and Imputeth it to us, requiring but this *Condition of us* (which also he worketh in us) by the Covenant of Grace; whereas perfect Obedience

dience *was required of us*, by the Law of Innocency. If we err in this explication, it had been better to confute us than deny God's Word.

Scriptures besides the former.   *Declaration.*

1 Joh. 2. 29. *Every one which doth Righteousness is born of God.* —— & 3. 7, 10. *He that doth Righteousness is Righteous, even as he is Righteous.* —— *Whosoever doth not righteousness is not of God.*
2 Tim. 4. 8. *He hath laid up for us a Crown of Righteousness.*
Heb. 11. 23. *Through Faith they wrought Righteousness.* —— Heb. 12. *The peaceable fruit of Righteousness.* —— Jam. 3. 18. *The fruit of Righteousness is sown in Peace.* —— 1 Pet. 2. 24. *That we being dead to sin, should live unto righteousness,* Mat 5. 20. *Except your Righteousness exceed the Righteousness of the Scribes and Pharisees, &c.*——Luk. 1. 71. *In Holiness and Righteousness before him all the days of our Life.* —— Act. 10. 35. *He that feareth God, and worketh Righteousness is accepted of him,* —— Rom. 6. 13, 16, 18, 19, 20. *Whether of sin unto death, or of Obedience unto Righteousness.* —— 1 Cor. 15. 34. *Awake to Righteousness and sin not.* —— Eph. 5. 9. *The fruit of the Spirit is in all Goodness, and Righteousness.* —— Dan. 12. 3. *They shall turn many to Righteousness.* ——Dan. 4. 27. *Break off thy sins by Righteousness.* —— Eph. 4. 24. *The new-man which after God is created in Righteousness.* —— Gen. 7. 1. *Thee have I seen Righteous before me.* —— Gen. 18. 23, 24, 25, 26. *Far be it from thee, to destroy the Righteous with the Wicked.* —— Prov. 24. 24. *He*

[2 For their sole Righteousness.]

that

that saith to the Wicked thou art Righteous, him shall the people Curse, Nations shall abhor him. —— Isa. 3. 10. *Say to the Righteous, it shall be well with him,* Isa. 5. 23. *That take away the Righteousness from the Righteous.* —— Mat. 25. 37, 46. *Then shall the Righteous answer.* —— *The Righteous into life eternal.* —— Luk. 1. 6. *They were both Righteous before God.* —— Heb. 11. 4, 7. *By Faith Abel offered to God a more excellent Sacrifice than Cain, by which he obtained witness that he was righteous, God testifying of his Gifts. By Faith Noah being warned of God of things not seen as yet, moved with fear, prepared an Ark,* —— *by which he became heir of the Righteousness by Faith,* 1 Pet. 4. 18. *If the Righteous be scarcely saved.* —— Math. 10. 41. *He that receiveth a Righteous man in the name of a Righteous man, shall have a Righteous mans reward.* —— 1 Tim. 1. 9. *The Law is not made for a Righteous man, but for*—— Many score of texts more mention a Righteousness distinct from that of Christ imputed to us.

Judg now, Whether he that believeth God should believe that he Imputeth Christs Obedience and Suffering to us, [for our *Sole Righteousness*.]

That which is not our *sole Righteousness*, is not so Reputed by God nor Imputed: But Christs Obedience and Suffering is not our *sole Righteousness*. —— See *Davenant's* many arguments to prove that we have an Inherent Righteousness.

Obj. *But, they mean,* [*our Sole Righteousness by which we are Justified.*]

Answ. 1. We can tell no mans meaning but by his words, especially not contrary to them, especially in an accurate Declaration of Faith. 2. Suppose it had been so said, we maintain on the contrary, 1. That

That we are Juſtified by more ſorts of Righteouſneſs than one, in ſeveral reſpects. We are juſtified *only by Chriſts Righteouſneſs* as the Purchaſing and Meritorious Cauſe of our Juſtification freely given by that new Covenant. We are Juſtified by the Righteouſneſs of God the Father, as performing his Covenant with Chriſt and us, (efficiently). We are juſtified efficiently by the Righteouſneſs of Chriſt as our Judg, paſſing a juſt ſentence according to his Covenant: Theſe laſt are neither *Ours* nor Imputed to us: But we are juſtified alſo againſt the Accuſation, of being finally Impenitent Unbelievers or unholy, by the perſonal particular Righteouſneſs of our own Repentance, *Faith and Holineſs*.

For 2. We ſay, that there is an univerſal Juſtification or Righteouſneſs, and there is a particular one. And this *particular* one may be the *Condition* and *Evidence* of our Title to all the reſt. And this is our caſe. The Day of Judgment is not to try and *Judg Chriſt*, or *his Merits, but us :* He will judg us himſelf by his new Law or Covenant, the ſum of which is, [*Except ye Repent, ye ſhall all periſh: and, He that believeth, ſhall be ſaved : and he that believeth not, ſhall be condemned.* If we be not accuſed of *Impenitence* or *Unbelief*, but only of *not-fulfilling the Law of Innocency*, that will ſuppoſe that we are to be *tryed* only by *that Law*, which is not true: And then we *refer the Accuſer only to Chriſt's Righteouſneſs*, and to the *Pardoning Law of Grace*, and to nothing in our ſelves to anſwer that charge ; And ſo it would be *Chriſt's part* only that would be judged. But *Matth.* 25. and all the Scripture aſſureth us of the contrary, that it's *Our part that it is to be tryed* and *judged*, and that we

ſhall

shall be all judged according to what we have done. And no man is in danger there of any other accusation, but that he did not truly *Repent* and *Believe*, and live *a holy life to Christ*: And shall the *Penitent Believer* say, *I did never Repent and Believe, but Christ did it for me*; and so use *two Lyes*, one of Christ, and another of himself, that he may be justified? Or shall the *Unholy, Impenitent Infidel* say, It's true I was never a *Penitent Believer, or holy*, but Christ was for me, or Christs Righteousness is my sole Righteousness? that is a fashood; For Christs Righteousness is none of his. So that there is a *particular personal Righteousness*, consisting in *Faith and Repentance*, which by way of *Condition* and *Evidence* of our title to Christ and his Gift of Pardon and Life, is of absolute necessity in our Justification. Therefore Imputed Righteousness is not the *sole Righteousness* which must justifie us.

I cited abundance of plain Texts to this purpose in my Confession, pag. 57. &c. Of which book I add, that when it was in the press, I procured those three persons whom I most highly valued for judgment, Mr. *Gataker*, (whose last work it was in this World) Mr. *Vines*, and lastly Arch-Bishop *Usher* to read it over, except the Epistles (Mr. *Gataker* read only to *pag.* 163.) and no one of them advised me to alter one word, nor signified their dissent to any word of it. But I have been long on this: to proceed in the History. ——

The same year that I wrote that book, that most Judicious excellent man *Joshua Placæus* of *Saumours* in *France*, was exercised in a Controversie conjunct with this; How far *Adams* sin is imputed to us. And to speak truth, at first in the *Theses Salmurienf.*

Vol.

Vol. 1. he seemed plainly to dispute against the Imputation of *Adam's* actual sin, and his arguments I elsewhere answer.) And *Andr. Rivet* wrote a Collection of the Judgment of all sorts of Divines for the contrary. But after he vindicated himself, & shewed that his Doctrine was, that *Adam's fact* is not *immediately* imputed to each of us, as if our *persons* as *persons* had been all fully represented in *Adam's* person (by an arbitrary Law or Will of God) or reputed so to be: But that our Persons being *Virtually* or *Seminally* in *him*, we derive from him first our *Persons*, and in them a corrupted nature; and that nature corrupted and justly deserted by the Spirit of God, because it is derived from *Adam* that so sinned: And so that *Adams* fact is imputed to us mediately, *mediante natura & Corruptione*, but not primarily and immediately.

This doctrine of the Good and Judicious man was thought too new to escape sharp censures, so that a rumour was spread abroad that he denied all Imputation of *Adams* fact, and placed original guilt only in the Guilt of Coruption, for which indeed he gave occasion. A Synod being called at *Charenton*, this opinion without naming any Author was condemned; & all Ministers required to subscribe it: *Amyraldus* being of *Placeus* mind, in a speech of two hours vindicated his opinion. *Placeus* knowing that the Decree did not touch him, took no notice of it. But *Gerissolius* of *Montauban* wrote against him, pretending him condemned by the Decree, which *Drelincourt* one that drew it up, denied, professing himself of *Placeus* his judgment. And *Rivet* also, *Maresius*, *Carol. Daubuz* and others, misunderstanding him wrote against him.

For my part I confess that I am not satisfied in his distinction of *Mediate* and *Immediate Imputation:* I see not, but our *Persons* as derived from *Adam*, being supposed to be in Being, we are at once Reputed to be such as Virtually sinned in him, and such as are deprived of God's Image. And if either must be put first, me-thinks it should rather be the former, we being therefore deprived of God's Immage (not by God, but by *Adam*) because he sinned it away from himself. It satisfieth me much more, to distinguish of our *Being* and so *sinning* in *Adam Personally* and *Seminally,* or *Virtually*: we were not *Persons* in *Adam* when he sinned; therefore we did not so sin in him: And it is a fiction added to God's Word, to say that God (because he would do it) reputed us to be what we were not. But we were Seminally in *Adam* as in *Causâ naturali*, who was to produce us out of his very essence: And therefore that kind of being which we had in him, could not be innocent when he was guilty: And when we had our *Natures* and *Persons* from him, we are justly reputed to be as we are, the off-spring of one that actually sinned: And so when our *Existence* and *Personality* maketh us capable Subjects, we are guilty *Persons* of his sin; though not with so *plenary a sort of Guilt as he.*

And I fear not to say, that as I lay the ground of this Imputation in Nature it self, so I doubt not but I have elsewhere proved that there is more participation of all Children in the guilt of their parents sins by nature, than is sufficiently acknowledged or lamented by most, though Scripture abound with the proof of it: And that the overlooking it, and laying all upon God's arbitrary Covenant

venant and Imputation, is the great temptation to *Pelagians* to deny Original sin: And that our misery no more increaseth by it, is, because we are now under a Covenant that doth not so charge all culpability on mankind, as the Law of Innocency did alone. And there is something of Pardon in the Case. And the *English Litany*, (after *Ezra*, *Daniel* and others) well prayeth, Remember not, Lord, our offences, nor the offences of our Forefathers, &c.

This same *Placeus* in *Thes: Salmurienf. Vol.* 1. hath opened the doctrine of Justification so fully, that I think that one Disputation might spare some the reading of many contentious Volumes.

The rigid assertors of Imputation proved such a stumbling-block to many, that they run into the other extreme, and not only denyed it, but vehemently loaded it with the Charges of over-throwing all Godliness and Obedience. Of these *Parker* (as is said) with some others wrote against it in an answer to the Assemblies Confession: Dr. *Gell* often reproacheth it in a large Book in *Folio*. And lastly and most sharply and confidently *Herbert Thorndike*, (to mention no more.)

The History of this Controversie of Imputation, I conclude, though disorderly, with the sense of all the Christian Churches, in the Creeds and Harmony of Confessions, because they were too long to be fitly inserted by the way.

The Consent of Christians, and specially Protestants, about the Imputation of Christs Righteousness in Justification; How far and in what sence it is Imputed.

I. SEeing *Baptism* is our visible initiation into Christianity, we must there begin; and see what of this is there contained. Mat. 28. 19. *Baptizing them into the name of the Father, the Son, and the Holy Ghost,* Mar. 16. 16. *He that believeth, and is baptized, shall be saved,* Act 2. 38. *Repent, and be Baptized every one of you in the name of Jesus Christ for the Remission of sins, and ye shall receive the gift of the Holy Ghost.* See Acts 8. 36, 37, 38. The Eunuch's Faith and Baptism. Act. 22. 16. *Arise, and be baptized, and wash away thy sins, having called on the name of the Lord.* Rom. 6. 3. *So many as were baptized into Jesus Christ, were baptized into his death.* Gal. 3. 27. *As many as have been baptized into Christ, have put on Christ.* 1. Pet. 3. 21. *The like whereunto, Baptism doth also now save us, (not the putting away the filth of the flesh, but the answer of a good Conscience towards God) by the Resurrection of Jesus Christ.* Rom. 4. 24, 25. *But for us also to whom it shall be imputed, if we believe on him that raised up Jesus our Lord from the dead: who was delivered for our offences, and was raised again for our Justification.* [Quær. *How far Christ's Resurrection is imputed to us.*]

II. The Creed, called the Apostles, hath but [*I believe —— the forgiveness of sins.*]

III. The Nicene and Constantinopolitane Creed,

I acknowledg one Baptism for the Remission of sins; (Chrift's Death, Burial, and Refurrection premifed.)

IV. Athanafius's Creed [*Who suffered for our Salvation, defcended into Hell, rofe again the third day.* —— *At whofe coming all men shall rife again with their bodies, and shall give account for their own works; and they that have done good, shall go into everlafting life, and they that have done evil into everlafting Fire.*] (*Remission* is contained in *Salvation*.)

V. The Fathers fence I know not where the Reader can fo eafily and furely gather, without reading them all, as in *Laurentius* his Collection *de Juftif.* after the *Corpus Confessionum*; and that to the beft advantage of the Proteftant Caufe. They that will fee their fence of fo much as they accounted neceffary to Salvation, may beft find it in their Treatifes of Baptifm, and Catechizings of the Catechumens; Though they fay lefs about our Controverfie than I could wifh they had. I will have no other Religion than they had. The Creed of *Damafus* in *Hieron. op. Tom.* 2. hath but (*In his Death and Blood we believe that we are cleanfed* —— *and have hope that we shall obtain the reward of good merit*, (meaning our own); which the *Helvetians* own in the end of their Confeffion.

VI. The Auguftane Confeffion, Art. 3, 4. *Chrift died* —— *that he might reconcile the Father to us, and be a facrifice, not only for original fin, but alfo for all the actual fins of men.* —— *And that we may obtain thefe benefits of Chrift, that is, Remission of fins, juftification and life eternal, Chrift gave us the Gofpel in which thefe benefits are propounded.* —— *To preach Repen-*

Repentance in his Name, and Remiſſion of ſins among all Nations. For when men propagated in the natural manner have ſin, and cannot truly ſatisfie Gods Law, the Goſpel reproveth ſin, and ſheweth us Chriſt the Mediator, and ſo teacheth us about Pardon of ſins ——*That freely for Chriſt's ſake are given us, Remiſſion of ſins, & Juſtification by Faith,* by which we muſt confeſs that theſe are given us for Chriſt, who was made a Sacrifice for us, and appeaſed the Father. Though the Goſpel require Penitence; yet that pardon of ſin may be ſure, it teacheth us that it is freely given us; that is, that it dependeth not on the Condition of our worthyneſs, nor is given for any precedent works, or worthyneſs of following works. —— For Conſcience in true fears findeth no work which it can oppoſe to the Wrath of God; and Chriſt is propoſed and given us, to be a propitiator. This honour of Chriſt muſt not be transferred to our works. Therefore Paul ſaith, ye are ſaved freely, (or of Grace,) And it is of grace, that the promiſe might be ſure; that is, Pardon will be ſure; when we know that it dependeth not on the Condition of our worthineſs, but is given for Chriſt. —— In the Creed this Article [*I believe the Forgiveneſs of ſins,*] is added to the hiſtory: And the reſt of the hiſtory of Chriſt muſt be referred to this Article: For this benefit is the end of the hiſtory, Chriſt therefore ſuffered and roſe again, that for him might be given us Remiſſion of ſins, and life everlaſting.

Art. 6. *When we are Reconciled by Faith, there muſt needs follow the Righteouſneſs of good works.* —— But becauſe the infirmity of mans nature is ſo great, that no man can ſatisfie the Law, it is neceſſary to teach men, not only that they muſt obey the Law, but alſo how this Obedience pleaſeth, leſt Conſciences fall into

into desperation, *when they understand that they satisfie not the Law. This Obedience then pleaseth, not because it satisfieth the Law, but because the person is in Christ, reconciled by Faith, and believeth that the relicts of his Sin are pardoned. We must ever hold that we obtain remission of sins, and the person is pronounced Righteous, that is, is accepted freely for Christ, by Faith: And afterward that Obedience to the Law pleaseth, and is reputed a certain Righteousness, and meriteth rewards.*] Thus the first Protestants.

VII. The 11th Article of the Church of England (to which we all offer to subscribe) is [*Of the Justification of Man. We are accounted Righteous before God, only for the Merit of our Lord and Saviour Jesus Christ by Faith; and not for our own works or deservings. Wherefore that we are justified by Faith only, is a most wholsome doctrine, and very full of Comfort, as more largely is expressed in the Homily of Justification.*]

The said Homilies (of Salvation and Faith) say over and over the same thing. As pag. 14. [*Three things go together in our Justification: On Gods part his great Mercy and Grace, on Christs part, Justice, that is, the Satisfaction of Gods Justice, or the Price of our Redemption, by the offering of his body, and shedding of his blood, with fulfilling of the Law perfectly and throughly; And on our part true and lively Faith in the Merits of Jesus Christ: which yet is not ours, but by Gods working in us.*

And pag. [*A lively Faith is not only the common belief of the Articles of our Faith, but also a true trust and confidence of the mercy of God through our Lord Jesus Christ, and a steadfast hope of all good things to be received at Gods hand; and that although we through*

infirmity

infirmity or temptation —— do fall from him by sin, yet if we return again to him by true repentance, that he will forgive and forget our offences, for his Sons sake our Saviour Jesus Christ, and will make us inheritors with him of his everlasting Kingdom —— Pag. 23. *For the very sure and lively* Christian Faith, *is, to have an earnest trust and confidence in God, that he doth regard us, and is careful over us, as the Father is over the Child whom he doth love; and that he will be merciful unto us, for his only Sons sake; and that we have our Saviour Christ our perpetual Advocate and Prince, in whose only merits, oblation and suffering, we do trust that our offences be continually washed and purged, whensoever we repenting truely do return to him with our whole heart, steadfastly determining with our selves, through his grace to obey and serve him, in keeping his Commandments, &c.]* So also the Apology. This is our doctrine of Imputation.

VIII. The Saxon Confession oft insisteth on the *free Pardon of sin, not merited by us, but by Christ.* And expoundeth *Justification* to be [*Of unjust, that is, Guilty and disobedient, and not having Christ: to be made Just, that is, To be Absolved from Guilt for the Son of God, and an apprehender by Faith of Christ himself, who is our Righteousness;* (as *Jeremiah* and *Paul* say) *because by his Merit we have forgiveness, and God imputeth righteousness to us, and for him, reputeth us just, and by giving us his Spirit quickeneth and regenerateth us.* —— *By being Justified by Faith alone we mean, that freely for our Mediator alone, not for our Contrition, or other Merits, the pardon of sin and reconciliation is given us.* —— *And before, It is certain, when the mind is raised by this Faith, that the pardon of sin, Reconciliation and Imputation of Righteousness*

ousness, are given for the Merit of Christ himself ──
And after [*By Faith is meant Affiance, resting in the Son of God the Propitiator, for whom we are received and please* (God) *and not for our virtues and fulfilling of the Law.*

IX. The Wittenberge Confession, (In Corp. Conf. pag. 104.) *A man is made Accepted of God, and Reputed just before him, for the Son of God our Lord Jesus Christ alone, by Faith. And at the Judgment of God we must not trust to the Merit of any of the Virtues which we have, but to the sole Merit of our Lord Jesus Christ, which is made ours by Faith. And because at the bar of God, where the case of true eternal Righteousness and Salvation will be pleaded, there is no place for mans Merits, but only for God's Mercy, and the Merits of our Lord Jesus Christ, whom we receive by Faith: therefore we think our Ancestors said rightly, that we are justified before God by Faith only.*

X. The Bohemian Confession, making Justification the principal Article, goeth the same way. [Pag. 183, 184. *By Christ men are Justified, obtain Salvation and Remission of sin, freely by Faith in Christ, through mercy, without any Work and Merit of man. And his death and blood alone is sufficient, to abolish & expiate all the sins of all men. All must come to Christ for pardon and Remission of Sin, Salvation and every thing. All our trust and hope is to be fastened on him alone. Through him only and his merits God is appeas'd and propitious; Loveth us, and giveth us Life eternal.*

XI. The Palatinate Confession ib. pag. 149. [*I believe that God the Father for the most full Satisfaction of Christ, doth never remember any of my sins, and that pravity which I must strive against while I live, but contrarily will rather of grace give me the righteous-*
ness

ness of *Christ*, *so that I have no need to fear the judgment of God.* —— And pag. 155. *If he merited, and obtained Remission of all our sins, by the only and bitter passion, and death of the Cross, so be it we embracing it by true Faith, as the satisfaction for our sins, apply it to our selves.* ——] I find no more of this.

XII. The Polonian Churches of Lutherans and Bohemians agreed in the Augustane and Bohemian Confession before recited.

XIII. The Helvetian Confession, [*To Justifie signifieth to the Apostle in the dispute of Justification, To Remit sins, to Absolve from the fault and punishment, to Receive into favour, and to Pronounce just.* —— *For Christ took on himself, and took away the sins of the World, and satisfied Gods Justice. God therefore for the sake of Christ alone, suffering and raised again, is propitious to our sins, and imputeth them not to us, but imputeth the righteousness of Christ for ours; so that now we are not only cleansed and purged from sins, or Holy, but also endowed with the Righteousness of Christ, and so absolved from sins, Death and Condemnation, and are righteous and heirs of life eternal. Speaking properly, God only justifieth us, and justifieth only for Christ, not imputing to us sins, but imputing to us his Righteousness.*] This Confession speaketh in terms neerest the opposed opinion: But indeed faith no more than we all say; Christs Righteousness being given and imputed to us as the *Meritorious Cause of our pardon and right to life.*

XIV. The Basil Confession, Art. 9. [*We confess Remission of sins by Faith in Jesus Christ crucified. And though this Faith work continually by Love, yet Righteousness and Satisfaction for our Sins, we do not attribute to works, which are fruits of Faith; but only ly to true affiance & faith in the blood shed of the Lamb of God. We ingenuously profess, that in Christ, who is our Righteousness, Holiness, Redemption, Way, Truth, Wisdom, Life, all things are freely given us.* The works therefore of the faithful are done, not that they may satisfie for their sins, but only that by them, they may declare that they are thankful to God for so great benefits given us in Christ.

XV. The Argentine Confession of the four Cities, Cap. 3. ib. pag. 179. hath but this hereof: *When heretofore they delivered, that a mans own proper Works are required to his Justification, we teach that this is to be acknowledged wholly received of God's benevolence and Christ's Merit, and perceived only by Faith.* C. 4. *We are sure that no man can be made Righteous or saved, unless he love God above all, and most studiously imitate him. We can no otherwise be Justified, that is, become both Righteous and Saved (for our Righteousness is our very Salvation) than if we being first indued with Faith, by which believing the Gospel, and perswaded that God hath adopted us as Sons, and will for ever give us his fatherly benevolence, we wholly depend on his beck (or will.)*

XVI. The Synod of Dort, mentioneth only Chrifts death for the pardon of sin and Justification. The Belgick Confession § 22. having mentioned Christ and his merits made ours, § 23. addeth, [*We believe that our blessedness consisteth in Remission of our sins for Jesus Christ; and that our Righteousness before God is therein contained, as* David *and* Paul *teach; We are justified freely, or by Grace, through the Redemption that is in Christ Jesus. We hold this Foundation firm, and give all the Glory to God—presuming nothing of our selves, and our merits,*

but

but we rest on the sole Obedience of a Crucified Christ; which is ours when we believe in him.] Here you see in what sence they hold that Christs merits are ours; Not to justifie us by the Law, that saith, (*Obey perfectly and Live*) but as the merit of our *pardon,* which they here take for their whole Righteousness.

XVII. The Scottish Confession, Corp. Conf. pag. 125. hath but [that true Believers *receive in this life Remission of Sins, and that by Faith alone in Christs blood : So that though sin remain —— yet it is not Imputed to us, but is remitted, and covered by Christs Righteousness.*] This is plain and past all question.

XVIII. The French Confession is more plain, § 18. ib. pag. 81. [*We believe that our whole Righteousness lyeth in the pardon of our sins; which is also as David witnesseth our only blessedness. Therefore all other reasons by which men think to be justified before God, we plainly reject; and all opinion of Merit being cast away; we rest only in the Obedience of Christ, which is Imputed to us, both that all our sins may be covered, and that we may get Grace before God.*] So that Imputation of Obedience, they think is but for *pardon of sin, and acceptance.*

Concerning Protestants Judgment of Imputation, it is further to be noted; 1. That they are not agreed whether Imputation of Christ's perfect Holiness and Obedience, be before or after the Imputation of his Passion in order of nature. Some think that our sins are first in order of nature done away by the Imputation of his sufferings, that we may be free from punishment; and next, that his *perfection* is Imputed to us, to merit the Reward of life eternal : But the most learned Confuters of the Papists

pists hold, that Imputation of Christs *Obedience* and *Suffering* together, are in order of nature before our Remission of sin and Acceptance, as the meritorious cause: And these can mean it in no other sence than that which I maintain. So doth *Davenant* de Just.hab. et act.& Pet.Molinæus Thes.Sedan.Vol.1. pag. 625. *Imputatio justitiæ Christi propter quam peccata remittuntur, & censemur justi coram Deo.* Maresius Thes. Sedan. Vol. 2. pag. 770, 771. § 6 & 10. *maketh the material cause of our Justification to be the Merits and Satisfaction of Christ, yea the Merit of his Satisfaction, and so maketh the formal Cause of Justification to be the Imputation of Christs Righteousness, or which is the same, the solemn Remission of all sins, and our free Acceptance with God.* Note that he maketh *Imputation* to be the same thing with *Remission and Acceptance*; which is more than the former said.

2. Note, that when they say that Imputation is the *Form* of Justification, they mean not of Justification Passively as it is ours, but Actively as it is *Gods Justifying act*; so *Maresius ibidem.* And many deny it to be the form: And many think that saying improper.

3. Note, that it is ordinarily agreed by Protestants, that Christs Righteousness is imputed to us in the same sence as our sins are said to be imputed to him; (even before they are committed many Ages;) which cleareth fully the whole Controversie to those that are but willing to understand, and blaspheme not Christ; so *Maresius ubi supra: Quemadmodum propter deliquia nostra ei imputata punitus fuit Christus in terris; ita & propter ejus Justitiam nobis imputatam coronamur in Cælis.* And *Joh. Crocius*

Crocius Disput. 10. p. 502. And *Vasseur* in his solid Disp. *Thes. Sedan. Vol.* 2. pag. 1053, 1054. While he mentioneth only *Satisfaction* for our Justification, yet § 27. saith that *Satisfaction* is *imputed to us*, and placeth Chrifts Imputed Righteousness in his Obedience *to the* death; and saith that this *satisfying Obedience, in suffering*, is our Imputed Righteousness. *Ea igitur Obedientia Christi qua Patri paruit usque ad mortem crucis, qua coram Patre comparuit ut voluntatem ejus perficeret, qua a Patre missus, ut nos sui sanguinis effusione redimeret, justitiæ ejus pro peccatis nostris abunde satisfecit; ea inquam obedientia ex gratia Patris imputata & donata, illa justitia est qua justificamur.* And they ordinarily use the similitude of the Redemption of a Captive, and Imputing the Price to him. He addeth (*Hence we may gather that as Chrift was made sin, so we are made the Righteousness of God, that is by Imputation*] which is true.

The plain truth in all this is within the reach of every sound Chriftian, and self-conceited wranglers make difficulties where there are none. Yea, how far the Papifts themselves grant the Proteftant doctrine of Imputation, let the following words of *Vasseur* on *Bellarmine* be judg. [*Bellarm. ait; Si solum vellent hæretici nobis imputari Merita Chrifti, quia nobis donata sunt, & possumus ea Deo Patri offerre pro peccatis nostris, quoniam Chriftus suscepit super se onus satisfaciendi pro nobis, nosque Deo Patri reconciliandi, recta esset eorum Sententia :* I doubt some will say, it is false, becaufe *Bellarmine* granteth it; but *Vasseur* addeth [*Hæc ille: sed an nostra longe abest ab illâ, quam in nobis requireret sententia.*] And I wish the Reader that loveth Truth and Peace

to

to read the words of *Pighius, Caſſander, Bellarmine*, &c. ſaying as the Proteſtants, cited by *Joh. Crocius de Juſtificat. Diſput. 9. pag. 458. &c.* And of *Morton Apolog* eſpecially *Tho. Waldenſis*.

Nazianzen's ſentence prefixed by the great *Baſil*-Doctors to their Confeſſion, I do affectionately recite, [*Sacred Theologie and Religion is a ſimple and naked thing; conſiſting of Divine Teſtimonies, without any great artifice: which yet ſome do naughtily turn into a moſt difficult Art*.

The Hiſtory of the *Socinians* oppoſing Chriſts *Satisfaction* and *Merits* I overpaſs, as being handled by multitudes of Writers.

If any impartial man would not be troubled with needleſs tedious writings, and yet would ſee the Truth clearly, about Juſtification and Imputation, in a very little room, let him read, 1. Mr. *Bradſhaw*, 2. Mr. *Gibbon's* Sermon in the Exerciſes at *Giles*'s in the Fields. 3. Mr. *Truman's* great Propitiation. 4. *Joſhua Placeus*, his *Diſput. de Juſtif.* in *Theſ. Salmur. Vol.* 1. 5. And *Le Blank's* late *Theſes*; Which will ſatisfie thoſe that have any juſt capacity for ſatisfaction. And if he add *Wotton de Reconciliatione*, and *Grotius de Satisfactione*, he need not loſe his labour: no nor by reading *John Goodwin* of Juſtification, though every word be not approveable. And Dr. *Stillingfleet's* Sermons of Satisfaction, coming laſt, will alſo conduce much to his juſt information.

So much of the Hiſtorical part.

CHAP.

CHAP. II.

Of the true stating of the Controversie, and the explication of the several points contained or meerly implyed in it.

I take explication to be here more useful than argumentation: And therefore I shall yet fullier open to you the state of our differences, and my own judgment in the point, with the reasons of it, in such necessary Distinctions, and brief Propositions, as shall carry their own convincing light with them. If any think I distinguish too much, let him prove any to be needless *or* unjust, *and then reject it and spare not. If any think I distinguish not accurately enough, let him add what is wanting, and but suppose that I have elsewhere done it, and am not now handling the whole doctrine of Justification, but only that of Imputation, and what it necessarily includeth.*

Though a man that readeth our most Learned Protestants, professing that they agree even with *Bellarmine* himself in the stating of the case of Imputation, would think that there should need no further stating of it. I cited you *Bellarmine's* words

words before with *Vasseurs* consent : I here add Johan. Crocius de Justif. Disp. 16. pag. 500. 501. *Vide hominis sive vertiginem sive improbitatem, clamat fieri non posse ut Justitia Christi nobis imputetur eo sensu qui hæreticis probetur* —— *Et tamen rectam vocat sententiam, quam suam faciunt Evangelici. Quod enim cum recta ratione pugnare dicit, nos per Justitiam Christi formaliter justos nominari & esse, nos non tangit : Non dicimus ; Non sentimus : Sed hoc totum proficiscitur e Sophistarum officinâ, qui phrasin istam nobis affingunt, ut postea eam exagitent tanquam nostram:* (yet some of our own give them this pretence.) *Nos sententiam quam ille rectam judicat, tenemus, tuemur ; sic tamen ut addamus, quod Genti adversariæ est intolerabile, non alia ratione nos justos censeri coram Deo.*] But by Justification the Papists mean Sanctification : And they count it not intolerable to say that the penalty of our sins is remitted to us, by that Satisfaction to the Justice of God according to the Law of Innocency, which Christ only hath made. But though many thrust in more indeed, and most of them much more in words; yet you see they are forced to say as we say whether they will or not : For they seem unwilling to be thought to agree with us, where they agree indeed.] And the following words of *Joh. Crocius pag.* 506, 507. *&c.* shew the common sence of most Protestants, [*When* Bellarmine *observeth that Imputation maketh us as righteous as Christ*, he saith, [*If we said that we are Justified by Christs essential righteousness.* —— *But we say it not. Yea above all we renounce that which the Sophister puts in of his own, even that which he saith of Formal Righteousness : For it is not our opinion, that we are constituted formally Righteous by*

E

Christ's

Christ's Righteousness, which we rather call the Material cause. —— § 32. *Christs satisfaction is made for all : But it is imputed to us, not as it is made for all, but as for us. I illustrate it by the like. The Kings Son payeth the debt of a Community deeply indebted to the King, and thence bound to perpetual slavery. This payment gets liberty for this, and that, and the other member of the Community : For it is imputed to them by the King as if they had paid it. But this Imputation transferreth not the honour to them, but brings them to partake of the Benefit. So when the price paid by Christ for all, is imputed to this or that man, he is taken into the society of the Benefit,* —— Pag. 503. *Distinguish between the Benefit, and the Office of Christ. The former is made ours, but not the latter,* —— Pag. 542. *The Remission of sin is nothing but the Imputation of Christs Righteousness.* Rom. 4. *Where Imputation of Righteousness, Remission of Iniquities, and non-imputation of sin, are all one,* —— Pag. 547. *God imputeth it as far as he pleaseth,* —— Pag. 548. *Princes oft impute the merits of Parents so unworthy Children,* —— Pag. 551. *He denyeth that we have Infinite Righteousness in Christ, because it is imputed to us in a finite manner, even so far as was requisite to our absolution.*

But I will a little more distinctly open and resolve the Case.

1. We must distinguish of *Righteousness* as it relateth to the Preceptive part of the Law; and as it relateth to the Retributive part : The first *Righteousness*, is *Innocency* contrary to *Reatus Culpæ* : The second is *Jus ad impunitatem & ad præmium (seu donum,)Right to Impunity and to the Reward.*

2. We must distinguish of *Christs Righteousness,*
which

which is either so called, *formally* and *properly*, which is the *Relation of Chrifts perfon* to his *Law of Mediation* impofed on him, 1. As *Innocent* and a perfect obeyer ; 2. As one that *deferved not punifhment, but deferved Reward.* Or it is fo called *materially* and *improperly* ; which is, Thofe *fame Habits, Acts and Sufferings* of Chrift, from which *his Relation of Righteous* did refult.

3. We muft diftinguifh of *Imputation*, which fignifyeth (here) 1. To repute us *perfonally* to have been the *Agents of Chrifts Acts*, the *fubjects* of his *Habits and Paffion* in a Phyfical fence. 2. Or to repute the fame *formal Relation* of *Righteoufnefs* which was in Chrifts perfon, to be in *ours* as the *fubject*. 3. Or to repute us to have been the very *fubjects of Chrift's Habits and Paffion*, and the Agents of his *Acts* in a *Political* or *Moral fenfe*, (and not a phyfical) ; as a man payeth a debt by his Servant, or Attorney, or Delegate. 4. And confequently to repute a *double formal Righteoufnefs* to refult from the faid *Habits, Acts,* and *Paffions*; one to *Chrift* as the *natural Subject* and *Agent*, and *another to us* as the *Moral, Political*, or *reputed Subject* and *Agent* (And fo his *Formal Righteoufnefs* not to be imputed to us *in it felf as ours*, but *another* to refult from the fame *Matter*.) 5. Or elfe that we are reputed both the *Agents* and *Subjects* of the *Matter* of his Righteoufnefs, morally, and alfo of the *Formal Righteoufnefs* of *Chrift himfelf.* 6. Or elfe by Imputation is meant here, that Chrift being truly reputed to have taken the Nature of finful man, and become a Head for all true Believers, in that undertaken *Nature* and *Office* in the *Perfon* of a *Mediator*, to have fulfilled *all the Law impofed on him*, by perfect *Holinefs* and

and *Obedience*, and *Offering* himself on the Cross a *Sacrifice for our sins*, voluntarily suffering in our stead, as if he had been a sinner, (guilty of all our sins) As soon as we believe we are pardoned, justified, adopted for *the sake and merit* of this Holiness, Obedience and penal Satisfaction of Christ, with as full demonstration of divine *Justice*, at least, and more full demonstration of his *Wisdom* and *Mercy*, than if we had suffered our selves what our sins deserved (that is, been damned) or had never sinned: And so *Righteousness is imputed to us*, that is, *we are accounted or reputed righteous*, (not in relation to the Precept, that is, *innocent*, or *sinless*, but in relation to the *Retribution*, that is, *such as have Right to Impunity and Life*,) because Christ's foresaid perfect Holiness, Obedience and Satisfaction, *merited our Pardon, and Adoption, and the Spirit*; or merited the *New-Covenant*, by which, as an Instrument, *Pardon, Justification and Adoption* are given to Believers, and the *Spirit* to be given to sanctifie them: And when we believe, we are justly *reputed* such as have *Right* to all these purchased Gifts.

4. And that it may be understood how far Christ did *Obey* or *Suffer* in our *stead*, or *person*, we must distinguish, 1. Between his taking the *Nature* of *sinful* man, and taking the Person of sinners. 2. Between his taking the *Person* of a *sinner*, and taking the *Person* of *you* and *me*, and each particular sinner. 3. Between his taking our sinful persons *simply, & ad omnia*, and taking them only, *secundum quid, in tantum, & ad hoc*. 4. Between his *suffering* in the *Person* of sinners, and his *obeying* and *sanctity in the Person* of sinners, or of us in particular. 5. Between his *Obeying* and *Suffering* in *our Person*, and

and our *Obeying* and *Suffering* in his Perſon (*Natural or Political.*) And now I ſhall make uſe of theſe diſtinctions, by the Propoſitions following.

Prop. 1. The phraſe of [*Chriſt's Righteouſneſs imputed to us*] is not in the Scripture.

2. Therefore when it cometh to Diſputation, to them that deny it, ſome Scripture-phraſe ſhould be put in ſtead of it; becauſe, 1. The Scripture hath as good, if not much better, phraſes, to ſignifie all in this that is neceſſary. 2. And it is ſuppoſed that the Diſputants are agreed of all that is expreſs in the Scripture.

3. Yet ſo much is ſaid in Scripture, as may make this phraſe [*of Imputing Chriſt's Righteouſneſs to us*] juſtifiable, in the ſound ſence here explained: For the thing meant by it is true, and the phraſe intelligible.

4. Chriſt's Righteouſneſs is imputed to Believers, in the ſixth ſence here before explained; As the Meritorious cauſe of our Pardon, Juſtification, Righteouſneſs, Adoption, Sanctification and Salvation, &c. as is opened.

5. Chriſt did not ſuffer all in kind (much leſs in duration) which ſinful man deſerved to ſuffer: As *e.g.* 1. He was not hated of God; 2. Nor deprived or deſerted of the ſanctifying Spirit, and ſo of its Graces and Gods Image; Nor had 3. any of that permitted penalty by which ſin it ſelf is a miſery and puniſhment to the ſinner. 4. He fell not under the Power of the Devil as a deceiver and ruler, as the ungodly do. 5. His Conſcience did not accuſe him of ſin, and torment him for it. 6. He did not totally deſpair of ever being ſaved. 7. The fire

fire of Hell did not torment his body. More such instances may be given for proof.

6. Christ did not perform all the same obedience in kind, which many men, yea all men, are or were bound to perform. As 1. He did not dress and keep that Garden which *Adam* was commanded to dress and keep. 2. He did not the conjugal offices which *Adam*, and millions more, were bound to. 3. Nor the Paternal Offices to Children. 4. Nor all the offices of a King on Earth, or Magistrate: nor of a Servant, &c. Nor the duty of the Sick. 5. He did not repent of sin, nor turn from it to God, nor mortifie or resist in himself any sinful lust; nor receive a Saviour by Faith, nor was circumcised or baptized for the Remission of his sins; nor loved God or thanked him for redeeming or pardoning him; nor obeyed God in the use of any Ordinance or Means, for the subduing of sin, and healing or saving of his Soul from any sin or deserved wrath of God; with much more such.

7. Christ did perform much which no man else was bound to do: As to redeem Souls, to work his Miracles and the rest of the works, peculiar to the Mediator.

8. That Law which bound us to Suffering, (or made it our due) bound not Christ to it, (as being innocent); But he was bound to it by the Fathers Law of Mediator, and by his own voluntary sponsion.

9. The Law obliging every sinner himself to suffer, was not *fulfilled* by the *Suffering* of Christ our Sponsor: But only the *Lawgiver satisfied* by attaining its Ends. For neither the letter nor sence of it said, [*If thou sin, thou or thy surety shall suffer.*]

10. Christ

10. Christ *satisfied Justice* and *obeyed* in *Humane Nature*, which also was *Holy* in him.

11. He did not this as a *Natural* Root, or Head to man, as *Adam* was; to convey *Holiness* or *Righteousness* by *natural propagation*, as *Adam* should have done; and did by sin: For Christ had no Wife or natural Children; But as a *Head, by Contract* as a Husband to a Wife, and a King to a Kingdom, and a *Head of Spiritual Influx*.

12. No as being *Actually* such a Head to the Redeemed when he *Obeyed* and *Suffered*; but as a Head by *Aptitude* and *Office*, *Power* and *Virtue*, who was to *become a Head actually* to every one when they *Believed* and *Consented*; Being before a *Head for them*, and *over those that did exist*, but not a *Head to them*, in act.

13. Therefore they were not Christs members Political, (much less Natural) when he obeyed and died.

14. A Natural Head being but a *part of a person*, what it doth the *Person doth*. But seeing a *Contracted Head*, and all the *members* of his *Body Contracted* or *Politick*, are every one a *distinct Person*, it followeth not that each person did really or reputatively what the *Head did*. Nay it is a good consequence that [*If he did it as Head, they did it not* (numerically) as *Head* or *Members*.]

15. Christ *Suffered* and *Obeyed* in the Person of the Mediator between God and man; and as a *subject* to the Law of Mediation.

16. Christ may be said to suffer *in the person of a sinner*, as it meaneth *his own person reputed and used as a sinner* by his persecutors, and as he was one who stood before God as an Undertaker to suffer for Man's sin.

17. Christ

17. Christ suffered in the *place* and *stead* of *sinners*, that they might be delivered, though in the *person* of a *Sponsor*.

18. When we are agreed that the *Person* of the *Sponsor*, and of every *particular sinner* are divers; and that Christ had not suffered, if we had not sinned, and that he as a *Sponsor suffered in our stead*, and so bore the punishment, which *not he, but we deserved*; If any will here instead of a *Mediator* or *Sponsor* call him our *Representative*, and say that he suffered *even in all our Persons reputatively*, not *simpliciter*, but *secundùm quid, & in tantum* only; that is, not representing our *Persons simply* and in all *respects*, and to *all ends*, but *only so far* as to be a *sacrifice* for *our sins*, and suffer in our *place* and *stead* what he suffered; we take this to be but *lis de nomine*, a question about the *name* and *words*: And we will not oppose any man that thinketh those words fittest, as long as we agree in the matter signified. And so many Protestant Divines say that Christ suffered in the person of every sinner, (at least Elect,) that is, so far only and to such effects.

19. Christ did not suffer strictly, simply, absolutely, in the *person* of any one elect sinner, much less in the millions of persons of them all, in Law-sence, or in Gods esteem. God did not esteem Christ to be *naturally*, or as an *absolute Representer, David, Manasseh, Paul*, and every such other sinner, but only a Mediator that suffered in their stead.

20. God did make Christ *to be sin* for us; that is, A *Sacrifice for our sin*, and one that by *Man* was reputed, and by *God and Man* was *used*, as *sinners are*, and deserve to be.

21. Christ was not our *Delegate* in *Obeying* or
Suffering;

Suffering : We did not commission him, or depute him to do what he did in our stead : But he did it by God's Appointment and his own Will.

22. Therefore he did it on God's terms, and to what effects it pleased God, and not on our terms, nor to what effects we please.

23. God did not suppose or repute Christ, to have committed all or any of the sins which we all committed, nor to have had all the wickedness in his nature which was in ours, nor to have deserved what we deserved : Nor did he in this proper sence *impute our sins* to Christ.

24. The false notion of God's strict imputing all our sins to Christ, and esteeming him the greatest sinner in the World, being so great a Blasphemy both against the Father and the Son, it is safest in such Controversies to hold to the plain and ordinary words of Scripture. And it is not the *Wisdom* nor *Impartiality* of some men, who greatly cry up the Scripture-perfection, and decry the addition of a Ceremony or Form in the Worship of God ; that yet think Religion is endangered, if our Confession use not the phrases of [*God's Imputing our sin to Christ, and his Imputing Christ's Righteousness to us*] when neither of them is in the Scripture ; As if all God's Word were not *big* or *perfect* enough to make us a Creed or Confession in such phrases as it is fit for Christians to take up with: Countenancing the Papists, whose Faith is swelled to the many Volumes of the Councils, and no man can know how much more is to be added, and when we have all.

25. God doth not repute or account us to have *suffered* in our Natural persons what Christ suffered for us, nor Christ to have suffered in our Natural persons. 26. Though

26. Though Christ *suffered in our stead*, and in a large sence, to certain uses and in *some respects*, as the *Representer*, or in the *Persons* of sinners; yet did he not so far *represent* their persons in his *Habitual Holiness and Actual Obedience* (no not in the *Obedience* of his *Suffering*,) as he did in the *suffering it self*. He obeyed not in the *Person* of a *sinner*, much less of millions of sinners; which were to say, *In the person of sinners he never sinned*. He suffered, to save us from suffering; but he *obeyed not to save us from obeying*, but to bring us to Obedience. Yet his *Perfection* of *Obedience* had this *end*, that *perfect Obedience* might not be *necessary* in us to our Justification and Salvation.

27. It was not *we our selves* who did *perfectly obey*, or were *perfectly holy*, or suffered for sin in the *Person* of *Christ*, or by *Him*: Nor did we (*Naturally* or *Morally*) *merit* our own Salvation by obeying in Christ; nor did *we satisfie Gods Justice for our sins*, nor purchase pardon of Salvation to our selves, by our *Suffering* in and *by Christ*; All such phrase and sence is contrary to Scripture. But Christ did this for us.

28. Therefore God doth not repute us to have done it, seeing it is not true.

29. It is impossible for the *individual* formal *Righteousness* of Christ, to be our *Formal personal Righteousness*. Because it is a *Relation* and *Accident*, which cannot be translated from subject to subject, and cannot be in divers subjects the same.

30. Where the question is, Whether Christs *Material Righteousness*, that is, his *Habits*, *Acts* and *Sufferings* themselves, be *Ours*, we must consider how a man can have *Propriety in Habits*, *Acts and Passions*.

Paſſions who is the *ſubject* of them : and in *Actions*, who is the *Agent* of them. To *Give the ſame Individual Habit or Paſſion* to another, *is an Impoſſibility*; that is, to make him by Gift the ſubject of it. For it is not the ſame, if it be in another ſubject. To *make* one *man really* or *phyſically* to have been the *Agent* of *anothers Act*, even that *Individual Act*, if he was not ſo, is a contradiction and impoſſibility; that is, to make it true, that I did that which I did not. To be ours by *Divine Imputation*, cannot be, *to be ours by a falſe Reputation*, or ſuppoſition that we did what we did not : For God cannot err or lie. There is therefore but one of theſe two ways left, Either *that we our ſelves in perſon, truly had the habits which Chriſt had, and did all that Chriſt did, and ſuffered all that he ſuffered, and ſo ſatisfied and merited Life in and by him, as by an Inſtrument, or Legal Repreſenter of our perſons in all this* ; Which I am anon to Confute : or elſe, That *Chriſts Satisfaction,* Righteouſneſs, and the *Habits*, *Acts* and *Sufferings* in which it lay, are imputed to us, and made ours ; not rigidly in the very thing it ſelf, but in the *Effects* and *Benefits* ; In as much as we are as really *Pardoned, Juſtified, Adopted* by them, as the Meritorious cauſe, by the inſtrumentality of the Covenants Donation, as if we our ſelves had done and ſuffered all that Chriſt did, as a Mediator and Sponſor, do and ſuffer for us : I ſay, As *really* and *certainly,* and with a fuller demonſtration of Gods Mercy and Wiſdom, and with a ſufficient demonſtration of his Juſtice. But not that our propriety in the benefits is in all reſpects the ſame, as it ſhould have been if we had *been, done, and ſuffered our ſelves* what Chriſt did. Thus Chriſts Righteouſneſs is ours.

31. Chriſt

31. Christ is truly *The Lord our Righteousness*; in more respects than one or two: 1. In that he is the *meritorious Cause* of the *Pardon of all our sins*, and our full Justification, Adoption, and right to Glory: and by his Satisfaction and Merits only, our Justification by the Covenant of Grace against the Curse of the Law of Works is purchased. 2. In that he is the Legislator, Testator and Donor of our Pardon, and Justification by this new-Testament or Covenant. 3. In that he is the Head of Influx, and King and Intercessor, by and from whom the *Spirit* is given, to sanctifie us to God, and cause us sincerely to perform the Conditions of the Justifying and saving Covenant, in Accepting and Improving the mercy then given. 4. In that he is the Righteous Judge and Justifyer of Believers by sentence of Judgment. In all these Respects he is *The Lord our Righteousness*.

32. We are said *to be made the Righteousness of God in him*: 1. In that, as he was *used like a sinner* for us, (but not esteemed one by God) so we are used *like Innocent persons* so far as to be *saved* by him. 2. In that through his *Merits*, and upon our *union with him*, when we believe and consent to his Covenant, we are *pardoned* and *justified*, and so made *Righteous* really, that is, such as are not to be *condemned* but to be glorified. 3. In that the *Divine Nature* and *Inherent Righteousness*, to them that are *in him by Faith*, are for his Merits, given by the Holy Ghost. 4. In that God's Justice and Holiness Truth, Wisdom, and Mercy, are all wonderfully demonstrated in this way of pardoning and justifying sinners by Christ. Thus are we made the Righteousness of God in him.

33. For

33. For *Righteousness to be imputed to us*, is all one as to be accounted *Righteous*, Rom. 4. 6, 11. notwithstanding that we be not Righteous as fulfillers of the Law of Innocency.

34. For *Faith to be imputed to us for Righteousness*, Rom. 4. 22, 23, 24. is plainly meant, that God who under the Law of Innocency required perfect Obedience, of us to our Justification and Glorification, upon the *satisfaction* and *merits* of Christ, hath freely given a full *Pardon* and *Right* to *Life*, to all true Believers; so that now by the Covenant of Grace nothing is required *of us*, to our Justification, but *Faith*: all the rest being done by Christ: And so Faith in God the Father, Son and Holy Ghost, is reputed truly to be the condition on our part, on which Christ and Life, by that Baptismal Covenant, are made ours.

35. Justification, Adoption, and Life eternal are considered; 1. *Quoad ipsam rem*, as to the thing it self in value. 2. *Quoad, Ordinem Conferendi & Recipiendi*, as to the *order* and *manner* of *Conveyance* and *Participation*. In the first respect, *It is a meer free-gift to us, purchased by Christ*: In the second respect, It is a *Reward* to Believers, who thankfully accept the free-Gift according to its nature and uses.

36. It is an error contrary to the scope of the Gospel to say, that *the Law of Works, or of Innocency*, doth justifie us, as performed either by our selves, or by Christ. For that Law condemneth and curseth us; And we are not efficiently justified by it, but *from or against it*.

37. Therefore we have no Righteousness in *Reality* or *Reputation formally ours*, which consisteth

in the first *species*; that is, in a *Conformity to the Preceptive part of the Law of Innocency*; we are not *reputed Innocent*: But only a Righteousness which consisteth in *Pardon of all sin, and right to life,* (with *sincere performance of the Condition of the Covenant of Grace,* that is, *True Faith.*)

38. Our pardon puts not away our *Guilt of Fact* or *Fault,* but our *Guilt of, or, obligation to Punishment.* God doth not repute us such as never sinned, or such as by our Innocency merited Heaven, but such as are not to be *damned,* but to be *glorified,* because *pardoned* and *adopted* through the Satisfaction and Merits of Christ.

39. Yet the *Reatus Culpæ* is remitted to us Relatively as to the punishment, though not in it self; that is, It shall not procure our Damnation: Even as Christ's Righteousness is, though not in it self, yet respectively as to the Benefits said to be *made ours,* in as much as we shall have those benefits by it.

40. Thus both the *Material* and the *Formal Righteousness* of *Christ are made ours*; that is, Both the *Holy Habits* and *Acts,* and his *Sufferings, with the Relative formal Righteousness of his own Person,* because these are altogether one Meritorious cause of our Justification, commonly called the Material Cause.

Obj. *But though Forma Denominat; yet if Christs Righteousness in Matter and Form, be the Meritorious Cause of ours, and that be the same with the Material Cause,* it is a *very tolerable speech to say, that His Righteousness is Ours in it self, while it is the very matter of ours.*

*Ans.*1. When any man is *Righteous Immediately by*
any

t action is called *the Matter* of his
in such an Analogical sense as Action,
ιy be called *Matter*, because the *Re-
eous* is founded or subjected first or
Action. And so when Christ perfectas the *Matter of his Righteousness*. But
s and to *Merit* are not all one notion:
itious to meer Righteousness. Now
Actions in themselves that our Righ-
teth from iinmediately as his own
e is first his *Action*, then his *formal*
ereby; and *thirdly*, *his Merit* by that
hich goes to procure the *Covenant-*
ghteousness to us, by which Cove-
ciently made Righteous. So that the
rial Cause is much more properly gi-
Actions, as to his *own formal Righte-*
to *ours*. But yet this is but *de nomine*.
:onsider what that *Righteousness* is
erited for us, (which is the heart of
iie.) It is not of the same *species* or
ωn. His Righteousness was a per-
ocency, and *Conformity* to the *precep-*
Law of Innocency in Holiness. Ours
: dissenters think it is such by *Imputa-*
is the difference. Ours is but in re-
nd or *retributive part* of the *Law*; a
ity *and Life, and a Justification* not at
, *but from its curse or condemnation*.
saith, *Obey perfectly and live*, sin
not justifie us as persons that have
d it, really or imputatively; But its
ishment is dissolved, not by it self,
of *Grace*. It is then by the Law
of

of Grace that we are judged and juſtified. According to it, 1. We are not *really* or *reputatively ſuch* as have *perfectly fulfilled* all *its Precepts :* 2. But we are ſuch as by Grace do *ſincerely perform* the *Condition* of its promiſe. 3. By which promiſe of Gift, we are ſuch as have right to Chriſts own *perſon,* in the Relation and Union of a Head and Saviour, and with him the pardon of all our ſins, and the *right of Adoption to the Spirit, and the Heavenly Inheritance* as *purchaſed by Chriſt.* So that beſides our Inherent or Adherent Righteouſneſs of ſincere *Faith, Repentance and Obedience,* as the performed condition of the Law of Grace, we have no other Righteouſneſs our ſelves, but *Right to Impunity and to Life* : and not any *imputed ſinleſs Innocency* at all. God *pardoneth* our ſins and *adopteth* us, for the ſake of Chriſts ſufferings and *perfect Holineſs* : But he doth not account us *perfectly Holy* for it, nor *perfectly Obedient.* So that how-ever you will call it, whether a *Material Cauſe* or a *Meritorious,* the thing is plain.

Obj. *He is made of God Righteouſneſs to us.*

Anſ. True : But that's none of the queſtion. But how is he ſo made ? 1. As he is made Wiſdom, Sanctification and Redemption as aforeſaid. 2. By Merit, Satisfaction, Direction, Preſcription and Donation. He is the Meritorious Cauſe of our Pardon, of our Adoption, of our Right to Heaven, of that new Covenant which is the Inſtrumental Deed of Gift, confirming all theſe : And he is alſo our Righteouſneſs in the ſenſe that *Auſtin* ſo much ſtandeth on, as all our Holineſs and Righteouſneſs of Heart and Life, is not of our natural endeavour, but his gift, and operation by his Spirit ; cauſing us

to

to obey his Holy precepts and Example. All thefe ways he is made of God our Righteoufnefs: Befides the Objective way of fenfe; as he is *Objectively* made our *Wifdom*, becaufe it is the trueft wifdom to know him; So he is objectively made our *Righteoufnefs*, in that it is that Gofpel-Righteoufnefs which is required *of our felves*, by his grace, to believe in him and obey him.

41. Though Chrift fulfilled not the Law by Habitual Holinefs and Actual Obedience, ftrictly in the Individual perfon of each particular finner; yet he did it in the nature of Man: And fo humane nature, (confidered *in fpecie*, and in Chrift perfonally, though not confidered as *a totum*, or as perfonally in each man,) did fatisfie and fullfil the Law and Merit. As Humane Nature finned in *Adam* actually in *fpecie*, and in his individual perfon, and all our *Perfons* were *feminally* and *virtually* in him, and accordingly finned, or are reputed finners, as having no nature but what he conveyed who could convey no better than he had (either as to Relation or Real quality): But not that God reputed us to have been *actually exiftent*, as really *diftinct perfons* in *Adam* (which is not true.) Even fo Chrift obeyed and fuffered in our *Nature*, and in our nature as it was in him; and humane finful nature in *fpecie* was Univerfally pardoned by him, and *Eternal life freely given to all men* for his merits, thus far imputed to them, their fins being not imputed to hinder this Gift; which is made in and by the Covenant of Grace: Only the Gift hath the Condition of mans Acceptance of it according to its nature, 2 *Cor.* 5. 19, 20. And all the individuals that fhall in time by Faith accept the Gift, are there and thereby made

F   such

such as the Covenant for his merits doth justifie, by that General Gift.

42. As *Adam* was a Head by *Nature*, and therefore conveyed Guilt by natural Generation; so Christ is a Head (not by nature but) by Sacred Contract; and therefore conveyeth Right to Pardon, Adoption and Salvation, not by Generation, but by Contract, or Donation. So that what it was to be *naturally* in *Adam*, seminally and virtually, though not personlly in existence; even that it is, in order to our benefit by him to be *in Christ by Contract or the new Covenant*, virtually, though not in personal existence when the Covenant was made.

43. They therefore that look upon Justification or Righteousness, as coming to us immediately by Imputation of Christs Righteousness to us, without the Instrumental Intervention and Conveyance or Collation by this Deed of Gift or Covenant, do confound themselves by confounding and overlooking the Causes of our Justification. That which Christ did by his merits was to procure the new Covenant. The new Covenant is a free Gift of pardon and life with Christ himself, for his merits and satisfaction sake.

44. Though the Person of the Mediator be not really or reputatively the very *person of each sinner*, (nor so *many persons* as there are *sinners* or *believers*,) yet it doth belong to the *Person of the Mediator*, so far (limitedly) to *bear the person of a sinner*, and to stand in the place of the *Persons of all Sinners*, as to bear the punishment they deserved, and to suffer for their sins.

45. Scripture speaking of moral matters, usually speaketh rather in Moral than meer Physical phrase:

phrase: And in strict Physical sence, Christs very personal Righteousness (Material or Formal) is not so given to us, as that we are proprietors of the very thing it self, but only of the effects (Pardon, Righteousness and Life,) yet in a larger Moral phrase that very thing is oft said to be given to us, which is given to another, or done or suffered for our benefit. He that ransometh a Captive from a Conquerer, Physically giveth the Money to the Conquerer & not to the Captive, & giveth the Captive only the Liberty purchased: But *morally* and reputatively he is said to give the Money to the Captive, because he gave it *for him*. And it redeemeth him as well as if he had given it himself. He that giveth ten thousand pounds to purchase Lands, & freely giveth that land to another; physically giveth the *Money* to the *Seller* only, and the Land only to the other. But morally and reputatively we content our selves with the metonymical phrase, and say, he gave the other ten thousand pound. So morally it may be said, that Christs Righteousness, Merits and Satisfaction, was given to us, in that the thing purchased by it was given to us; when the Satisfaction was given or made to God. Yea when we said it was made to God, we mean only that he was passively the *Terminus* of active Satisfaction, being the party satisfyed; but not that he himself was made the Subject and Agent of Habits and Acts, and Righteousness of Christ as in his humane nature, except as the Divine Nature acted it, or by Communication of Attributes.

46. Because the words [*Person*] and [*Personating*] and [*Representing*] are ambiguous (as all humane language is,) while some use them in a *stricter sense*

sense than others do, we must try by other explicatory terms whether we agree in the matter, and not lay the stress of our Controversy upon the bare words. So some Divines say that Christ suffered in the *Person of a sinner*, when they mean not that he represented the Natural person of any one particular sinner; but that his own *Person* was reputed the Sponsor of sinners by God, and that he was judged a real sinner by his persecuters; and so suffered as if he had been a sinner.

47. As Christ is less improperly said to have Represented our Persons in his satisfactory Sufferings, than in his personal perfect *Holiness* and *Obedience*; so he is less improperly said to have *Represented all mankind as newly fallen in Adam, in a General sense, for the purchasing of the universal Gift of Pardon and Life, called, The new Covenant*; than to have *Represented in his perfect Holiness and his Sufferings, every Believer considered as from his first being to his Death.* Though it is certain that he dyed for all their sins from first to last. For it is most true; 1. That Christ is as a second *Adam*, the Root of the Redeemed; And as we derive sin from *Adam*, so we derive life from Christ, (allowing the difference between a Natural and a Voluntary way of derivation.) And though no mans *Person* as a *Person* was actually *existent* and *offended* in *Adam*, (nor was by God reputed to have been and done) yet all mens Persons were *Virtually* and *Seminally* in *Adam* as is aforesaid; and when they *are existent persons*, they are no better either by *Relative Innocency*, or by *Physical Disposition*, than he could propagate: and are truly and justly reputed by God to be *Persons Guilty of Adams fact*, so far as they were by nature

semi-

seminally and virtually in him: And Christ the second *Adam* is in a sort the root of *Man as Man*, (though not by propagation of us, yet) as he is the *Redeemer* of *Nature* it self from destruction, but more notably the *Root* of *Saints as Saints*, who are to have no real sanctity but what shall be derived from him by Regeneration, as Nature and Sin is from *Adam* by Generation. But *Adam* did not represent all his posterity as to all the Actions which they should do themselves from their Birth to their Death; so that they should all have been taken for perfectly obedient to the death, if *Adam* had not sinned at that time, yea or during his Life. For if any of them under that Covenant had ever sinned afterward in their own person, they should have died for it. But for the time past, they were Guiltless or Guilty in *Adam*, as he was Guiltless or Guilty himself, so far as they were in *Adam*: And though that was but in *Causâ, & non extra causam*; Yet a Generating Cause which propagateth essence from essence, by self-multiplication of form, much differeth from an *Arbitrary facient Cause* in this. If *Adam* had obeyed, yet all his posterity had been nevertheless bound to perfect personal persevering Obedience on pain of Death. And Christ the second *Adam* so far bore the person of fallen *Adam*, and suffered in the nature and room of Mankind in General, as without any condition on their part at all; to give man by an act of Oblivion or new Covenant a pardon of *Adams* sin, yea and of all sin past, at the time of their consent, though not disobliging them from all future Obedience. And by his perfect Holiness and Obedience and Sufferings, he hath merited that new Covenant, which *Accepteth* of sincere, though imperfect, Obedience, and maketh no more in us necessary to Salvation. When I say he did this *without* any *Condition* on mans part, I mean, He *absolutely without Condition*, merited and gave us the *Justifying Testament* or *Covenant*. Though that Covenant give us not Justification absolutely, but on Condition of *believing, fiducial Consent*. 2. And so as this *Universal Gift* of Justification upon Acceptance, is actually given to all fallen mankind as such; so Christ might be said to suffer instead of all, yea and merit too, so far as to procure them this Covenant-gift.

48. The sum of all lyeth in applying the distinction of giving Christs Righteousness *as such in it self*, and as *a cause of our Righteousness*, or in the *Causality of it*. As our sin is not reputed Christs sin *in it self*, and in the culpability of it (for then it must needs make Christ odious to God) but in its *Causality of punishment*: so Christ's Material or Formal Righteousness, is not by God reputed to be properly and absolutely *our own* in *it self as such*, but the *Causality* of it as it produceth such and such effects.

49. The Objections which are made against Imputation of Christs Righteousness in the sound sense, may all be answered as they are by our Divines; among whom the chiefest on this subject are *Davenant de Justit. Habit. & Actual. Johan. Crocius de Justif. Nigrinus de Impletione Legis*, Bp. *G. Downam of Justif. Chamier, Paræus, Amesius* and *Junius* against *Bellarm*. But the same reasons against the unsound sence of Imputation are unanswerable. Therefore if any shall say concerning my following Arguments, that most of them are used, by *Gregor.*

de

de Valent. by *Bellarm. Becanus,* or other Papists, or by Socinians, and are answered by *Nigrinus, Crocius, Davenant,* &c. Such words may serve to deceive the simple that are led by Names and Prejudice; but to the Intelligent they are contemptible, unless they prove that these objections are made by the Papists against the same sence of Imputation against which I use them, and that it is that sense which all those Protestants defend in answering them: For who-ever so answereth them, will appear to answer them in vain.

50. How far those Divines who do use the phrase of *Chrifts suffering in our person,* do yet limit the sense in their exposition, and deny that we are reputed to have fulfilled the Law in Christ: because it is tedious to cite many, I shall take up now with one, even Mr. *Lawson* in his *Theopolitica,* which (though about the office of Faith he some-what differ from me) I must needs call an excellent Treatise, as I take the Author to be one of the most Knowing men yet living that I know.) Pardon me if I be large in transcribing his words.

"Pag. 100, 101. [If we enquire of the manner
" how Righteousness and Life is derived from Christ,
" being one unto so many, it cannot be, except
" Christ be a general Head of mankind, and one
" Person with them, as *Adam* was. We do not read of
" any but two who were general Heads, and in some
" respect virtually, *All mankind*; the
" *first* and *second Adam,* ──── The Mark, *Virtually.*
" principal cause of this Representation
" whereby he is one person with us, is
" the will of God, who as Lord made him such,
" and as Lawgiver and Judge did so account him.
"But

"But, 2. How far is he *One person with us?* Ans.

"1. In general so far as it pleased God
Not abso- "to make him so, and no further. 2. In
lutely. "particular, He and we are one so far

"1. As to make him liable to the pe-
"nalty of the Law for us. 2. So far as to free us
"from that obligation, and derive the benefit of his
"death to us. Though Christ be so far one with us
"as to be lyable unto the penalty of the Law, and
"to suffer it, and upon this suffering we are freed;
"yet Christ is not the sinner, nor the sinner Christ.
"Christ is the Word made flesh, innocent without
"sin, an universal Priest and King : but we are none

"of these. Though we be accounted
Mark by a "as one person in Law with him, by a
Trope. "Trope; yet in proper sence it cannot
"be said *that in Christ's Satisfying we*
"*satisfied for our own sins.* For then we should have
"been the Word made flesh, able to plead Innocen-

"cy, &c. All which are false, impos-
Mark how "sible, blasphemous if affirmed by any.
far. "It's true, we are so one with him, that
"he satisfied for us, and the benefit of
"this Satisfaction redounds to us, and is communi-
"cable to all, upon certain termes; though not
"actually communicated to all : From this Unity
"and Identity of person in Law (if I may so
"speak) it followeth clearly that Christ's suffer-
"ings were not only Afflictions, but Punishments
"in proper sense. ——*Pag.* 102, 103. That Christ
"died for all in some sence must needs be granted,
"because the Scripture expresly affirms it *(vid.*
"*reliqua.)* ——

"There is another question unprofitably hand-
"led,

the *Propitiation* which includeth
on and Merit, be to be afcribed to the
ive Obedience of Chrift? *Anf.* 1.
ve, Perfonal, Perfect and Perpetual
ich by reafon of his humane nature
ubjection unto God was due, and al-
:nce to the great and tranfcendent
f fuffering the death of the Crofs,
s Caufes of Remiffion and Juftificati-
ptures ufually afcribe it to the Blood,
ifice of Chrift, and never to the Perfo-
edience of Chrift's to the Moral Law.
ctive Obedience is neceffary, becaufe
1e could not have offered that great
imfelf without fpot to God. And if
:en without fpot, it could not have
tory and effectual for Expiation. 4. If
Surety had performed for us perfect
al Obedience, fo that we might have
I to have perfectly and fully kept
him, then no fin could have been
1pon us, and the Death of Chrift had
s and fuperfluous. 5. Chrifts Propi-
1 the Believer not only from the obli-
punifhment of fenfe, but of lofs;
:d for him not only deliverance from
I, but the enjoyment of all good ne-
ir full happinefs. Therefore, there is
of Scripture for that opinion, that the
irift and his Sufferings free us from pu-
and by his Active Obedience imputed
e made righteous, and the heirs of life.
ift was bound to perform perfect and
)bedience for us, and he alfo performed
" it

"it for us, then we are freed not only from sin, but
"Obedience too: And this Obedience as distinct and
"separate from Obedience unto death, may be plea-
"ded for Justification of Life, and will be sufficient
"to carry the Cause. For the tenor of the Law
"was this, *Do this and live:* And if man do this
"by himself or Surety, so as that the Lawgiver and
"supreme Judg accept it, the Law can require no
"more. It could not bind to perfect Obedience and
"to punishment too. There was never any such
"Law made by God or just men. Before I conclude
"this particular of the extent of Chrifts Merit and
"Propitiation, I thought good to inform the Rea-
"der, that as the Propitiation of Christ maketh no
"man absolutely, but upon certain terms pardon-
"able and savable; so it was never made, either
"to prevent all sin, or all punishments: For it pre-
"supposeth man both sinful and miserable: And
"we know that the Guilt and Punishment of
"*Adams* sin, lyeth heavy on all his posterity to this
"day. And not only that, but the guilt of actual
"and personal sins lyeth wholly upon us, whilest
"impenitent and unbelieving and so out of Christ.
"And the Regenerate themselves are not fully freed
"from all punishments till the final Resurrection
"and Judgment. So that his Propitiation doth not
"altogether prevent but remove sin and punish-
"ment by degrees. Many sins may be said to be
"Remissible by vertue of this Sacrifice, which ne-
"ver shall be remitted.] So far Mr. *Lawson.*

Here I would add only these Animadversions.
1. That whereas he explaineth *Chrifts personating
us* in suffering by the similitude of a Debtor and his
Surety who are the same person in Law: I note 1.
That

That the cafe of Debt much differeth from the cafe of Punifhment. 2. That a Surety of Debt is either antecedently fuch, or confequently: Antecedently, either firft one that is bound equally with the Debtor; 2. or one that promifeth to pay if he do not. I think the Law accounteth neither of thefe to be the *Perfon* of the principal Debtor (as it doth a Servant by whom he fends the Debt.) But Chrift was neither of thefe: For the Law did not beforehand oblige him with us, nor did he in Law-fence undertake to pay the Debt, if we failed. Though God decreed that he fhould do fo; yet that was no part of the fence of the Law. But confequently, if a friend of the Debtor when he is in Jayl will, without his requeft or knowledg, fay to the Creditor, I will pay you all the Debt; but fo that he fhall be in my power, and not have prefent liberty (left he abufe it) but on the terms that I fhall pleafe; yea not at all if he ungratefully reject it] This *Confequent* Satisfyer, or Sponfor, or Paymafter, is not in Law-fence the fame *Perfon* with the Debtor: But if any will call him fo, I will not contend about a word, while we agree of the thing (the terms of deliverance.) And this is as near the Cafe between Chrift and us, as the fimilitude of a Debtor will allow.

2. I do differ from Mr. *Lawfon* and *Paræus*, and *Urfine*, and *Olevian*, and *Scultetus* and all that fort of worthy Divines in this; that whereas they make Chrifts Holinefs and perfect Obedience to be but *Juftitia perfonæ*, neceffary to make his Sacrifice fpotlefs and fo effectual: I think that *of it felf* it is as directly the caufe of our Pardon, Juftification and Life, as Chrifts Paffion is; The Paffion being fatisfactory

factory and so meritorious, and the personal Holiness Meritorious and so Satisfactory. For the truth is, The Law that condemned us was not fulfilled by Chrifts suffering for us, but the *Lawgiver* satisfied instead of the fulfilling of it: And that Satisfaction lyeth, in the substitution of that which as fully (or more) attaineth the ends of the Law as our own suffering would have done. Now the ends of the Law may be attained by immediate Merit of Perfection as well as by Suffering; but best by both. For 1. By the perfect Holiness and Obedience of Chrift, the Holy and perfect will of God is *pleased*: whence [*This is my beloved Son, in whom I am well pleased.*] 2. In order to the ends of Government, Holiness and perfect Obedience, is honoured and freed from the contempt which sin would cast upon it; and the holiness *of the Law* in its *Precepts* is publickly honoured in this grand Exemplar; In whom only the will of God was done on Earth, as it is done in Heaven. And such a Specimen to the World is greatly conducible to the ends of Government: So that Christ voluntarily taking humane nature, which as such is obliged to this Perfection, He first highly merited of God the Father hereby, and this with his Suffering, went to attain the ends that our suffering should have attained, much better. So that at least as *Meritorious*, if not secondarily as *satisfactory*, I see not but *Chrifts Holiness* procureth the *Justifying Covenant* for us, equally with his Death. A Prince may pardon a Traitor for *some noble service of his Friend*, as well as for his suffering: much more for both. This way go *Grotius de satisf.* Mr. *Bradshaw* and others.

3. When Mr *Lawson* saith that the Law binds

not

not to Obedience and Punishment both, he meaneth as to the same Act: which contradicts not what *Nigrinus* and others say, that it binds a sinner to punishment for sin past, and yet to Obedience for the time to come: (which cannot be entire and perfect.)

So pag. 311. *Cap.* 22. *Qu.* 2. Whether there be two parts of Justification, Remission and Imputation of Christs Righteousness. 1. He referreth us to what is aforecited against Imputation of Christs Active Righteousness, separated or abstracted for Reward from the Passive. 2. He sheweth that *Paul* taketh *Remission of sin and Imputation of Righteousness for the same thing.*] So say many of ours.

In conclusion I will mind the Reader, that by reading some Authors for Imputation, I am brought to doubt whether some deny not all true Remission of sin, that is, Remission of the deserved punishment. Because I find that by *Remission* they mean *A non-Imputation of sin under the formal notion of sin*; that God taketh it not to be our sin, but Christs; and Christs Righteousness and perfection to be so ours, as that God accounteth us not as truly sinners. And so they think that the *Reatus Culpæ* as well as *Pœnæ* simply in it self is done away. Which if it be so, then the *Reatus Pœnæ*, the obligation to punishment, or the *dueness* of punishment, cannot be said to be dissolved or remitted, because it was never contracted. Where I hold, that it is the *Reatus ad Pœnam*, the *Dueness* of punishment only that is remitted, and the *guilt* of *sin* not as in it self, but in its *Causality* of punishment. And so in all common language, we say we forgive a man his fault, when we forgive him all the penalty positive and privative. Not esteeming him, 1. Never to have done the fact. 2. Or that fact not to have been a fault,*and his fault*;3.but that punishment for that fault, is forgiven him, and the fault so far as it is a cause of punishment. We must not feign God to judg falsly.

This maketh me think of a saying of Bp. *Ushers* to me, when I mentioned the Papists placing Justification and Remission of sin conjunct, he told me that the Papists ordinarily acknowledg no Remission. And on search I find that *Aquinas* and the most of them place no true Remission of sin, in Justification : For by *Remission* (which they make part of Justification,) they mean *Mortification, or destroying sin it self* in the act or habit. But that the *pardon* of the punishment is a thing that we all need, is not denyable;nor do they deny it,though they deny it to be part of our Justification. For it's strange if they deny Christ the pardoning power which they give the Pope. And as *Joh. Crocius de Justif.* oft tells them, They should for shame grant that Chrifts Righteousness may be as far imputed to us, as they say a Saints or Martyrs redundant merits and supererogations are.

But if the *Guilt* of *Fact and Guilt of Fault* in it self considered, be not both imputed first to us,that is, If we be not judged sinners, I cannot see how we can be judged *Pardoned sinners* ; For he that is judged to have no sin, is judged to deserve no punishment. Unless they will say that to prevent the *form and desert* of *sin*, is *eminenter*, though not *formaliter*, to forgive. But it is another (even Actual) forgiveness which we hear of in the Gospel, and pray for daily in the Lords prayer. Of all which see the full Scripture-proof in Mr. *Hotchkis* of *Forgiveness of sin*.

CHAP.

CHAP. III.

A further explication of the Controverſie.

I am afraid leſt I have not made the ſtate of the Controverſie plain enough to the unexerciſed Reader, and leſt the very explicatory diſtinctions and propoſitions, though needful and ſuitable to the matter, ſhould be unſuitable to his capacity; I will therefore go over it again in a ſhorter way, and make it as plain as poſſibly I can; being fully perſwaded, that it is not ſo much Argumentation, as help to underſtand *the* matter, *and our* own *and* other mens ambiguous words, *that is needful to end our abominable Contentions.*

1. THE Righteouſneſs of a Perſon is formally a moral Relation of that Perſon.
§ 2. This moral Relation, is the Relation of that ſon to the *Rule* by which he is to be judged.
§ 3. And it is his Relation to ſome *Cauſe*, or ſuppoſed Accuſation or Queſtion to be decided by that Judgment.
§ 4. The Rule of Righteouſneſs here is Gods w, naturally or ſupernaturally made known.
§ 5. The

§ 5. The Law hath a Preceptive part, determining what shall be due from us, and a Retributive part determining what shall be due to us.

§ 6. The Precept instituting Duty, our Actions and Dispositions, which are the Matter of that duty, are physically considered, conform or disconform to the Precept.

§ 7. Being Physically, they are consequently so Morally considered, we being Moral Agents, and the Law a Rule of Morality.

§ 8. If the *Actions* be righteous or unrighteous, consequently the Person is so, in reference to those Actions, supposing that to be his *Cause*, or the *Question* to be decided.

§ 9. Unrighteousness as to this Cause, is *Guilt*, or *Reatus Culpæ*; and to be unrighteous is to be *Sons*, or Guilty of sin.

§ 10. The *Retributive* part of the Law is, 1. Premiant, for Obedience; 2. Penal, for Disobedience.

§ 11. To be Guilty or Unrighteous as to the reward, is, to have no right to the reward (that being supposed the Question in judgment): And to be Righteous here, is to have *right* to the *reward*.

§ 12. To be *Guilty* as to the penalty, is to be *jure puniendus*, or *Reus pœnæ*, or *obligatus ad pœnam*. And to be righteous here, is to have *Right* to *impunity*, (*quoad pœnam damni & sensus*.)

§ 13. The first Law made *personal*, *perfect*, *persevering Innocency* both mans duty, and the Condition of the Reward and Impunity, and any sin the condition of punishment.

§ 14. Man broke this Law, and so lost his Innocency, and so the Condition became naturally impossible to him, *de futuro*.

§ 15. There-

§ 15. Therefore that Law as a Covenant, that is, the Promissory part with its Condition, ceased; *cessante capacitate subditi*; and so did the preceptive part. 1. As it commanded absolute Innocency (of act and habit.) 2. And as it commanded the seeking of the Reward on the Condition and by the means of personal Innocency. The Condition thus passing into the nature of a sentence; And punishment remaining due for the sin.

§ 16. But the Law remained still an obliging Precept for future perfect Obedience, and made punishment due for all future sin: and these two parts of it, as the Law of lapsed Nature, remained in force, between the first sin, and the new-Covenant promise or Law of Grace.

§ 17. The eternal Word interposing, a Mediator is promised, and Mercy maketh a Law of Grace, and the Word becometh mans Redeemer by undertaking, and by present actual reprieve, pardon and initial deliverance: and the fallen world, the miserable sinners, with the Law and obligations which they were under, are now become the Redemers *jure Redemptionis*, as before they were the Creator's *jure Creationis*.

§ 18. The Redeemers Law then hath two parts; 1. The said Law of lapsed nature (binding to future perfect obedience or punishment) which he found man under (called vulgarly the Moral Law.) 2. And a pardoning Remedying Law of Grace.

§ 19. Because man had dishonoured God and his Law by sin, the Redeemer undertook to take mans nature without sin, and by perfect Holiness and Obedience, and by becoming a Sacrifice for sin, to bring that Honour to God and his Law which we should have done, and to attain the Ends of Law and Government instead of our *Perfection* or *Punishment*, that for the Merit hereof we might be delivered and live.

§ 20. This he did in the third person of a Mediator, who as such had a Law or Covenant proper to himself, the Conditions of which he performed, (by perfect keeping, 1. The Law of Innocency; 2. Of *Moses*; 3. And that proper to himself alone) and so merited all that was promised to him, for Himself and Us.

§ 21. By his Law of Grace (as our Lord-Redeemer) he gave first to all mankind (in *Adam*, and after in *Noah*, and by a second fuller edition at his Incarnation) a free Pardon of the destructive punishment (but not of all punishment) with right to his Spirit of Grace, Adoption and Glory, in Union with Himself their Head, on Condition initially of Faith and Repentance, and progressively of sincere Obedience to the end, to be performed by his Help or Grace.

§ 22. By this Law of Grace (supposing the Law of lapsed nature aforesaid, inclusively) all the World is ruled, and shall be judged, according to that edition of it (to *Adam* or by *Christ*) which they are under. And by it they shall be Justified or Condemned.

§ 23. If the question then be, Have you kept or not kept the Conditions of the Law of Grace, Personal Performance or nothing must so far be our Righteousness, and not Christs keeping them for us, or Satisfaction for our not keeping them. And this is the great Case (so oft by Christ described *Mat.* 7. & 25. &c.) to be decided in judgment; and therefore the word *Righteous* and *Righteousness* are used for

what

what is thus perfonal hundreds of times in Scripture.

§ 24. But as to the queftion, *Have we kept the Law of Innocency?* we muft confefs guilt and fay, No: neither Immediately by our felves, nor Mediately by another, or Inftrument : for *Perfonal Obedience* only is the performance required by that Law; Therefore we have no *Righteoufnefs* confifting in fuch Performance or Innocency; but muft confefs fin, and plead a pardon.

§ 25. Therefore no man hath a proper *Univerfal Righteoufnefs*, excluding all kind of Guilt whatfoever.

§ 26. Therefore no man is juftified by the Law of Innocency (nor the Law Mofaical as of works;) either by the Preceptive or Retributive part: for we broke the Precept, and are by the Threatning heirs of death.

§ 27. That Law doth not juftifie us, becaufe Chrift fulfilled it for us: For it faid not (in words or fenfe) [Thou or one for thee fhall *Perfectly Obey*, or *Suffer*:] It mentioned no Subftitute : But it is the Law-giver (and not that Law) that juftifieth us by other means.

§ 28. But we have *another Righteoufnefs imputed to us inftead of that Perfect Legal Innocency* and *Rewardablenefs*, by which we fhall be *accepted of God*, and *glorified* at laft as furely and fully (at leaft) as if we had never finned, or had perfectly kept that Law; which therefore may be called our *Pro-legal Righteoufnefs*.

§ 29. But this Righteoufnefs is not yet either OURS by fuch a propriety as a Perfonal performance would have bin, nor OURS to all the fame ends

ends and purpofes: It faveth us not from all pain, death or penal defertion, nor conftituteth our Relation juft the fame.

§ 30. It is the Law of Grace that Juftifieth us, both as giving us Righteoufnefs, and as *Virtually judging* us Righteous when it hath made us fo, and it is Chrift as Judg according to that Law (and God by Chrift) that will *fentence* us juft, and *executively* fo ufe us.

§ 31. The Grace of Chrift firft giveth us *Faith* and *Repentance* by effectual Vocation: And then the Law of Grace by its *Donative* part or Act doth give us a *Right* to *Union* with Chrift as the Churches Head (and fo to his Body) and with him a right to Pardon of paft fin, and to the Spirit to dwell and act in us for the future, and to the Love of God, and Life eternal, to be ours in poffeffion, if we fincerely obey and perfevere.

§ 32. The total Righteoufnefs then which we have (as an Accident of which we are the Subjects,) is 1. A right to Impunity, by the free Pardon of all our fins, and a right to Gods Favour and Glory, as a free gift *quoad valorem*, but as a *Reward* of our Obedience, *quoad Ordinem conferendi & rationem Comparativam* (why one rather than another is judged meet for that free gift.) 2. And the *Relation* of one that hath by grace performed the Condition of that free Gift, without which we had been no capable recipients: which is initially [Faith and Repentance] the Condition of our Right begun, and confequently, fincere Obedience and Perfeverance (the Condition of continued right.)

§ 33. Chrifts perfonal Righteoufnefs is no one of thefe, and fo is not our *Conftitutive Righteoufnefs*.

for-

formally and strictly so called: For *Formally* our Righteousness is a *Relation*, (of right;) and it is the Relation of our own Persons: And a Relation is an accident: And the numerical Relation (or Right) of one person cannot be the same numerical Accident of another person as the subject.

§ 34. There are but three sorts of *Causes*; *Efficient*, *Constitutive*, and *Final*.

1. Christ is the efficient cause of all our Righteousness: (1. Of our Right to Pardon and Life; 2. And of our Gospel-Obedience:) And that many waies: 1. He is the Meritorious Cause: 2. He is the *Donor* by his Covenant; 3. And the Donor or Operator of our Inherent Righteousness by his Spirit: 4. And the moral efficient by his Word, Promise, Example, &c.

2. And Christ is partly the final cause.

3. But all the doubt is whether his personal Righteousness be the *Constitutive Cause*.

§ 35. The *Constitutive Cause* of natural bodily substances consisteth of *Matter disposed*, and *Form*. Relations have no *Matter*, but instead of *Matter* a *Subject* (and that is *Our own persons* here, and not Christ.) and a *terminus* and *fundamentum*.

§ 36. The *Fundamentum* may be called both the *Efficient Cause* of the *Relation* (as commonly it is) and the *Matter* from which it *resulteth*: And so Christs Righteousness is undoubtedly the *Meritorious* efficient Cause, and undoubtedly not the *Formal* Cause of our personal Relation of Righteousness: Therefore all the doubt is of the Material Cause.

§ 37. So that all the Controversie is come up to a bare *name* and Logical term, of which Logicians agree not as to the aptitude. All confess that Relalations have no proper *Matter*, besides the subject: all confess that the *Fundamentum* is *loco efficientis*, but whether it be a fit name to call it the *Constitutive Matter* of a Relation, there is no agreement.

§ 38. And if there were, it would not decide this Verbal Controversie: For 1. *Titulus est fundamentum Juris*: The *fundamentum* of our *Right to Impunity and Life* in and with Christ, is the *Donative act* of our Saviour in and by his Law or Covenant of Grace: that is our *Title*; And from that our Relation resulteth, the *Conditio tituli vel juris* being found in our selves. 2. And our Relation of *Performers* of that Condition of the Law of Grace, resulteth from our own performance as the *fundamentum* (compared to the Rule.) So that both these parts of our Righteousness have a nearer *fundamentum* than Christs personal Righteousness.

§ 39. But the *Right* given us by the Covenant (and the Spirit and Grace) being a Right merited first by Christs personal Righteousness, this is a *Causa Causæ, id est, fundamenti, seu Donationis*: And while this much is certain, whether it shall be called a *Remote fundamentum* (viz. *Causa fundamenti*) and so a Remote Constitutive Material Cause, or only (properly) a Meritorious Cause, may well be left to the arbitrary Logician, that useth such notions as he pleases; but verily is a Controversie unfit to tear the Church for, or destroy Love and Concord by.

§ 40. Quest. 1. *Is Christs Righteousness OURS?* *Ans.* Yes; In some sense, and in another not.

§ 41. Quest. 2. *Is Christs Righteousness OURS?* *Ans.* Yes; In the sense before opened; For *all things are ours*; and his righteousness more than lower Causes. § 2. Quest.

§ 42. Queft. 3. *Is Chrift's Righteoufnefs OURS as it was or is His own, with the same sort of propriety?* Anf. No.

§ 43. Queft. 4. *Is the formal Relation of Righteous as an accident of our persons, numerically the same Righteoufnefs?* Anf. No; It is impoffible: Unlefs we are the same perfon.

§ 44. Queft. 5. *Is Chrift and each Believer one political perfon?* Anf. A political perfon is an equivocal word: If you take it for *an Office* (as the King or Judg is a political perfon) I fay, No: If for a *Society, Yea;* But *noxia & noxa caput fequuntur:* True *Guilt* is an accident of natural perfons, and of Societies only as conftituted of fuch; and fo is Righteoufnefs; Though Phyfically Good or Evil may for fociety-fake, befal us without perfonal defert or confent.

But if by [*Perfon*] you mean a certain *State or Condition* (as to be a *fubject of God*, or one that is to *fuffer for fin*) fo Chrift may be faid to be the fame *perfon* with us *in fpecie*, but not *numerically*, becaufe that Accident whence his *Perfonality* is named, is not in the fame fubject.

§ 45. Queft. 6. *Is Chrifts Righteoufnefs imputed to us?* Anf. Yes; If by imputing you mean reckoning or reputing it ours, fo far as is aforefaid, that is fuch a Caufe of ours.

§ 46. Queft. 7. *Are we reputed our felves to have fulfilled all that Law of Innocency in and by Chrift, as reprefenting our perfons, as obeying by him?* Anf. No.

§ 47. Queft. 8. *Is it Chrifts Divine, Habitual, Active or Paffive Righteoufnefs which Juftifieth us?* Anf. All: viz, the Habitual, Active and Paffive exalted in Meritoriousnefs by Union with the Divine.

§ 48. Queſt. 9. *Is it Chriſts Righteouſneſs, or our Faith which is ſaid to be imputed to us for Righteouſneſs?* Rom. 4. *Anſ.* 1. The text ſpeaketh of imputing Faith, and by Faith is meant Faith, and not *Chriſts* Righteouſneſs in the word: But that Faith is *Faith in Chriſt* and his Righteouſneſs; and the Object is *quaſi materia actus*, and covenanted.

2. *De re*, both are Imputed: that is, 1. Chriſts Righteouſneſs is reputed the meritorious Cauſe. 2. The *free-gift* (by the Covenant) is reputed the *fundamentum juris* (both oppoſed to our Legal Merit.) 3. And our Faith is *reputed* the *Conditio tituli*, and all that is required in us to our Juſtification, as making us *Qualified Recipients* of the *free-Gift* merited by Chriſt.

§ 49. Queſt. 10. *Are we any way Juſtified by our own performed Righteouſneſs?* Anſ. Yes; Againſt the charge of non-performance, (as Infidels, Impenitent, Unholy,) and ſo as being uncapable of the free-gift of Pardon and Life in Chriſt.

CHAP.

CHAP. IV.

The Reasons of our denying the fore-described rigid Sence of Imputation.

Though it were most accurate to reduce what we deny to several Propositions, and to confute each one argumentatively by it self, yet I shall now choose to avoid such prolixity; and for brevity and the satisfaction of such as look more at the force of a Reason, than the form of the Argument, I shall thrust together our denyed Sence, with the manifold Reasons of our denyal.

"WE deny, that God doth so Impute Chrifts
" Righteousness to us, as to repute or ac-
" count us to have been Holy with all that Habitu-
" al Holiness which was in Christ, or to have done
" all that he did in obedience to his Father, or in
" fulfilling the Law, or to have suffered all that he
" suffered, and to have made God satisfaction for
" our own sins, and merited our own Salvation and
" Justification, in and by Christ; or that he *was*,
" *did* and *suffered*, and *merited*, all this strictly in
" the *person* of every sinner that is saved; Or that
" Christs very individual Righteousness Material or
" Formal, is so made ours in a strict sense, as that
" we are Proprietors, Subjects, or Agents of the
"   very

" very thing it self simply and absolutely, as it is
" distinct from the effects; or that Christs Indivi-
" dual Formal Righteousness, is made our Formal
" Personal Righteousness; or that as to the *effects*,
" we have any such Righteousness Imputed to us,
" as formally ours, which consisteth in a perfect Ha-
" bitual and Actual Conformity to the Law of In-
" nocency; that is, that we are reputed perfectly
" Holy and sinless, and such as shall be Justified by
" the Law of Innocency, which saith, *Perfectly Obey*
" and *Live*, or *sin and die.*] All this we deny.

Let him that will answer me, keep to my words, and not alter the sense by leaving any out. And that he may the better understand me, I add, 1. I take it for granted that the Law requireth Habitual Holiness as well as Actual Obedience, and is not fulfilled without both. 2. That Christ loved God and man with a perfect constant Love, and never sinned by Omission or Commission. 3. That Christ died not only for our Original sin, or sin before Conversion, but for all our sin to our lives end. 4. That he who is supposed to have no sin of Omission, is supposed to have done all his duty. 5. That he that hath done all his duty, is not condemnable by that Law, yea hath right to all the Reward promised on Condition of that duty. 6. By Christs Material Righteousness, I mean, those Habits, Acts and Sufferings in which his Righteousness did consist, or was founded. 7. By his and our *Formal Righteousness*, I mean the *Relation* it self of being *Righteous*. 8. And I hold that Christs Righteousness, did not only *Numerically* (as aforesaid) but also thus *totâ specie*, in kind differ from ours, that his was a *perfect Habitual and Actual Conformity to the Law*

Law of Innocency, together with the peculiar *Laws* of *Mediator-ship*, by which he merited Redemption for *us*, and Glory for himself and *us*: But *ours* is the Pardon of *sin*, and Right to Life, Purchased, Merited and freely given us by *Christ* in and by a new *Covenant*, whose condition is *Faith with Repentance*, as to the gift of our *Justification now*, and sincere Holiness, Obedience, Victory and Perseverance as to our *possession* of *Glory*.

Now our Reasons against the denyed sence of Imputation are these.

1. In general this opinion setteth up and introduceth all Antinomianism or Libertinism, and Ungodliness, and subverteth the Gospel and all true Religion and Morality.

I do not mean that all that hold it, have such effects in themselves, but only that this is the tendency and consequence of the opinion: For I know that many see not the nature and consequences of their own opinions, and the abundance that hold damnable errors, hold them but notionally in a peevish faction, and therefore not dammingly, but hold practically and effectually the contrary saving truth. And if the Papists shall perswade Men that our doctrine, yea theirs that here mistake, cannot consist with a godly life, let but the lives of Papists and Protestants be compared. Yea in one of the Instances before given; Though some of the Congregational-party hold what was recited, yet so far are they from ungodly lives, that the greatest thing in which I differ from them is, the overmuch unscriptural strictness of some of them, in their Church-admissions and Communion, while they fly further from such as they think not godly, than I think God would

would have them do, being generally persons fearing God themselves: (Excepting the sinful alienation from others, and easiness to receive and carry false reports of Dissenters, which is common to all that fall into sidings.) But the errors of any men are never the better if they be found in the hands of godly men: For if they be practised they will make them ungodly.

2. It confoundeth the *Person* of the *Mediator*, and of the *Sinner*: As if the Mediator who was proclaimed the Beloved of the Father, and therefore capable of reconciling us to him, because he was still *well-pleased* in him, had (not only suffered in the room of the sinner by voluntary Sponsion, but also) in suffering and doing, been *Civilly* the very person of the sinner himself; that sinner I say, who was an enemy to God, and so esteemed.

3. It maketh Christ to have *been Civilly* as *many persons* as there be elect sinners in the World: which is both beside and contrary to Scripture.

4. It introduceth a false sence and supposition of our sin imputed to Christ, as if Imputatively it were his as it is ours, even the *sinful Habits*, the *sinful Acts*, and the *Relation* of *evil*, *Wicked*, *Ungodly* and *Unrighteous* which resulteth from them: And so it maketh Christ really *hated of God*: For God cannot but *hate* any one whom he reputeth to be truly ungodly, a Hater of God, an Enemy to him, a Rebel, as we all were: whereas it was only the Guilt of Punishment, and not of *Crime*, as such that Christ assumed: He undertook to suffer in the room of sinners; and to be reputed one that had so undertaken; But not to be reputed really a sinner, an ungodly person, hater of God, one that had the Image of the Devil.

5. Nay

5. Nay it maketh Chrift to have been incomparably the worſt man that ever was in the World by juſt reputation; and to have been by juſt imputation guilty of all the ſins of all the Elect that ever lived, and reputed one of the Murderers of himſelf, and *one* of the Perſecutors of his Church, or rather *many*: and the language that *Luther* uſed Catechreſtically, to be ſtrictly and properly true.

6. It ſuppoſeth a wrong ſence of the Imputation of *Adams* ſin to his poſterity: As if we had been juſtly reputed *perſons exiſtent* in *his perſon*, and ſo in him to have been *perſons that commited the ſame ſin*; whereas we are only reputed to be *now* (not *then*) *perſons* who have a *Nature* derived from him, which being then *ſeminally only* in him, deriveth by propagation an anſwerable *Guilt* of his ſinful fact, together with *natural Corruption.*

7. It ſuppoſeth us to be Juſtifiable and Juſtified by the Law of Innocency, made to *Adam*, as it ſaith [*Obey perfectly and Live.*] As if we fulfilled it by Chriſt: which is not only an addition to the Scripture, but a Contradiction. For it is only the Law or Covenant of Grace that we are Juſtified by.

8. It putteth, to that end, a falſe ſence upon the Law of Innocency: For whereas it commandeth *Perſonal Obedience*, and maketh *Perſonal* puniſhment *due* to the offender: This ſuppoſeth the Law to ſay or mean [*Either thou, or one for thee ſhall Obey*; or, *Thou ſhalt obey by thy ſelf, or by another: And if thou ſin thou ſhalt ſuffer by thy ſelf, or by another.*]

Whereas the Law knew no Subſtitute or Vicar, no nor Sponſor; nor is any ſuch thing ſaid of it in the Scripture: ſo bold are men in their additions.

9. It falſly ſuppoſeth that we are not Judged and Juſti-

Juftified by the new Covenant or Law of Grace, but (but is faid) by the Law of Innocency.

10. It fathereth on God an erring judgment, as if he reputed, reckoned or accounted things to be what they are not, and us to have done what we did not. To repute Chrift a Sponfor for finners who undertook to obey in their natures, and fuffer in their place and ftead, as a Sacrifice to redeem them, is all juft and true: And to repute *us thofe* for whom Chrift did this. But to repute Chrift to have been really and every one of us, or a finner, or guilty of fin it felf; or to repute us to have been habitually as Good as Chrift was, or actually to have done what he did, either Naturally or Civilly and by Him as our fubftitute, and to repute us Righteous by poffeffing his formal perfonal Righteoufnefs in it felf; All thefe are untrue, and therefore not to be afcribed to God. To Impute it to us, is but to Repute us as verily and groundedly Righteous by his Merited and freely-Given Pardon, and Right to Life, as if we had merited it our felves.

11. It feigneth the fame Numerical Accident [their *Relation* of *Righteoufnefs*] which was in one fubject to be in another, which is Impoffible.

12. It maketh us to have fatisfied Divine Juftice for our felves, and merited Salvation (and all that we receive) for our felves, in and by another: And fo that we may plead our own Merits with God for Heaven and all his benefits.

13. The very making and tenor of the new Covenant, contradicteth this opinion: For when God maketh a Law or Covenant, to convey the effects of Chrifts Righteoufnefs to us, by degrees and upon certain Conditions, this proveth that the very

Righ-

Righteousness in it self simply was not ours: else we should have had these effects of it both presently and immediately and absolutely without new Conditions.

14. This opinion therefore maketh this Law of Grace, which giveth the benefits to us by these degrees and upon terms, to be an *injury* to Believers, as keeping them from their own.

15. It seemeth to deny Chrifts Legiflation in the Law of Grace, and confequently his Kingly Office. For if we are reputed to have fulfilled the whole Law of Innocency in Chrift, there is no bufinefs for the Law of Grace to do.

16. It feemeth to make internal Sanctification by the Spirit needlefs, or at leaft, as to one half of its ufe: For if we are by juft Imputation in Gods account perfectly Holy, in Chrifts Holinefs the firft moment of our believing, nothing can be added to Perfection; we are as fully *Amiable* in the fight of God, as if we were fanctified in our felves; Becaufe by Imputation it is all our own.

17. And so it seemeth to make our after-Obedience unneceffary, at leaft as to half its ufe: For if in Gods true account, we have perfectly obeyed to the death by another, how can we be required to do it all or part again by our felves? If all the debt of our Obedience be paid, why is it required again?

18. And this feemeth to Impute to God a nature lefs holy and at enmity to fin, than indeed he hath; if he can repute a man laden with hateful fins, to be as perfecty Holy, Obedient and Amiable to him as if he were really fo in himfelf, becaufe another is such for him.

19. If we did in our own perfons Imputatively
what

what Christ did, I think it will follow that we *sinned*; that being unlawful to us which was Good in him. It is a sin for us to be Circumcised, and to keep all the Law of *Moses*, and send forth Apostles, and to make Church-Ordinances needful to Salvation. Therefore we did not this in Christ: And if not this, they that distinguish and tell us what we did in Christ, and what not, must prove it. I know that Christ did somewhat which is a common duty of all men, and somewhat proper to the *Jews*, and somewhat proper to himself: But that one sort of men did one part in Christ, and another sort did another part in him, is to be proved.

20. If Christ suffered but in the Person of sinful man, his sufferings would have been in vain, or no Satisfaction to God: For sinful man is obliged to perpetual punishment; of which a temporal one is but a small part: *Our persons* cannot make a temporal suffering equal to that perpetual one due to man: but the transcendent person of the Mediator did.

Obj. *Christ bore both his own person and ours: It belongeth to him as Mediator to personate the guilty sinner.*

Ans. It belongeth to him as Mediator to undertake the sinners punishment in his own person. And if any will improperly call that, the *Personating and Representing* of the *sinner*, let them limit it, and confess that it is not *simply*, but *in tantum*, so far, and to such uses and no other, and that yet *sinners did it not in* and *by Christ*, but only Christ for them to convey the benefits as he pleased; And then we delight not to quarrel about mere words; though we like the phrase of Scripture better than theirs.

21. If

21. If Christ was perfectly Holy and Obedient in our persons, and we in him, then it was either in the Person of Innocent man before we sinned, or of sinful man. The first cannot be pretended: For man as Innocent had not a Redeemer. If of *sinful man*, then his perfect Obedience could not be meritorious of our Salvation: For it supposeth him to do it in the person of a sinner: and he that hath once sinned, according to that Law, is the Child of death, and uncapable of ever fulfilling a Law, which is fulfilled with nothing but sinless perfect perpetual Obedience.

Obj. *He first suffered in our stead and persons as sinners, and then our sin being pardoned, he after in our persons fulfilled the Law, instead of our after-Obedience to it.*

Ans. 1. Christs Obedience to the Law was before his Death. 2. The sins which he suffered for, were not only before Conversion, but endure as long as our lives: Therefore if he fulfilled the Law in our persons after we have done sinning, it is in the persons only of the dead. 3. We are still obliged to Obedience our selves.

Obj. *But yet though there be no such difference in Time, God doth first Impute his sufferings to us for pardon of all our sins to the death, and in order of nature, his Obedience after it, as the Merit of our Salvation.*

Ans. 1. God doth Impute or Repute his sufferings the satisfying cause of our Pardon, and his Merits of Suffering and the rest of his Holiness and Obedience, as the meritorious cause of our *Pardon* and our Justification and Glory without dividing them. But 2. that implyeth that we did not our selves re-

H   puta-

putatively do all this in Chrift: As fhall be further proved.

22. Their way of Imputation of the Satisfaction of Chrift, overthroweth their own doctrine of the Imputation of his Holinefs and Righteoufnefs. For if all fin be fully pardoned by the Imputed Satisfaction, then fins of *Omiffion* and of habitual Privation and Corruption are pardoned; and then the whole punifhment both of *Senfe* and *Lofs* is remitted: And he that hath no fin of Omiffion or Privation, is a perfect doer of his duty, and holy; and he that hath no punifhment of Lofs, hath title to Life, according to that Covenant which he is reputed to have perfectly obeyed. And fo he is an heir of life, without any Imputed Obedience upon the pardon of all his Difobedience.

Obj. *But Adam muft have obeyed to the Death if he would have Life eternal: Therefore the bare pardon of his fins did not procure his right to life.*

Anf. True; if you fuppofe that only his firft fin was pardoned. But 1. *Adam* had right to heaven as long as he was finlefs. 2. Chrift dyed for all *Adams* fins to the laft breath, and not for the firft only. And fo he did for all ours. And if all the fins of omiffion to the death be pardoned, Life is due to us as righteous.

Obj. *A Stone may be finlefs, and yet not righteous nor have Right to life.*

Anf. True: becaufe it is not a capable fubject. But a man cannot be finlefs, but he is Righteous, and hath right to life by Covenant.

Obj. *But not to punifh is one thing and to Reward is another?*

Anf. They are diftinct formal Relations and Notions:

Reward only for the *terms* and *order* of Collation, and where *Iunocency* is the same with *perfect Duty*, and is the title-Condition; there to be punished is to be *denyed* the *Gift*, and to be *Rewarded* is to have that *Gift* as qualified persons: and not to *Reward*, is materially to *punish*; and to be reputed innocent is to be reputed a Meriter. And it is impossible that the most Innocent man can have any thing from God, but by way of free-Gift as to the *Thing* in Value; however it may be merited in point of Governing Paternal Justice as to the *Order* of donation.

Obj. *But there is a greater Glory merited by Christ, than the Covenant of works promised to man.*

Ans. 1. That's another matter, and belongeth not to Justification, but to Adoption. 2. Christs Sufferings as well as his Obedience, considered as meritorious, did purchase that greater Glory. 3. We did not purchase or merit it in Christ, but Christ for us.

23. Their way of Imputation seemeth to me to leave no place or possibility for Pardon of sin, or at least of no sin after Conversion. I mean, that according to their opinion who think that we fulfilled the Law in Christ as we are elect from eternity, it leaveth no place for any pardon: And according to their opinion who say that we fulfilled it in him as *Believers*, it leaveth no place for pardon of any sin after Faith. For where the Law is reputed perfectly fulfilled (in Habit & Act) there it is reputed that the person hath no sin. We had no sin before we had a Being; and if we are reputed to have perfectly obeyed in Christ from our first Being, we are reputed sinless. But if we are reputed to have obeyed in him

him only since our believing, then we are reputed to have no sin since our Believing. Nothing excludeth sin, if perfect Habitual and Actual Holiness and Obedience do not.

24. And consequently Christs blood shed and Satisfaction is made vain, either as to all our lives, or to all after our first believing.

25. And then no believer must confess his sin, nor his desert of punishment nor repent of it, or be humbled for it.

26. And then all prayer for the pardon of such sin is vain, and goeth upon a false supposition, that we have sin to pardon.

27. And then no man is to be a partaker of the Sacrament as a Conveyance or Seal of such pardon; nor to believe the promise for it.

28. Nor is it a duty to *give thanks* to God or Christ for any such pardon.

29. Nor can we expect Justification from such *guilt* here or at *Judgment*.

30. And then those in Heaven praise Christ in errour, when they magnifie him that washed them from such sins in his blood.

31. And it would be no lie to say that we have no sin, at least, since believing.

32. Then no believer should *fear sinning*, because it is *Impossible* and a *Contradiction*, for the same person to be perfectly innocent to the death, and yet a sinner.

33. Then the Consciences of believers have no work to do, or at least, no examining, convincing, self-accusing and self-judging work.

34. This chargeth God by Consequence of wronging all believers whom he layeth the least punishment

nishment upon: For he that hath perfectly obeyed, or hath perfectly satisfied, by himself or by another in his person, cannot justly be punished. But I have elsewhere fully proved, that Death and other Chastisements are punishments, though not destructive, but corrective: And so is the permission of our further sinning.

35. It intimateth that God wrongeth believers, for not giving them immediately more of the Holy Ghost, and not present perfecting them and freeing them from all sin: For though Christ may give us the fruits of his own merits in the time and way that pleaseth himself; yet if it be *we our selves* that have perfectly satisfied and *merited in Christ*, we have present Right to the thing merited thereupon, and it is an injury to deny it us at all.

36. And accordingly it would be an injury to keep them so long out of Heaven, if they themselves did merit it so long ago.

37. And the very *Threatning* of Punishment in the Law of Grace would seem injurious or incongruous, to them that have already reputatively obeyed perfectly to the death.

38. And there would be no place left for any Reward from God, to any act of obedience done by our selves in our natural or real person: Because having reputatively fulfilled all Righteousness, and deserved all that we are capable of by another, our own acts can have no reward.

39. And I think this would overthrow all Humane Laws and Government: For all true Governours are the Officers of God, and do what they do in subordination to God; and therefore cannot justly

juftly punifh any man, whom he pronounceth erfectly Innocent to the death.

40. This maketh every believer (at leaft) as Righteous as Chrift himfelf, as having true propriety in all the fame numerical Righteoufnefs as his own. And if we be as Righteous as Chrift, are we not as amiable to God? And may we not go to God in our Names as Righteous?

41. This maketh all believers (at leaft) *equally Righteous* in degree, and every one *perfect*, and no difference between them. David and Solomon as Righteous in the act of finning as before, and every weak and fcandalous believer, to be as Righteous as the beft. Which is not true, though many fay that Juftification hath no degrees, but is perfect at firft; as I have proved in my *Life of Faith* and elfewhere.

42. This too much levelleth Heaven and Earth; For in Heaven there can be nothing greater than perfection.

43. The Scripture no-where calleth our Imputed Righteoufnefs by the name of Innocency, or finlefs Perfection, nor Inculpability Imputed. Nay when the very phrafe of *Imputing Chrifts* Righteoufnefs is not there at all, to add all thefe wrong defcriptions of Imputation, is fuch Additions to Gods words as tendeth to let in almoft any thing that mans wit fhall excogitate, and ill befeemeth them, that are for Scripture-fufficiency and perfection, and againft Additions in the general. And whether fome may not fay that we are Imputatively Chrift himfelf, Conceived by the Holy Ghoft, Born of the Virgin Mary, fuffered under Pontius Pilate, Crucified, &c. I cannot tell.

ſtead, and ſatisfied the Juſtice of God: That he hath by his perfect Holineſs and Obedience with thoſe ſufferings, merited our pardon and life: That he never hereby intended to make us Lawleſs or have us Holy, but hath brought us under a **Law of Grace**: which is the Inſtrument by which he pardoneth, juſtifieth and giveth us Right to life: That by this Covenant he requireth of us Repentance and true Faith to our firſt Juſtification, and ſincere Obedience, Holineſs and Perſeverance to our Glorification, to be wrought by his Grace and our Wills excited and enabled by it: That Chriſts Sufferings are to ſave us from ſuffering; but his Holineſs and Obedience are to merit Holineſs, Obedience & Happineſs for us, that we may be like him, and ſo be made perſonally amiable to God: But both his Sufferings and Obedience, do bring us under a Covenant, where Perfection is not neceſſary to our Salvation.

H 4 CHAP.

CHAP. V.

The Objections Answered.

"*Obj.* 1. YOU *confound a Natural and a Politi-*
"*cal person: Christ and the several be-*
"*lieving sinners are not the same natural Person, but*
"*they are the same Political. As are with us,* saith
"Dr. Tullie, *the Sponsor and the Debtor, the Attor-*
"*ney and the Clyent, the Tutor and the Pupil; so are*
"*all the faithful in Christ, both as to their Celestial*
"*regenerate nature, of which he is the first Father, who*
"*begetteth sons by his Spirit and seed of the Word to his*
"*Image, and as to Righteousness derived by Legal*
"*Imputation. Vid.* Dr. Tullie, Justif. Paul. p. 80, 81.
"*It's commonly said that Christ as our surety is our*
"*Person.*

Ans. 1. The distinction of a *Person* into *Natural* and *Political* or *Legal,* is *equivoci in sua equivocata:* He therefore that would not have contention cherished and men taught to damn each other for a word not understood, must give us leave to ask what these equivocals mean. What a *Natural Person* signifieth, we are pretty well agreed; but a *Political Person* is a word not so easily and commonly understood. *Calvin* tells us that *Persona definitur homo qui caput habet civile.* (For *omnis persona est homo, sed non vicissim: Homo cum est vocabulum naturæ; Persona juris civilis.*) And so (as *Albenius*) *civitas, municipium, Castrum, Collegium, Universitas, & quodlibet corpus, Personæ appellatione continetur; ut Spigel.*

gel. But if this Definition be commensurate to the common nature of a civil person, then a King can be none; nor any one that hath not a *civil head.* This therefore is too narrow. The same *Calvin* (*in n. Personæ*) tells us, that *Seneca Personam vocat, cum præ se fert aliquis, quod non est*; A Counterfeit: But sure this is not the sence of the Objectors. In general saith *Calvin, Tam hominem quam qualitatem hominis, seu Conditionem significat.* But it is not sure every *Quality* or *Condition*: *Calvin* therefore giveth us nothing satisfactory, to the decision of the Controversie which these Divines will needs make, whether each believer and Christ be the same Political Person. *Martinius* will make our Controversie no easier by the various significations gathered out of *Vet. Vocab. Gel. Scaliger, Valla*; Which he thus enumerateth. 1. *Persona est accidens conditio hominis, qualitas quâ homo differt ab homine, tum in animo, tum in corpore, tum in externis.* 2. *Homo qualitate dictâ proditus*: 3. *Homo insigni qualitate præditus habens gradum eminentiæ, in Ecclesia Dei, &c.* 4. *Figura, seu facies ficta, larva histrionica, &c.* 5. *Ille qui sub hujusmodi figura aliquam repræsentat, &c.* 6. *Figura eminens in ædificiis quæ ore aquam fundit, &c. Individua substantia humana, seu singularis homo.* 8. *Individua substantia Intelligens quælibet.* Now which of these is *Persona Politica vel Legalis.* Let us but agree what we mean by the word and I suppose we shall find that we are agreed of the Matter. When I deny the *Person* of Christ and the sinner to have been the same, or to be so reputed by God, I mean by *Person*, univocally or properly, An *Individual Intelligent substance.* And they that mean otherwise are obliged to Define; For *Analogum per se se positum stat pro suo significato famosiore.* If they mean that Chrift and the Believer are the fame as to fome *Quality,* or *Condition,* let them tell us what Quality or Condition it is, and I think we fhall be found to be of one mind.

But I think by the fimilitudes of a *Sponsor, Attorney,* and *Guardian,* that they mean by a *Political Person* (not as a *society,* nor fuch as agree *in Quality,* but) *A natural Person so related to another Natural person, as that what he doth and suffereth, Is or Hath, is limitedly to certain ends and uses as effectual as if that other person himself did and suffered, Were or Had numerically the same thing.* I obtrude not a fenfe on others, but muft know theirs before I can know where we differ. And if this be the meaning, we are agreed: Thus far (though I greatly diflike their way that lay much ftrefs on fuch humane phrafes,) I grant the thing meant by them. Chrifts Holinefs Habitual and Actual, and his Merits and Satisfaction are as effectual to a believers Juftification and Salvation upon the terms of the Covenant of Grace (which is fealed by baptifm) as if we had been, done and fuffered the fame our felves. But ftill remember that this is only [*limitedly*] to *these uses,* and on thefe *termes* and no other, and I think that this is the meaning of moft Divines that ufe this phrafe.

But the fenfe of thofe men that I differ from and write againft (the *Libertines* and *Antinomians,* and fome others that own not thofe names,) is this: that *A Legal Person is one so Related to anothers Natural person as that what he Hath, Doth, or Suffereth in such a case,* is (not only effectual as aforefaid to others, but) *is in itself simply Reputed or Imputed to be Morally, though not physically, the Habit, Act and Suffering,*

Suffering, the Merit and *satisfactory* Sacrifice of the other *person*: And *so* being the reputed Haver, Doer or Sufferer, *Meriter* or *Satisfyer* himself, he hath absolute right to all the proper refults or benefits.

And so a man may indeed many ways among us *Represent* or *Personate* another. If I by Law am Commanded to do this or that fervice *per meipsum aut per alium*, I do it in the Moral or Law-fence, becaufe the other doth it in my name and I am allowed fo to do it. So if I appear or anfwer by any Proctor or Attorney; if the Law make it equal to my perfonal appearance and anfwer, it is faid that *I did it by him*: (but only fo far as he doth it as my *Representer* or *in my name*): So if I pay a debt by the hand of *my Servant* or any Meffenger, if fo allowed, I do it by that other. So indeed a Pupil, doth by his Guardian what his Guardian doth, only fo far as the Law obligeth him to confent or ftand to it.

We did not thus our felves fulfil all the Law in and by Chrift : Nor are we *thus* the *Proprietors* of his *Habitual* perfection, *Merits or Satisfaction*.

The common reafon given by the contrary-minded is, that he was our *Surety*, or *Sponfor*, or *fidejuffor*: and fo we tranflate ἐγγυῷ Heb. 7. 22. and I remember not any other text of Scripture allegable for that title. But this word doth not neceffarily fignifie any fuch *Representer of our Perfons* as aforefaid. Nay when he is called thus the *fidejuffor of a better Covenant*, it feemeth plain that it is Gods Covenant as fuch, and fo Gods *Sponfor* that is meant ; and as *Grotius* faith *Mofes pro Deo fpofpondit in Lege Veteri: Jefus pro Deo in Lege Novi: Lex utraque & pactum continet, promiffa habet. Sponforem dare folent minùs nati: & Mofes & Deus hominibus*

bus melius nati erant quam Deus qui inconspicuus. So also Dr. Hamond [*He was Sponsor and Surety for God, that it should be made good to us on Gods part, on Condition that we performed that which was required of us* :] And here they that translate διαθήκη a Testament, never intended that it was our *Part* of the Covenant that is meant by a *Testament*: But (the most Judicious expositor,) " Mr. *Lawson* on the
" text, truly faith [The Scriptures of *Moses* and the
" Prophets translated into Greek will tell us; That
" διαθήκη always signifieth a Law or a Covenant,
" and for the most part both: so it doth in the
" writings of the Apostles and Evangelists where it
" seldom signifieth the last Will and Testament of a
" man. The same thing is a Law in respect of the
" precepts, &c. Ἐγγυος turned Surety, signifieth
" one that undertaketh for another to see something
" paid or performed: And though the word is not
" found in the New Testament except in this place,
" &c. But *Varnius* tells us that Ἐγγυος is μεσίτης,
" a Mediator; and so it is taken here as it's ex-
" pounded by the Apostle in the Chapter following:
" And because a Priest doth undertake to procure
" from God, both the Confirmation and performance
" of the promises to the people, and to that end me-
" diates between both; therefore he is a Surety and
" Mediator of the Covenant, and in this respect the
" Surety and Mediator of the Covenant is a Priest.]

So *Calvin* (though almost passing it by) seemeth to intimate that which I think is the truth, that Christ is called Ἐγγυος of Gods Covenant from the *sacerdotal appropinquation*, mentioned *vers.* 19. &c.

" And *Marlorate* after *Theophilact, Sponsorem pro Me-*
" *diatore & intercessore posuit.*

" So

" So *Paræus in loc. Est novi fæderis Sponsor Christus,*
" *quia novum fædus sanguine & morte sua obsignavit.*

So the *Dutch Annot.* and many others, besides the Ancients, by a *Sponsor*, tell us is meant a *Mediator.*

And we grant that a Mediator is *not of one*, but doth somewhat on the behalf of *both parties*. But that as Mediator he Is, Hath, Doth, Suffereth, Meritteth, Satisfyeth; so as the Representer or person of each believer, as that every such Person is supposed in Law to have *Been, Done, Suffered, Merited*, thus in and by the *Mediator*, is neither signified by this or any other text.

2. And they that distinguish of a Natural and Political Person, do but darken the case by an ill-expressed distinction, which indeed is not of two sorts of *Persons*, but between *Reality* and *Acceptation*, taking *Person* properly for *a Natural Person*: It's one thing to be such a *Person*, and another thing to have the *Act, Passion, Merit*, &c. *Accepted* for that other *Person*: And this latter signifieth, either 1. That it was done by *the other person mediately*, as being *a cheif Cause acting by his Instrument*. 2. Or that it was *done for that other Person* by another. The first is our denyed sence, and the second our affirmed sence.

Among us *Sureties* and *Sponsors* are of several sorts: *Grotius de Jure Belli* tells you of another sense of *Sponsion* in the Civil Law, than is pertinent to the objectors use: And in Baptism the same word, hath had divers senses as used by persons of different intentions. The time was when the Sponsor was not at all taken for the *Political Person* (as you call it) of *Parent* or *Child*, nor spake as *their Instrument*, in *their name*: But was a Third person,

who

who (becauſe many parents *Apoſtatized*, and more *Died* in the Childs minority) did paſs his word, 1. *That the Parent was a credible Perſon*, 2. That if he *Dyed* ſo ſoon or *Apoſtatized*, he himſelf would undertake the Chriſtian Education of the Child. But the *Parent* himſelf was *Sponſor for the Child* in a ſtricter ſenſe, (as alſo Adopting Pro-parents were, & as ſome take God-fathers to be now,) that is, they were taken for ſuch, whoſe Reaſon, will and word, we authoriſed to diſpoſe of the Child as obligingly, as if it had been done by his own reaſon will and word, ſo be it, it were but *For his good*, and the Child did own it when he came to age: And ſo they were to ſpeak as in the Childs name, as if Nature or Charity made them his Repreſenters, in the Judgment of many. (Though others rather think that they were to ſpeak as in their own perſons, *e.g.* I dedicate this Child to God, and enter him into the Covenant as obliged by my Conſent.) But this ſenſe of *Sponſion* is nothing to the preſent Caſe.

They that lay all upon the very Name of a *Surety* as if the word had but one ſignification, and all *Sureties* properly repreſented the perſon of the Principal obliged perſon, do deal very deceitfully: There are *Sureties* or *Sponſors*, 1. For ſome Duty, 2. For Debt, 3. For Puniſhment. 1. It is one thing to undertake that another ſhall do a Commanded duty: 2. It's another thing to undertake that elſe I will do it for him: 3. It's another thing to be Surety that he ſhall pay a Debt, or elſe I will pay it for him: 4. It's another thing to undertake that he ſhall ſuffer a penalty, or elſe to ſuffer for him, or make a Valuable Compenſation.

1. And it's one kind of Surety that becometh a
ſecond

second party in the bond, and so maketh *himself a debtor*; 2. And its another sort of Surety that *undertaketh only the Debt afterward voluntarily as a Friend*; who may pay it on such Conditions as he and the Creditor think meet, without the Debtors knowledg. Every Novice that will but open *Calvin* may see that *Fidejussor* and *Sponsor* are words of very various signification; and that they seldom or never signifie the *Person Natural* or *Political* (as you call it) of the *Principal*: *Sponsor est qui sponte & non rogatus pro alio promittit, ut Accurs. vel quicunque spondet, maxime pro aliis: Fidejubere est suo periculo fore id, de quo agitur, recipere: Vel, fidem suam pro alio obligare*. He is called *Adpromissor*, and he is *Debtor*, but not the same *person* with the *Principal*; but his promise is *accessoria obligatio, non principalis*. Therefore *Fidejussor sive Intercessor non est conveniendus, nisi prius debitore principali convento: Fidejussores a correis ita differunt, quod hi suo & proprio morbo laborant, illi vero alieno tenentur: Quare fideijussori magis succurrendum censent: Venia namque digni sunt qui aliena tenentur Culpa, cujusmodi sunt fidejussores pro alieno debito obligati, inquit* Calv.

There must be somewhat more than the bare name ἐγγύος once used of Christ as Mediator of Gods Covenant, or the name of a *Surety* as now used among men, that must go to prove that the Mediator and the several sinners are the same *Legal Persons* in Gods account.

But seeing *Legal-Personality* is but a *Relation* of our *Natural person*, to another *Natural person*, that we may not quarrel and tear the Church when really we we differ not 1. Let our agreement be noted. 2. Our difference intelligibly stated.

1. It is granted (not only by *Dr. Tullie*, but others that accurately handle the Controversie,) 1. That Christ and the Believer never were nor are our Natural person; and that no union with him maketh us to be Christ, or God, nor him to be *Peter*, *John* or *Paul*, &c. That we know of no third sort of *Natural person*, (which is neither Jesus, nor Peter, John, &c.) But composed of both united, which is constituted by our Union. For though it be agreed on, that the same Spirit that is in Christ is (operatively) also in all his Members, and that therefore our *Communion* with him is more than *Relative*, and that from this *Real-Communion*, the name of a *Real-Union* may be used; yet here the *Real-Union* is not *Personal* (as the same Sun quickeneth and illuminateth a Bird and a Frog and a Plant, and yet maketh them not our person:) Therefore he that will say we are *Physically* one with Christ, and not only Relatively; but tell us [*ONE What?*] and make his words Intelligible; and must deny that we are ONE PERSON: and that by that time we are not like to be found differing. But remember that while *Physical Communion*, is confessed by all, what *UNION* we shall from thence be said to have (this Foundation being agreed on) is like to prove but a question, *de realitione & nomine*.

2. Yea all the world must acknowledg that the whole Creation is *quoad præsentiam & derivationem* more dependant on God than the fruit is on the *Tree*, or the Tree on the Earth, and that God is the inseperate Cause of our *Being*, *Station*, and *Life*;

And

dent of our *natural Persons*; (and an *Accident* it is) *unless* it can be reduced to that of *Relation*. 1. The *Habits* of our Person, cannot possibly be the habits of another inherently. 2. The *actions* of one *cannot* possibly be the *actions* of another, as the Agent, unless as that other as a *principal Cause*, acteth by the other as his *Instrument* or second Cause. 3. The same *fundamentum relationis* inherent in One Person, is not inherent in another if it be a personal Relation: And so the same individual Relation that is one Mans, cannot numerically be another Mans, by the same sort of in-being, propriety, or adherence. Two Brothers have a Relation in *kind the same*, but not *unmerically*.

4. And it is agreed that God judgeth not falsly, and therefore taketh not Christ's Righteousness to be any more or otherwise *ours*, than indeed it is; nor imputeth it to us erroneously.

5. Yet it is commonly agreed, that *Christ's Righteousness* is O U R S in some sense; And so far is justly *reputed Ours*, or *imputed* to us as being *Ours*.

6. And this ambiguous syallable [O U R S] (enough to set another Age of Wranglers into bitter Church-tearing strife, if not hindred by some that will call them to explain an ambiguous word) is it that must be understood to end this Controversie. *Propriety* is the thing signified. 1. In the strictest sense that is called *Ours*, which inhereth in us,

a third person doth partly *instead* of what we should have done (*had, or suffered*) and partly for our *use,* or *benefit.* 4. In a yet larger sense that may be called *OURS,* which another *hath,* or *doth,* or *suffereth* for our *Benefit,* (though not in our stead) and which will be for our good, (as that which a Friend or Father hath, is his Friends or Childs, and *all things* are *Ours,* whether *Paul,* or *&c.* and the Godly are owners of the World, in as much as God *will use all for* their good).

7. It is therefore a *Relation* which Christ's Righteousness hath to us, or we to it, that must here be meant by the word [*OURS*]: Which is our *RIGHT* or *Jus*; And that is acknowledged to be no *Jus* or Right to it in the foresaid denied sense; And it is agreed that *some Right* it is. Therefore, to understand what it is, the *Titulus seu Fundamentum juris* must be known.

8. And here it is agreed; 1. That we are before Conversion or Faith related to Christ as part of the Redeemed World, of whom it is said, 2 *Cor.* 5. 19. *That God was in Christ, reconciling the World to himself, not imputing to them their sins,* &c. 2. That we are after Faith related to Christ as his Covenanted People, Subjects, Brethren, Friends, and Political Members; yea, as such that have *Right to,* and *Possession of* Real Communion with him by his Spirit: And that we have then Right to *Pardon,* Justification, and Adoption, (or have

Right

Right to *Impunity* in the promised degree, and to the *Spirits Grace*, and the *Love of God*, and *Heavenly Glory*). This Relation to *Christ* and this Right, to the *Benefits* of his *Righteousness* are agreed on: And consequently that his *Righteousness* is *OURS*, and so may be called, as far as the foresaid *Relations* and *Rights* import.

II. Now a Relation (as *Ockam* hath fully proved) having no real entity, beside the *quid absolutum*, which is the *Subject*, *Fundamentum*, or *Terminus*, he that yet raileth at his Brother as not saying enough, or not being herein so wise as he, and will maintain that yet *Christ's Righteousness* is further *OURS*, must name the *Fundamentum* of that *Right* or *Propriety*: What more is it that you mean? I think the make-bates have here little probability of fetching any more Fuel to their Fire, or turning Christ's Gospel into an occasion of strife and mutual enmity, if they will but be driven to a distinct explication, and will not make *confusion* and *ambiguous* words their defence and weapons. If you set your quarrelsome Brains on work, and study as hard as you can for matter of Contention, it will not be easie for you to find it, unless you will raze out the names of *Popery*, *Socinianism*, *Arminianism*, or *Solifidianism*, Heresie, &c. instead of real Difference. But if the *angriest* and *lowdest* Speakers be in the right, *Bedlam* and *Billingsgate* may be the most Orthodox places.

Briefly, 1. The foresaid Benefits of Christ's Righteousness, (Habitual, Active and Passive) as a Meritorious, Satisfactory, Purchasing Cause, are ours.

2. To

2. To say that the Benefits are *Ours*, importeth that the *Causal Righteousness* of Christ is related to us, *and the Effects* as *such a Cause:* and so is it self *OURS*, in that sense, that is, so related.

3. And Christ himself is *OURS*, as related to us as our Saviour; the Procurer and Giver of those Benefits. And do you mean any more by [*OURS*]?

If you say that we deny any *Benefits* of Christ's Righteousness which you assert, name what they are. If you say that we deny any true *Fundamentum juris*, or reason of our title, name what that is. If you say that we deny any true Relation to Christ himself, tell us what it is: If you cannot, say that you are agreed.

1. If you say that the Benefit denied by us, is that we are judged by God, as those that (habitually and actively) have perfectly fulfilled the Law of Innocency our selves, though not in our natural Persons, yet by Christ as representing us, and so shall be justified by that Law of Innocency as the Fulfiller of it, we do deny it, and say, That you subvert the Gospel, and the true Benefits which we have by Christ.

2. If you say that we deny that God esteemeth or reputeth us, to be the very Subjects of that Numerical Righteousness, in the Habits, Acts, Passion or Relation, which was in the Person of Christ, or to have *done, suffered,* or *merited our selves* in and by him, as the proper Representer of our Persons therein; and so that his Righteousness is thus imputed to us as truly in it self *our own propriety,* we do deny it, and desire you to do so also, lest you deny Christianity.

2. If

2. If you blame us for saying, That we had or have no such Relation to Christ, as to our Instrument, or the proper full Representer of each Believers particular Person, by whom we did truly fulfil the Law of Innocency, habitually and actively, and satisfied, merited, &c. We do still say so, and wish you to consider what you say, before you proceed to say the contrary.

But if you come not up to this, where will you find a difference.

Object. 2. *Christ is called The Lord our Righteousness, and he is made Righteousness to us, and we are made the Righteousness of God in him,* 2 Cor. 5. 21, &c. *And by the Obedience of one, many are made Righteous.*

Answ. And are we not all agreed of all this? But can his Righteousness be *Ours* no way but by the foresaid Personation Representating? How prove you that? He is *Our Righteousness*, and his *Obedience maketh us Righteous.*

1. Because the very Law of Innocency which we dishonoured and broke by sin, is perfectly fulfilled and honoured by him, as a Mediator, to repair the injury done by our breaking it.

2. In that he suffered to satisfie Justice for our sin.

3. In that hereby he hath merited of God the Father, all that *Righteousness* which we are truly the Subjects of, whether it be Relative, or Qualitative, or Active; that is, 1. Our Right to Christ in Union to the Spirit, to Impunity, and to Glory; And, 2. The Grace of the Spirit by which we are made Holy, and fulfil the Conditions of the Law

of Grace. We are the *Subjects of these*, and he is the *Minister*, and the *meritorious Cause* of our *Life*, is well called *Our Righteousness*, and by many the *material Cause*, (as our own perfect Obedience would have been) because it is the *Matter* of that Merit.

4. And also Christ's Intercession with the Father, still procureth all this as the Fruit of his Merits.

5. And we are Related as his Members (though not parts of his *Person* as such) to him that thus merited for us.

6. And we have the Spirit from him as our Head.

7. And he is our Advocate, and will justifie us as our Judg.

8. And all this is *God's Righteousness* designed for us, and thus far given us by him.

9. And the perfect Justice and Holiness of God, is thus glorified in us through Christ. And are not all these set together enough to prove, that we justly own all asserted by these Texts? But if you think that you have a better sense of them, you must better prove it, than by a bare naming of the words.

Object. 3. *If Christ's Righteousness be Ours, then we are Righteous by it as Ours; and so God reputeth it but as it is: But it is Ours; 1. By our Union with him. 2. And by his Gift, and so consequently by God's Imputation.*

Answ. 1. I have told you before that it is confessed to be *Ours*; but that this syllable *OURS* hath many senses; and I have told you in what sense, and

and how far it is *OURS*, and in that sense we are justified by it, and it is truly imputed to us, or reputed or reckoned as *OURS*: But not in their sense that claim a strict ·Propriety in the same numerical Habits, Acts, Sufferings, Merits, Satisfaction, which was in Christ, or done by him, as if they did become *Subjects* of the *same Accidents*; or, as if they did it by an instrumental second Cause. But it is *OURS*, as being done by a Mediator, instead of what we should have done, and as the Meritorious Cause of all our Righteousness and Benefits, which are freely given us for the sake hereof.

2. He that is made Righteousness to us, is also made Wisdom, Sanctification and Redemption to us: but that *sub genere Causæ Efficientis, non autem Causæ Constitutivæ:* We are the Subjects of the same numerical *Wisdom* and *Holiness* which is in Christ. Plainly the Question is, Whether Christ or his Righteousness, Holiness, Merits, and Satisfaction, be *Our Righteousness Constitutively*, or only *Efficiently?* The *Matter* and *Form* of Christ's Personal Righteousness is *OURS*, as an Efficient Cause, but it is neither the nearest *Matter*, or the *Form* of that Righteousness which is *OURS* as the Subjects of it; that is, It is not a Constitutive Cause nextly material, or formal of it.

3. If our Union with Christ were Personal, (making us the same Person) then doubtless the Accidents of his Person would be the Accidents of ours, and so not only Christ's Righteousness, but every Christians would be each of Ours: But that is not so. Nor is it so given us by him.

Object.

Object. 4. *You do seem to suppose that we have none of that kind of Righteousness at all, which consisteth in perfect Obedience and Holiness, but only a Right to Impunity and Life, with an imperfect Inherent Righteousness in our selves: The Papists are forced to confess, that a Righteousness we must have which consisteth in a conformity to the preceptive part of the Law, and not only the Retributive part: But they say, It is in our selves, and we say it is Christ's imputed to us.*

Answ. 1. The Papists (*e. g.* Learned *Vasquez* in *Rom.* 5.) talk so ignorantly of the differences of the Two Covenants, or the Law of Innocency and of Grace, as if they never understood it. And hence they 1. seem to take no notice of the Law of Innocency, or of Nature now commanding our perfect Obedience, but only of the Law of Grace. 2. Therefore they use to call those *Duties* but Perfections; and the Commands that require them, but *Counsels*, where they are not made Conditions of Life: and sins not bringing Damnation, some call Venial, (a name not unfit) and some expound that as properly *no sin*, but analogically. 3. And hence they take little notice, when they treat of Justification, of the *Remitting of Punishment*; but by *remitting Sin*, they usually mean the destroying the *Habits:* As if they forgot all *actual sin past*, or thought that it deserved no Punishment, or needed no Pardon: For a past Act in it self is now nothing, and is capable of no Remission but Forgiveness. 4. Or when they do talk of Guilt of Punishment, they lay so much of the Remedy on Man's *Satisfaction,* as if Christ's Satisfaction and

Merits

Merits had procured no pardon, or at least, of no temporal part of Punishment. 5. And hence they ignorantly revile the Protestants, as if we denied all *Personal Inherent Righteousness*, and trusted only to the Imputation of Christ's Righteousness as justifying wicked unconverted Men: The Papists therefore say not that we are innocent or sinless, (really or imputatively); no not when they dream of *Perfection* and *Supererrogation*, unless when they denominate *Sin* and *Perfection* only from the Condition of the Law of Grace, and not that of Innocency.

2. But if any of them do as you say, no wonder if they and you contend: If one say, We *are Innocent*, or *Sinless* in reality, and the *other, we are so* by *Imputation*, when we are so no way at all (but sinners *really*, and so reputed); what Reconciliation is there to be expected, till both lay by their Errour?

Object. 5. *How can God accept him as just, who is really and reputedly a Sinner? This dishonoureth his Holiness and Justice.*

Answ. Not so: Cannot God pardon sin, upon a valuable Merit and Satisfaction of a Mediator? And though he judg us not *perfect* now, and accept us not as such; yet 1. now he judgeth us Holy, 2. and the Members of a perfect Saviour; 3. and will make us perfect and spotless, and then so judg us, having washed us from our sins in the Blood of the Lamb.

Object. 6. *Thus you make the* Reatus Culpæ, *not pardoned at all, but only the* Reatus Pœnæ.

Answ.

Answ. 1. If by *Reatus Culpæ* be meant the Relation of a Sinner as he is *Revera Peccator*, and so to be *Reus*, is to be *Revera ipse qui peccavit*; then we must consider what you mean by *Pardon:* For if you mean the *nullifying* of such a *Guilt*, (or *Reality*) it is impossible, because *necessitate existentiæ*, he that hath once sinned, will be still the Person that sinned, while he is a Person, and the Relation of *one that sinned* will cleave to him: It will eternally be a true Proposition, [*Peter* and *Paul* did sin]; But if by *Pardon* you mean, the *pardoning* of all the *penalty* which for that sin is due, (*damni vel sensus*) so *it is pardoned*; and this is indeed the *Reatus pœnæ:* Not only the *Penalty*, but the *Dueness* of that Penalty, or the Obligation to it, is remitted and nullified.

2. Therefore if by *Reatus Culpæ* you mean an *Obligation* to *Punishment for that Fault*, this being indeed the *Reatus pœnæ*, as is said, is done away. So that we are, I think, all agreed *de re*; And *de nomine* you may say that the *Reatus Culpæ* is done away or remitted, or not, in several senses: *In se*, it is not nullified, nor can be: But as *Dueness* of Punishment followeth, that is pardoned.

Object. 7. *You have said, That though we were not personally but seminally in* Adam *when he sinned, yet when we are Persons, we are Persons guilty of his actual sin: And so we must be Persons that are Partakers of Christ's Actual Righteousness, and not only of its Effects, as soon as we are Believers. For Christ being the Second* Adam, *and publick Person, we have our part in his Righteousness, as truly and as much as in* Adam'*s sin.*

Answ

Answ. 1. We must first understand how far *Adam*'s sin is ours: And first I have elsewhere proved that our *Covenant-Union and Interest* supposeth our *Natural Union* and *Interest*; and that it is an adding to God's Word and Covenant, to say, That he covenanted that *Adam* should personate each one of his Posterity in God's imputation or account, any further than they were naturally in him; and so that his *innocency or sin* should be reputed theirs, *as far* as if they had been personally the Subjects and Agents. The *Person* of *Peter* never was in *Reality* or *God's Reputation*, the *Person of* Adam. (Nor *Adam*'s Person the Person of *Peter*): But *Peter* being virtually and seminally in *Adam*, when he sinned, his Person is derived from *Adam*'s Person: And so *Peter*'s Guilt is not numerically the same with *Adams*, but the Accident of another Subject, and therefore another Accident, derived with the Person from *Adam* (and from nearer Parents). The *Fundamentum* of that *Relation* (of Guilt) is the *Natural Relation* of the Person to *Adam*, (and so it is *Relatio in Relatione fundata*). The *Fundamentum* of that *natural Relation*, is *Generation*, yea a *series* of Generations from *Adam* to that Person: And *Adam*'s Generation being the Communication of a *Guilty Nature with personality* to his Sons and Daughters, is the *fundamentum* next following his *personal Fault and Guilt* charged on him by the Law: So that here is a long *series* of efficient Causes, bringing down from *Adam's Person and Guilt* a *distinct numerical Person* and *Guilt* of every one of his later Posterity.

2. And it is not the same sort of Guilt, or so plenary, which is on us, for *Adam*'s Act, as was on

on him, but a Guilt Analogical, or of another fort: that is, He was guilty of being the *wilful finning Perfon*, and fo are not we, but only of being *Perfons whofe Being is derived by Generation from the wilful finning Perfons*, (befides the guilt of our own inherent pravity): That is, *The Relation is fuch which our Perfons have to* Adam's *Perfon, as make it juft with God to defert us, and to punifh us for that and our pravity together.* This is our Guilt of Original fin.

3. And this Guilt cometh to us by Natural Propagation, and refultancy from our very Nature fo propagated. And now let us confider of our contrary Intereft in Chrift.

- And, 1. Our Perfons are not the fame as Chrift's Perfon, (nor Chrift's as ours) nor ever fo judged or accounted of God.

2. Our *Perfons* were not naturally, feminally, and virtually in Chrift's Perfon (any further than he is Creator and Caufe of all things) as they were in *Adams*.

3. Therefore we derive not Righteoufnefs from him by Generation, but by his voluntary Donation or Contract.

4. As he became not our Natural Parent, fo our Perfons not *being in Chrift* when he obeyed, are not *reputed to have been in him naturally*, or to have obeyed in and by him.

5. If Chrift and we are reputed one Perfon, either he *obeyed* in our *Perfon*, or we *in his*, or *both*. If he *obeyed* as a *Reputed Sinner* in the Perfon of each Sinner, his Obedience could not be meritorious, according to the Law of Innocency, which required finlefs Perfection; And he being fuppofed

sed to have broken the Law in our Persons, could not so be supposed to keep it. If we obeyed in his *Person*, we obeyed as *Mediators*, or Christ's, of which before.

6. But as is oft said, Christ our Mediator undertook in a middle Person to reconcile God and Man, (not by bringing God erroneously to judg that he or we were what we are not, or did what we did not, but) by *being*, *doing*, and *suffering* for us, that in *his own Person*, which should better answer God's Ends and Honour, than if we had done and suffered in our Persons, that hereby he might *merit* a free Gift of *Pardon* and *Life* (with himself) to be given by a Law of Grace to believing penitent Accepters. And so our Righteousness, as is oft opened, is a Relation resulting at once from all these Causes as fundamental to it, *viz.* Christ's Meritorious Righteousness, his free Gift thereupon, and our Relation to him as Covenanters or United Believers. And this is agreed on.

Object. 8. *As Christ is a Sinner by imputation of our sin, so we are Righteous, by the imputation of his Righteousness. But it is our sin it self that is imputed to Christ: Therefore it is his Righteousness it self that is imputed to us.*

Answ. 1. Christ's Person was not the Subject of our personal Relative *Guilt*, much less of our *Habits* or *Acts*.

2. God did not judg him to have been so.

3. Nay, Christ had no *Guilt* of the *same kind* reckoned to be on him; else those unmeet Speeches, used rashly by some, would be true, *viz.* That Christ was the greatest Murderer, Adulterer, Idolater, Blasphe-

Blasphemer, Thief, &c. in all the World, and consequently more hated of God, (for God must needs hate a sinner as such). To be guilty of sin as we are, is to be reputed truly to be the Person that committed it: But so was not Christ, and therefore not so to be reputed. Christ was but the Mediator that undertook to suffer for our sins, that we might be forgiven; and not for his *own* sin, real or justly reputed: Expositors commonly say that to be [*made sin for us*], is but to be made [*a Sacrifice for sin*]. So that Christ took upon him neither our *numerical guilt* of sin it self, nor any of the same *species*; but only our *Reatum Pœnæ*, or *Debt* of *Punishment*, or (lest the Wrangler make a verbal quarrel of it) our *Reatum Culpæ non qua talem & in se, sed quatenus est fundamentum Reatus pœnæ* : And so his *Righteousness* is ours; not *numerically* the same Relation that he was the Subject of made that Relation to us; nor yet a *Righteousness* of the same *Species* as Christ's is given us at all, (for his was a *Mediators Righteousness*, consisting in, 1. *perfect Innocency*; 2. And that in the *Works* of the *Jewish Law*, which bind us not; 3. And in doing his peculiar *Works*, as *Miracles*, *Resurrection*, &c. which were all *His Righteousness* as a conformity to *that Law*, and performance of that *Covenant*, which was made with, and to him *as Mediator*). But his Righteousness is the *Meritorious Cause* and *Reason* of another Righteousness or Justification (distinct from his) freely given us by the Father and himself by his Covenant. So that here indeed the Similitude much cleareth the Matter; And they that will not blaspheme Christ by making *guilt of sin it self* in its *formal Relation* to be his own, and so

Christ

Chrift to be *formally* as great a finner as all the Redeemed fet together, and they that will not overthrow the Gofpel, by making us formally as Righteous as Chrift in kind and meafure, muft needs be agreed with us in this part of the Controverfie.

Object. *9. When you infer, That if we are reckoned to have perfectly obeyed in and by Chrift, we cannot be again bound to obey our felves afterward, nor be guilty of any fin; you muft know that it's true, That we cannot be bound to obey to the fame ends as Chrift did, (which is to redeem us, or to fulfil the Law of Works) But yet we muft obey to other ends, viz. Ingratitude, and to live to God, and to do good, and other fuch like.*

Anfw. 1. This is very true, That we are not bound to obey to all the fame ends that Chrift did, as to redeem the World, nor to fulfil the Law of Innocency. But hence it clearly followeth that *Chrift obeyed not* in each of our Perfons legally, but in the Perfon of a Mediator, feeing his due Obedience and ours have fo different *Ends,* and a different formal Relation, (his being a conformity proximately to the Law, given him as Mediator) that they are not fo much as of the fame *fpecies,* much lefs numerically the fame.

2. And this fully proveth that we are not reckoned to have perfectly obeyed in and by him: For elfe we could not be yet obliged to obey, though to other ends than he was: For either this *Obedience of Gratitude* is a Duty or not; If not, it is not truly *Obedience,* nor the omiffion fin: If yea, then *that Duty* was made a Duty by fome Law: And if by a Law we are now bound to obey *in gratitude* (or
for

for what ends foever) either we do all that we are so bound to do, or not. If we do it (or any of it) then to say that we did it twice, once by Christ, and once by our selves, is to say that we were bound to do it twice, and then Christ did not all that we were bound to, but half: But what Man is he that sinneth not? Therefore seeing it is certain, that no Man doth all that he is bound to do by the Gospel, (in the time and measure of his *Faith, Hope, Love, Fruitfulness,* &c.) it followeth that he is a sinner, and that he is not supposed to have done all that by Christ which he failed in, both because he was bound to do it himself, and because he is a sinner for not doing it.

3. Yea, the Gospel binds us to that which Christ could not do for us, it being a Contradiction. Our great Duties are, 1. To believe in a Saviour. 2. To improve all the parts of his Mediation by a Life of Faith. 3. To repent of our sins. 4. To mortifie sinful Lusts in our selves. 5. To fight by the Spirit against our flesh. 6. To confess our selves sinners. 7. To pray for pardon. 8. To pray for that Grace which we culpably want. 9. To love God for redeeming us. 10. Sacramentally to covenant with Christ, and to receive him and his Gifts; with many such like; which Christ was not capable of doing in and on his own Person for us, though as Mediator he give us Grace to do them, and pray for the pardon of our sins, as in our selves.

4. But the Truth which this Objection intimateth, we all agree in, *viz.* That the Mediator perfectly kept the Law of Innocency, that the keeping of that Law might not be necessary to our Salvation,

on, (and so such Righteousness necessary in our selves) but that we might be pardoned for want of perfect Innocency, and be saved upon our sincere keeping of the Law of Grace, because the Law of Innocency was kept by our Mediator, and thereby the Grace of the New-Covenant merited, and by it Christ, Pardon, Spirit and Life, by him freely given to Believers.

Object. 10. *The same Person may be really a sinner in himself, and yet perfectly innocent in Christ, and by imputation.*

Answ. Remember that you suppose here the *Person* and *Subject* to be the same Man: And then that the two contrary Relations of *perfect Innocency*, or *guiltlesness*, and *guilt of any*, (yea much sin) can be consistent in him, is a gross contradiction. Indeed he may be guilty, and not guilty in several partial respects; but a *perfection* of *guiltlesness* excludeth all guilt. But we are guilty of many a sin after Conversion, and need a Pardon. All that you should say is this, *We are sinners our selves, but we have a Mediator that sinned not, who merited Pardon and Heaven for sinners.*

2. But if you mean that God reputeth us to be perfectly innocent when we are not, because that Christ was so, it is to impute Error to God: He reputeth no Man to be otherwise than he is: But he doth indeed first give, and then impute a Righteousness Evangelical to us, instead of perfect Innocency, which shall as certainly bring us to Glory; and that is, He giveth us both the Renovation of

K his

his Spirit, (to Evangelical Obedience) and a Right by free gift to Pardon and Glory for the Righteousness of Christ that merited it; And this thus given us, he reputeth to be an acceptable Righteousness in us.

CHAP. VI.

Animadversions on some of Dr. T. Tullies Strictures.

§. 1. I Suppose the Reader desireth not to be wearied with an examination of all Dr. *Tullies* words, which are defective in point of Truth, Justice, Charity, Ingenuity, or Pertinency to the Matter, but to see an answer to those that by appearance of pertinent truth do require it, to disabuse the incautelous Readers; Though somewhat by the way may be briefly said for my own Vindication. And this Tractate being conciliatory, I think meet here to leave out most of the *words*, and *personal* part of his contendings, and also to leave that which concerneth the *interest of Works* (as they are pleased to call *Man's performance of the Conditions of the Covenant of Grace*) in our Justification, to a fitter place, *viz.* To annex what I think needful to my friendly Conference with Mr. *Christopher Cartwright* on the Subject, which Dr. *Tullies* Assault perswadeth me to publish.

§. 2.

§. 2. *pag.* 71. *Justif. Paulin.* This Learned Doctor saith, [*The Scripture mentioneth no Justification in foro Dei at all, but that One, which is Absolution from the Maledictory Sentence of the Law.*

Answ. 1. If this be untrue, it's pity so worthy a Man should unworthily use it against peace and concord. If it be true, I crave his help for the expounding of several Texts.

Exod. 23. 6, 7. *Thou shalt not wrest the Judgment of thy Poor in his Cause: Keep thee far from a false Matter, and the Innocent and Righteous slay thou not; for I will not justifie the wicked*]. Is the meaning only, I will not absolve the wicked from the Maledictory Sentence of the Law (of Innocency)? Or is it not rather, [I will not misjudg the wicked to be just, nor allow his wickedness, nor yet allow thee so to do, nor leave thee unpunished for thy unrighteous judgment, but will condemn thee if thou condemn the Just].

Job 25. 4. *How then can Man be justified with God?* or, *How can he be clean that is born of a Woman?* Is the sense, [*How can Man be absolved from the Maledictory Sentence of the Law?*] Or rather, [How can he be maintained Innocent?]

Psal. 143. 2. *In thy sight shall no Man living be justified.* Is the sense, [*No Man living shall be absolved from the Maledictory sentence of the Law?* Then we are all lost for ever: Or rather no Man shall be found and maintained Innocent, and judged one that deserved not punishment]; (Therefore we are not judged perfect fulfillers of that Law by another or our selves).

Object. *But this is for us and against you: for it denyeth that there is any such Justification.*

K 2 *Answ.*

Answ. Is our Controversie *de re,* or only *de nomine,* of the sense of the word Justifie? If *de re,* then his meaning is to maintain, That God never doth judg a Believer to be a Believer, or a Godly Man to be Godly, or a performer of the Condition of Pardon and Life to have performed it, nor will justifie any believing Saint against the false Accusations, that he is an Infidel, a wicked ungodly Man, and an Hypocrite, (or else he writeth against those that he understood not). But if the Question be (as it must be) *de nomine,* whether the word *Justifie* have any sense besides that which he appropriateth to it, then a Proposition that denieth the *Existentiam rei,* may confute his denyal of any other sense of *the word.*

So *Isa.* 43. 9, 26. *Let them bring forth their Witnesses that they may justified: Declare thou that thou mayest be justified*; that is, proved Innocent.

But I hope he will hear and reverence the Son; Matth. 12. 37. *By thy words thou shalt be Justified, and by thy words thou shalt be Condemned*] (speaking of Gods Judgment) which I think meaneth *(de re & nomine) Thy Righteous or unrighteous words* shall be a part of the Cause of the day, or Matter, for or according to which, thou shalt be judged obedient or disobedient to the Law of Grace, and so far just or unjust, and accordingly sentenced to Heaven or Hell, as is described *Matth.* 25. But it seems this Learned Doctor understands it only, *By thy words thou shalt be absolved* from the Maledictory Sentence of the Law, and by thy words contrarily condemned.

Luk. 18. 14. The Publican [*went down to his House justified rather than the other*]; I think not only

only [from the *Maledictory Sentence of the Law* of *Innocency*] but [*by God approved a sincere Penitent*], and so a fit Subject of the other part of Justification.

Acts 13. 30. is the Text that speaketh most in the sense he mentioneth; And yet I think it includeth more, *viz. By Christ,* 1. *we are not* only absolved from that Condemnation due for our sins; 2. but also we are by his repealing or ending of the *Mosaick Law* justified against the Charge of Guilt for our not observing it; and 3. *Augustine* would add, That we are by Christ's Spirit and Grace made just (that is, sincerely Godly) by the destruction of those inherent and adherent sins, which the *Law* of *Moses* could not mortifie and save us from, but the Spirit doth.

Rom. 2. 13. *Not the Hearers of the Law are just before God, but the Doers of the Law shall be justified*]. Is it only, *The Doers shall be Absolved from the Maledictory Sentence, &c* ? Or first and chiefly, *They shall be judged well-doers, so far as they do well,* and so approved and justified, so far as they do keep the Law ? (which because no Man doth perfectly, and the Law of Innocency requireth Perfection, none can be justified absolutely, or to Salvation by it).

Object. *The meaning is,* (say some) *The Doers of the Law should be justified by it* ; were there any such.

Answ. That's true, of absolute Justification unto Life : But that this is not all the sense of the Text, the two next Verses shew, where the Gentiles are pronounced partakers of some of that which he meaneth inclusively in doing to Justification: Therefore it muſt include that their Actions and Perſons are ſo *far, juſtified*, (more or leſs) as they are *Doers* of the Law, as being ſo far actively juſt.

Rom. 8. 30. *Whom he juſtified, them he alſo glorified*; And 1 Cor. 6. 11. *Ye are juſtified in the Name of the Lord Jeſus, and by the Spirit of our God*. Many Proteſtants, and among them *Beza* himſelf, expound (in the Papiſts and *Auſtins* ſenſe of Juſtification) as including Sanctification alſo, as well as Abſolution from the Curſe: And ſo Arch Biſhop *Uſher* told me he underſtood them. As alſo *Tit.* 3. 7. *That being juſtified freely by his Grace*.

And many think ſo of *Rom.* 4. 5. he [*juſtifieth the Ungodly*] ſay they, by Converting, Pardoning, and Accepting them in Chriſt to Life.

And *Rom.* 8. 33. *Who ſhall condemn? it is God that juſtifieth*, ſeemeth to me more than barely to ſay, God *abſolveth us from the Curſe*, becauſe it is ſet againſt *Man's Condemnation*, (who reproached, ſlandered and perſecuted the Chriſtians as evil Doers, as they did Chriſt, to whom they were predeſtinated to be conformed). And ſo muſt mean, *God will not only abſolve us from his Curſe*, but alſo juſtifie our Innocency againſt all the falſe Accuſations of our Enemies.

And it ſeemeth to be ſpoken by the Apoſtle, with reſpect to *Iſa*. 50. 8. *He is near that juſtifieth me, who will contend with me?* Which my reverence to this Learned Man ſufficeth not to make me believe, is taken only in his ſenſe of Abſolution.

Rev. 22. 11. *He that is Righteous, let him be juſtified ſtill*, (δικαιωθήτω) which not only our Tranſlaters, but almoſt all Expoſitors take as incluſive

clusive of Inherent Righteousness, if not principally speaking of it.

To speak freely, I remember not one Text of Scripture that useth the word [*Justifie*] in this Doctor's sense; that is, *Only for the said absolution from the Curse of the Law*: For all those other Texts that speak for Justification by Christ's Grace, and Faith, *and not by the Works of the Law*, (as *Rom.* 3. 20, 24, 28, 30. and 4. 2, 5, 25. & 5. 1, 9, 16, 18. 1 *Cor.* 4. 4. *Gal.* 2. 16, 17. & 3. 8, 11, 24. & 5. 4, &c.) do all seem to me to mean, not only that [we are *absolved from the Maledictory Sentence of the Law*], but also that we are first made, and then accounted Persons first meet for Absolution, and next meet for God's Acceptance of us as just, and as Heirs of Life Eternal, and meet for the great *Reward in Heaven:* For when the Apostle denieth *Justification* by *Works*; it is not credible that he meaneth only, that [*By the Works of the Law no Man is absolved from the Curse of the Law*] ; But also, *No Man by the Works of the Law*, is before God taken for a Performer of the necessary Condition of Absolution and Salvation, nor fit for his Acceptance, and for the Heavenly Reward.

Answ. 2. But let the Reader here note, that the Doctor supposeth *James* to mean, that [*By Works a Man is absolved from the Maledictory Sentence of the Law, and not by Faith only*]. For that *James* speaks of Justification *in foro Dei* is past all doubt : And who would have thought that the Doctor had granted this of the Text of *James* ? But mistakes seldom agree among themselves.

Answ. 3. And would not any Man have thought that

that this Author had pleaded for such an Imputation of Christ's Righteousness, as justifieth not only from the Maledictory Sentence of the Law, but also from the very guilt of sin as sin, we being reputed, (not only pardoned sinners, but) perfect fulfillers of the Law by Christ, and so that we are in Christ conform to the *Fac hoc* or preceptive part commanding Innocency? Who would have thought but this was his drift? If it be not, all his angry Opposition to me, is upon a mistake so foul, as reverence forbids me to name with its proper Epithets: If it be, how can the same Man hold, That we are justified as in Christ, conform *to the Precept* of *perfect Innocency?* And yet that *The Scripture mentioneth no Justification at all*, in foro Dei, *besides that one, which is Absolution from the Maledictory Sentence of the Law*. But still mistakes have discord with themselves.

Answ. 4. It is the judgment indeed of Mr. *Gataker, Wotton, Piscator, Paraeus, Ursine, Wendeline*, and abundance other excellent Divines, that as sins of omission are truly sin, and *poena damni*, or privations truly punishment; so for a sinner for his sin to be denied God's Love and Favour, Grace and Glory, is to be punished; and to be pardoned, is to have this privative punishment remitted as well as the rest; and so that Justification containeth our Right to Glory, as it is the bare forgiveness of the penalty of sin; because Death and Life, Darkness and Light are such Contraries, as that one is but the privation of the other: But this Learned Doctor seemeth to be of the commoner Opinion, that the Remission of Sin is but one part of our Justification, and that by Imputation of perfect

Holiness

Holinefs and Obedience we muft have another part, which is our *Right to the Reward*; (and I think a little Explication would end that difference). But doth he here then agree with himfelf? And to contradict the common way of thofe with whom he joyneth? Do they not hold that Juftification is more than an *Abſolution from the Maledictory Sentence of the Law?*

Anſw. 5. But indeed his very Defcription by *Abſolution* is utterly ambiguous: 1. Abfolution is either by *Actual Pardon*, by the Law or Covenant of Grace; - which giveth us our *Right* to *Impunity:* 2. Or by *Sentence* of the Judg, who publickly *decideth* our Cafe, and declareth our Right determinatively : Or by execution of that Sentence in actual delivering us from penalty ; And who knoweth which of thefe he meaneth? This is but confufion, to defcribe by an unexplained equivocal word.

And who knoweth what Law he meaneth, whofe *Maledictory Sentence* Juftification abfolveth us from? Doth he think that the Law of Innocency, and of *Moſes*, and the Law of Grace are all one, which Scripture fo frequently diftinguifheth? Or that each of them hath not its *Malediction?* If he deny this, I refer him to my full proof of it, to Mr. *Cartwright* and elfewhere. If not, we fhould know whether he mean all, or which.

3. And what he meaneth by the Sentence of the Law is uncertain : Whether it be the Laws *Commination*, as obliging us to punifhment, which is not a *Sentence* in the ufual proper fenfe, but only a *virtual Sentence*, that is, the *Norma Judicis*; or whether he mean the *Sentence of God as Judg*, according to the *Law:* which is not the Sentence of the Law

pro-

properly, but of the Judg : It's more intelligible speaking, and diftinct, that muft edifie us, and end thofe Controverfies which ambiguities and confufion bred and feed.

Anfw. 6. But which-ever he meaneth, moft certainly it is not true that the Scripture mentioneth no other Juftification in *foro Dei*. For many of the fore-cited Texts tell us, that it oft mentioneth a Juftification, which is no Abfolution from the Maledictory Sentence, (neither of the Law of Innocency, of *Mofes*, or of Grace) but a Juftification of a Man's innocency in *tantum*, or *quoad Caufam hanc particularem, Viz.*

1. Sometimes a Juftifying the Righteous Man againft the flanders of the World, or of his Enemies.

2. Sometimes a juftifying a Man in fome one action, as having dealt faithfully therein.

3. Sometimes a judging a Man to be a faithful Godly Man, that performeth the Conditions of Life in the Law of Grace made neceffary to God's Acceptance.

4. Sometimes for making a Man fuch, or for making him yet more inherently juft, or continuing him fo.

5. Sometimes for Juftification by the Apology of an Advocate, (which is not *Abfolution*).

6. Sometimes for Juftification by *Witnefs*.

7. And fometimes, perhaps, by *Evidence*. As appeareth, *Ifa* 50. 8. *Rom.* 8. 33. (and fo God himfelf is faid to be juftified, *Pfal.* 51. 4. *Rom.* 3. 4. and Chrift, 1 *Tim.* 3. 16.) 1 *King.* 8. 32. *Hear thou in Heaven, and do, and judg thy Servants, condemning the Wicked to bring his way upon his Head ; and*

and justifying the Righteous, to give him according to his Righteousness, (where the *Sentence* is passed by the Act of Execution). Is this absolving him from the Curse of the Law? So 1 *Chron.* 6. 23. so *Mat.* 12. 37. & *Jam.* 2. 21, 24, 25. where Justification by our *Words* and by *Works* is asserted; and many other Texts so speak: Frequently to Justifie, is to *maintain* one, or *prove him* to be just. It's strange that any Divine should find but one sort or sense of Justification before God mentioned in the Scriptures.

I would give here to the Reader, a help for some excuse of the Author, *viz.* that by [*præter unam illam quæ est Absolutio*] he might mean, which is *partly Absolution,* and *partly Acceptation,* as of a fulfiller of the Precept of Perfection by Christ, and partly Right to the Reward, all three making up the whole; but that I must not teach him how to speak his own mind, or think that he knew not how to utter it; And specially, because the Instances here prove that even so it is very far from Truth, had he so spoken.

Answ. 7. But what if the word [*Justification*] had been found only as he affirmed? If *Justice,* (Righteousness) and *Just,* be otherwise used, that's all one in the sense, and almost in the word; seeing it is confessed, that *to Justifie,* is, 1. To make *Just;* 2. Or to *esteem Just;* 3. Or *sentence Just;* 4. Or to prove Just, and defend as Just; 5. Or to *use* as Just by execution. And therefore in so many senses as a Man is called *Just* in Scripture, he is inclusively, or by connotation, said to be *Justified,* and *Justifiable,* and *Justificandus.* And I desire no more of the Impartial Reader, but to

turn

turn to his *Concordances*, and peruse all the Texts where the words [Just, Justice, Justly, Righteous, Righteousness, Righteously] are used; and if he find not that they are many score, if not hundred times used, for that Righteousness which is the Persons Relation resulting from some Acts or Habits of his own, (as the Subject or Agent) and otherwise than according to his solitary sense here, let him then believe this Author.

§. 3. But he is as unhappy in his Proofs, as in his singular untrue Assertion: "[Rom. 8. 2, 4. "*The Law of the Spirit of Life, hath freed us from* "*the Law of Sin and of Death.* Gal. 3. 13. God "*sent his Son, that the Righteousness of the Law* "*might be fulfilled in us* ; *Christ hath redeemed us* "*from the Curse of the Law* ; and many more such: Here is no mention of any but *one Legal Justification*].

Answ. 1. Reader, do you believe that these two Texts are a perfect Enumeration. And that if these mention but one sense or sort of Justification, that it will follow that no more is mentioned in Scripture : Or if many hundred other Texts have the same sense?

2. Nay, he hath chosen only these Texts where the word [*Justification*] or [*Justifie*] is not at all found. By which I may suppose that he intendeth the Controversie here *de re*, and not *de nomine*. And is that so? Can any Man that ever considerately opened the Bible, believe that *de re* no such Thing is mentioned in Scripture. 1. As making a Man a believing Godly Man. 2. Or as performing the Conditions of Life required of us in the Covenant of Grace. 3. Nor esteeming a

Man

Man such. 4. Nor defending or proving him to be such. 5. Nor judging him such decisively. 6. Nor using him as such. 7. Nor as justifying a Man so far as he is Innocent and Just against all false Accusation of Satan or the World.

3. The first Text cited by him, *Rom.* 8.24. downright contradicts him: Not only *Augustine*, but divers Protestant Expositors suppose, that by the *Law of the Spirit of Life* is meant, either the *quickning Spirit it self* given to us that are in Christ, or the Gospel, as it *giveth that Spirit into us*; And that by *delivering* us from the *Law of Sin*, is meant either from that *sin which is* as a *Law within us*, or *Moses Law*, as it forbiddeth and commandeth all its peculiarities, and so maketh *doing* or *not doing* them sin; and as it declareth sin, yea, and accidentally irritateth it: Yea, that by the Law of Death is meant, not only that Law we are cursed by, and so guilty, but chiefly that Law, as it is said *Rom.* 7. to *kill Paul*, and to occasion the abounding of sin, and the Life of it: And that by [*the fulfilling of the Law in us, that walk not after the Flesh, but after the Spirit*], is meant [that by the Spirit and Grace of Christ, Christians do fulfil the Law, as it requireth sincere Holiness, Sobriety and Righteousness, which God accepteth for Christ's sake; which the Law of *Moses*, without Christ's Spirit, enabled no Man to fulfil]. Not to weary the Reader with citing Expositors, I now only desire him to peruse, *Ludov. de Dieu* on the Text.

And it is certain, that the Law that *Paul* there speaketh of, was *Moses* Law: And that he is proving all along, that the observation of it was not necessary to the Gentiles, to their *performance*, or

Justi-

Justification and Salvation, (*necessitate præcepti vel medii*); (for it would not justifie the Jews themselves). And sure, 1. all his meaning is not, [The Law will not absolve Men from the sense of the Law]. But also *its Works* will give no one the just title of a Righteous Man, accepted of God, and saved by him, as judging between the Righteous and the wicked: (as Christ saith, *Matth.* 25. *The Righteous shall go into Everlasting Life*, &c.) 2. And if it were only the *Maledictory Sentence* of *Moses Law*, as such, that *Paul* speaketh of Absolution from, as our only Justification, then none but Jews and Proselites who were under that Law, could have the Justification by Faith which he mentioneth; for it curseth none else: For what-ever the Law saith, it saith to them that are under the Law: The rest of the World were only under the Law of lapsed Nature, (the relicts of *Adam's* Law of Innocency) and the Curse for *Adam's* first Violation; and the Law of Grace made to *Adam* and *Noah*, and after perfected fullier by Christ in its second Edition.

2. His other Text [*Christ redeemed us from the Curse of the Law*] proveth indeed that all Believers are redeemed from the Curse of the first Law of Innocency, and the Jews from the Curse of *Moses Law* (which is it that is *directly* meant): But what's that to prove that these words speak the whole and the *only Justification?* and that the Scripture mentioneth no other?

§. 4. He addeth, [*Lex est quæ prohibet; Lex quæ pœnam decernit; Lex quæ irrogat: Peccatum est transgressio Legis: Pœna effectus istius trangressionis; Justificatio denique absolutio ab ista pœna: Itaque*
cum

cum Lex *nisi præstita neminem* Justificat, & *præstitam omnes in Christo agnoscunt, aut Legalis erit omnis* Justificatio coram Deo, *aut omnino nulla*].

Answ. 1. But doth he know but *one sort of Law* of God? Hath every Man incurred the Curse by *Moses* Law that did by *Adams*? Or every Man fallen under the peremptory irreversible condemnation which the Law of Grace passeth on them that never believe and repent? Doth this Law, [*He that believeth not shall be damned*] damn Believers? One Law condemneth all that are not Innocent. Another supposeth them under that defect, and condemneth peremptorily (not every Sinner) but the Wicked and Unbelievers.

2. Again here he saith, [*Justification is Absolution from that Penalty*]. But is a Man absolved (properly) from that which he was never guilty of? Indeed if he take *Absolution* so loosly as to signifie, the justifying a Man against a false Accusation, and pronouncing him *Not-Guilty*; So all the Angels in Heaven may possibly be capable of Absolution: Justification is ordinarily so used, but Absolution seldom by Divines. And his words shew that this is not his sense, if I understand them. But if we are reputed perfect fulfillers of the Law of Innocency by Christ, and yet Justification is our Absolution from the Curse, then no Man is justified that is Righteous by that Imputation.

3. And how unable is my weak Understanding, to make his words at peace with themselves? The same Man in the next lines saith, [*Lex nisi præstita neminem justificat :* and all *Justification before God must be legal or none*]; so that no Man is justified but as reputed Innocent, or a performer of the Law: And

And yet *Justification* is our Absolution from the Punishment and Malediction of the Law; As if he said, No Man is justified but by the pardon of that sin which he is reputed never to have had, and Absolution from that Curse and Punishment which he is reputed never to have deserved or been under. Are these things reconcileable? But if really he take *Absolution* for justifying or acquitting from a false Accusation, and so to be absolved from the Malediction of the Law, is to be reputed one that never deserved it, or was under it, then it's as much as to say, that there is no pardon of sin, or that no Man that is pardoned, or reputed to need a Pardon, is justified.

4. All this and such Speeches would perswade the Reader that this Learned Disputer thinketh that I took and use the word [Legal] generally as of that which is related to any Law *in genere,* and so take *Evangelical* contrarily for that which is related to no Law: whereas I over and over tell him, that (speaking in the usual Language that I may be understood) I take [Legal] *specially* (and not generally) for that Righteousness which is related to the *Law of Works* or *Innocency*, (not as if we had indeed such a Righteousness as that Law will justifie us for; But a *pro-Legal-Righteousness*, one instead of it, in and by our perfect Saviour, which shall effectually save us from that Laws condemnation): And that by [*Evangelical Righteousness*], I mean, that which is related to the *Law of Grace*, as the Rule of *Judgment*, upon the just pleading whereof that Law will not condemn but justifie us. If he knew this to be my meaning, in my weak judgment, he should not have written either as if he

did

did not, or as if he would perswade his Rsaders to the contrary: For Truth is moft congruoufly defended by Truth: But if he *knew it not*, I defpair of becoming intelligible to him, by any thing that I can write, and I fhall expect that this Reply be wholly loft to him and worfe.

5. His [*Lex nifi præstita neminem justificat*] is true; and therefore no Man is juftified by the Law, But his next words [*& præstitam omnes in Christo agnoscunt*] feemeth to mean that [*It was performed by us in Christ*]; Or that [*It justifieth us, because performed perfectly by Christ as such*]: Which both are the things that we moft confidently deny. It was not Phyfically, or Morally, or Politically, or Legally, or Reputatively, (take which word you will) *fulfilled by us in Christ*: it doth not juftifie us, becaufe it was fulfilled by Chrift, *(as such,* or immediately, and *eo nomine*). It juftified *Christ*, becaufe he fulfilled it; and fo their Law doth all the perfect Angels. But we did not perfonally fulfil it in Chrift; it never allowed *vicarium obedientiæ* to fulfil it by our *selves* or another: Therefore anothers *Obedience*, merely as fuch, (even a Mediators) is not our Obedience or Juftification: But that Obedience juftifieth us, as given us only in or to the effecting of our Perfonal Righteoufnefs, which confifteth in our right to Impunity, and to God's Favour and Life, freely given for Chrift's Merits fake, and in our performance of the Conditions of the Law of Grace, or that free Gift, which is therefore not a co-ordinate but a fub-ordinate Righteoufnefs (and Juftification) to qualifie us for the former. This is fo plain and neceffary, that if (in fenfe) it be not underftood by all that are admitted to the Sacra-

cramental Communion, (excepting Verbal Controverfies or Difficulties) I doubt we are too lax in our admiffions.

§. 5. Next he tells us of a *threefold respect of Justification* : 1. *Ex parte principii.* 2. *Termini.* 3. *Medii* : (I find my felf uncapeable of *teaching him*, that is a Teacher of fuch as I, and therefore prefume not to tell him how to diftinguifh more congruoufly, plainly, and properly, as to the terms). And *as to the Principle or Fountain whence it floweth*, that is, *Evangelical Grace in Chrift*, he faith; *It is thus neceffary, that in our lapfed State all Juftification be Evangelical*].

Anfw. Who would defire a *sharper* or a *softer*, a more *diffenting* or a more *confenting* Adverfary ? Very good : If then I mean it *ex parte principii*, I offend him not by afferting Evangelical Righteoufnefs : The Controverfie then will be only *de nomine*, whether it be congruous thus to call it. And really are his *Names* and *Words* put into our Creed, and become fo neceffary as to be worthy of all the ftrefs that he layeth on them, and the calling up the Chriftian World to arrive by their Zeal againft our Phrafe ? Muft the Church be awakened to rife up againft all thofe that will fay with Chrift, [*By thy words thou shalt be juftified*]. And with *James*, [*By Works a Man is juftified, and not by Faith only*], and [*we are judged by the Law of Liberty*]; and as Chrift, *Joh*. 5. 22. [*The Father judgeth no Man, but hath committed all Judgment to the Son*]; and that fhall recite the 25*th* Chapter of *Matthew*.

Even now he faid at once, [*There is no Juftification* in foro Dei, *but Abfolution*, &c. *The Law of the Spirit of Life hath freed us*, &c. *Here is no men-*

mention of any Juſtification but Legal]. And now [*All our Juſtification* ex parte principii, is *only Evangelical*]. So then *no Text* talks of *Evangelical Juſtification,* or of Juſtification *ex parte principii :* And *Abſolution* which defineth it, is named *ex parte principii.* And yet all *Juſtification* is *Evangelical.* Is this mode of Teaching worthy a Defence by a Theological War?

2. But Reader, Why may not I denominate Juſtification *ex parte principii ? Righteouſneſs* is formally a Relation : To juſtifie conſtitutively, is to *make Righteous.* To be Juſtified, (or Juſtification *in ſenſu paſſivo*) is to be made *Righteous ;* And *in foro,* to be *judged Righteous :* And what meaneth he by *Principium* as to a Relation, but that which other Men call the *Fundamentum,* which is *loco Efficientis,* or a remote efficient ? And whence can a Relation be more fitly named, than from the *fundamentum,* whence it hath its formal being ? Reader, bear with my Error, or correct it, if I miſtake. I think that as our *Righteouſneſs* is not all of one ſort, no more is the *fundamentum :* 1. I think I have no Righteouſneſs, whoſe immediate *fundamentum* is my ſinleſs Innocency, or fulfilling the Law of Works or Innocency, by my ſelf or another : and ſo I have no *fundamentum* of ſuch. 2. I hope I have a Righteouſneſs conſiſting in my perſonal *Right* to *Impunity* and *Life* ; and that *Jus* or *Right* is mine by the *Title* of *free Condonation* and *Donation* by the Goſpel-Covenant or Grant : And ſo that Grant or Goſpel is the *fundamentum* of it : But the Merits of Chriſt's Righteouſneſs purchaſed that Gift, and ſo thoſe Merits are the remote *fundamentum* or efficient : And thus my Juſtification,

L 2   by

by the Doctor's confession, is Evangelical. 3. I must perish if I have not also a subordinate personal Righteousness, consisting in my performance of those Conditions on which the New-Covenant giveth the former. And the *fundamentum* of this Righteousness is the Reality of that performance, as related to the Irrogation, Imposition, or Tenor of the Covenant, making this the Condition. This is my Heresie, if I be heretical; and be it right or wrong, I will make it intelligible, and not by saying and unsaying, involve all in confusion.

§. 6. He addeth, [*Ex parte Termini Legalis est, quia terminatur in satisfactione, Legi præstandâ: Liberavit me à Lege mortis, &c.* And hence, he saith, *the denomination is properly taken.*

Answ. 1. The Reader here seeth that all this Zeal is exercised in a *Game at Words*, or *Logical Notions*; and the Church must be called for the umpirage, to stand by in Arms to judg that he hath won the Day: What if the *denomination be properly to be taken from* the *Terminus?* Is it as dangerous as you frightfully pretend to take it *aliunde?* 2. But stay a little: Before we come to this, we must crave help to understand what he talketh of: Is it, 1. *Justificatio, Justificans (active sumpta)?* Or, 2. *Justificatio Justificati (passive)?* 3. Or *Justitia?*

1. The first is *Actio*, and the *Terminus* of that Action is two-fold. 1. The Object or Patient (a believing Sinner). 2. The Effect, *Justificatio passive*, neither of these is *the Law,* or its *Malediction*. But which of these is it that we must needs name it from?

2. The *passive* or *effective* Justification is in respect of the Subjects Reception called *Passio:* In respect

respect of the form received, it is as various as I before mentioned.

1. The Effect of the Donative Justification of the Law of Grace, is *Justitia data*; a Relation (oft described).

2. The Effect of the Spirits giving us *Inherent Righteousness*, is a *Quality given, Acts excited*, and a Relation thence resulting.

3. The Effect of *Justification per sententiam Judicis*, is immediately a Relation, *Jus Judicatum*.

4. The Effect of an Advocates Justification, is *Justitia & persona ut defensa seu vindicata*.

5. The Effect of *Executive Justification*, is Actual Impunity or Liberation. And are all these one *Terminus*, or hence one name then? These are the *Termini* of *Justificatio Justificantis, ut Actionis*; and nothing of this nature can be plainer, than that, 1. Remission of sin (passively taken) the *Reatus* or *Obligatio ad poenam*, (the first *ad quem*, and the second *à quo*) are both the immediate *Termini* of our Act of Justification: 2. That the *Terminus Justitiæ*, as it is the formal Relation of a Justified Person, as such, is the Law as *Norma Actionum*, as to Righteous Actions, and the Law or Covenant, as making the Condition of Life, as to those Actions, *sub ratione Conditionis & Tituli*. And the Promissory and Minatory part of the Law, as *Justitia* is *Jus præmii, & impunitatis*. First, The Actions, and then the Person are Just in Relation to the Law or Covenant, by which their Actions and they are to be judged. But the remoter *Terminus* is the *malum à quo*, and the *bonum ad quod*. And as *à quo*, it is not only the *evil* denounced, but also the

L 3 *Reatus*,

Reatus, or Obligation to it, and the efficacious Act of the Law thus cursing, and the *Accusation* of the Actor or Accuser, (real or possible) that is such a *terminus*.

II. But when he saith, *Ex parte Termini Legalis est*, either still he taketh *legal generally*, as comprehending the Law of *Innocency*, of *Works*, and of *Grace*, or not. If he do, I must hope he is more *intelligent* and *just*, than to insinuate to his Reader, that I ever mention an *Evangelical Justification* that is not so legal, as to be denominated from the Law of Grace, as distinct from that of Works: If not, he was indebted to his intelligent Reader for some proof, that no Man is justified against this false Accusation ; [Thou art by the Law of Grace the Heir of a far sorer punishment, for despising the Remedy, and not performing the Conditions of Pardon and Life. And also for this thou hast no right to Christ, and the Gifts of his Covenant of Grace]. But no such proof is found in his Writings, nor can be given.

III. But his [*Quia Terminatur in satisfactione Legi. præstanda*], I confess it is a Sentence not very intelligible or edifying to me. 1. *Satisfactio proprie & stricte sic dicta differt à solutione ejusdem quod sit, solutio æquivalentis alias indebite :* Which of these he meaneth, Satisfaction thus strictly taken, or *solutio ejusdem*, I know not : Nor know what it is that he meaneth by *Legi præstandâ :* Indeed *solutio ejusdem* is *Legi præstanda*, but not *præstita* by us (personally or by another) : For we neither kept the Law, nor bare the full Penalty ; And
the

the Law mentioned no *Vicarium Obedientiæ aut pœnæ*; Chrift *performed the Law*, as it obliged himfelf as Mediator, and as a Subject, but not as *it obliged us*; for it obliged us to *Perfonal performance only*: And Chrift by bearing that Punifhment (in fome refpects) which we deferved, fatisfied the *Law-giver*, (who had power to take a Commutation) but not *the Law*: unlefs fpeaking improperly you will fay that the *Law is fatisfied*, when the remote ends of the Law-giver and Law are obtained. For the Law hath but one fixed fenfe, and may be it felf changed, but changeth not it felf, nor accepteth a *tantundem*: And Chrift's fuffering for us, was a *fulfilling* of the Law, which peculiarly *bound him* to fuffer, and not a Satisfaction *loco folutionis ejufdem*: And it was no *fulfilling* the Penal part of the *Law* as it bound *us* to fuffer: For fo it bound none but us; fo that the *Law* as *binding* us to *Duty* or *Suffering*, was neither *fulfilled*, nor ftrictly *fatisfied* by Chrift; but the *Law-giver* fatisfied, and the remote ends of the Law attained, by Chrift's perfect fulfilling all that Law which bound himfelf as Mediator.

Now whether he mean the Law as binding us to *Duty*, or to *Punifhment*, or both, and what by *fatisfaction* I am not fure: But as far as I can make fenfe of it, it feemeth to mean, that *Pœna* is *fatisfactio loco obedientiæ*, and that Punifhment being our Due, this was *fatisfactio Legi præftandæ*, (for he faith not *Præftita*). But then he muft judge that we are juftified only from the *penal Obligation* of the Law, and not from the *preceptive Obligation* to perfect Obedience. And this will not ftand with the fcope of other Paffages, where he endureth not my Opinion, that we are not *justified* by the *fac hoc*, the Precept as fulfilled, or from the *Reatus Culpæ in se*, but by Chrift's whole Righteoufnefs from the *Reatus ut ad pænam*.

2. But if this be his fenfe, he meaneth then that it is only the *Terminus à quo*, that *Justification* is properly denominated from. And why fo? 1. As *Juftitia* and *Juftificatio paffive fumpta, vel ut effectus*, is *Relatio*, it hath neceffarily no *Terminus à quo*; And certainly is *in specie*, to be rather denominated from its own proper *Terminus ad quem*. And as *Juftification* is taken for the Juftifiers *Action*; why is it not as well to be denominated from the *Terminus ad quem*, as *à quo*? *Juftificatio efficiens fic dicitur, quia Juftum facit*: *Juftificatio apologetica, quia Juftum vindicat vel probat. Juftificatio per fententiam, quia Juftum aliquem effe Judicat*: *Juftificatio executiva, quia ut Juftum eum tractat*.

But if we muft needs denominate from the *Terminus à quo*, how ftrange is it that he fhould know but of *one* fenfe of *Juftification*?

3. But yet perhaps he meaneth, [*In fatisfactione Legi præftitâ*, though he fay *præftandâ*, and fo denominateth from the *Terminus à quo*: But if fo, 1. Then it cannot be true: For *fatisfacere & Juftificare* are not the fame thing, nor is *Juftifying giving Satisfaction*; nor were we juftified when Chrift had fatisfied, but long after: Nor are we juftified *eo nomine*, becaufe Chrift fatisfied, (that is, immediately) but becaufe he gave us that *Jus ad impunitatem & vitam & spiritum fanctum*, which is the *Fruit* of his Satisfaction. 2. And as is faid, if it be only *in fatisfactione*, then it is not in that *Obedience which fulfileth* the preceptive part as it

bound

bound us: for to satisfie for not fulfilling, is not to fulfil it. 3. And then no Man is justified, for no Man hath satisfied either the Preceptive or Penal Obligation of the Law, by himself or another: But Christ hath satisfied the Law-giver by Merit and Sacrifice for sin.

His *Liberavit nos à Lege Mortis*, I before shewed impertinent to his use, Is *Liberare & Justificare*, or *Satisfacere* all one? And is *à Lege Mortis*, either from all the Obligation to Obedience, or from the sole malediction? There be other Acts of *Liberation* besides *Satisfaction*: For it is [*The Law of the Spirit of Life*] that doth it: And we are freed both from the *power* of *indwelling-sin*, (called a Law) and from the Mosaical Yoak, and from the Impossible Conditions of the Law of Innocency, though not from its bare Obligation to future Duty.

§. 7. He addeth a Third, *Ex parte Medii, quod est Justitia Christi Legalis nobis per fidem Imputata: Omnem itaque Justificationem proprie Legalem esse constat.*

Answ. 1. When I read that he will have but one sense or sort of Justification, will yet have the Denomination to be *ex termino*, and so justifieth my distinction of it, according to the various *Termini*; And here how he maketh the Righteousness of Christ to be but the MEDIUM of our Justification, (though he should have told us which sort of *Medium* he meaneth) he seemeth to me a very favourable consenting Adversary: And I doubt those Divines who maintain that Christ's Rignteousness is the *Causa Formalis* of our Justification, (who are no small ones, nor a few, though other in answer to the Papists disclaim it) yea, and those that make it

but

but *Causa Materialis*, (which may have a sound sense) will think this Learned Man betrayeth their Cause by prevarication, and seemeth to set fiercly against me, that he may yeeld up the Cause with less suspicion. But the truth is, we all know but in part, and therefore err in part, and Error is inconsistent with it self. And as we have conflicting Flesh and Spirit in the *Will*, so have we conflicting *Light* and *Darkness*, *Spirit* and *Flesh* in the Understanding; And it is very perceptible throughout this Author's Book, that in one line the *Flesh* and *Darkness* saith one thing, and in the next oft the *Spirit* and *Light* saith the contrary, and seeth not the inconsistency: And so though the *dark* and *fleshy* part rise up in wrathful striving Zeal against the Concord and Peace of Christians, on pretence that other Mens Errors wrong the Truth, yet I doubt not but Love and Unity have some interest in his lucid and Spiritual part. We do not only grant him that Christ's Righteousness is a *Medium* of our Justification, (for so also is *Faith* a *Condition*, and *Dispositio Receptiva* being a *Medium*); nor only some *Cause*, (for so also is the *Covenant-Donation*); but that it is an *efficient meritorious Cause*, and because if Righteousness had been that of our own, *Innocency* would have been founded in *Merit*, we may call Christ's Righteousness the *material Cause* of our Justification, remotely, as it is *Materia Meriti*, the Matter of the *Merit* which procureth it.

2. But for all this it followeth not that all Justification is only *Legal*, as *Legal* noteth its respect to the Law of Innocency: For 1. we are justified from or against the Accusation of being non-performers of the Condition of the Law of Grace;

2. And

2. And of being therefore unpardoned, and lyable to its forer Penalty. 3. Our particular fubordinate Perfonal Righteoufnefs confifting in the faid performance of thofe Evangelical Conditions of Life, is fo denominated from its conformity to the Law of Grace, (as it inftituteth its own Condition) as the meafure of it, (as *Rectitudo ad Regulam*). 4. Our *Jus ad impunitatem & vitam*, refulteth from the *Donative* Act of the Law or Covenant of Grace, as the *Titulus qui est Fundamentum Juris*, or fuppofition of our Faith as the Condition. 5. This Law of Grace is the *Norma Judicis*, by which we fhall be judged at the Laft Day. 6. The fame Judg doth now *per sententiam conceptam* judg of us, as he will then judg *per sententiam prolatam*. 7. Therefore the Sentence being *virtually* in the Law, this fame Law of Grace, which in *primo instanti* doth make *us Righteous*, (by *Condonation* and *Donation* of Right) doth *in secundo instanti*, *virtually* juftifie us as containing that regulating ufe, by which we are to be fententially juftified. And now judg Reader, whether no Juftification be Evangelical, or by the Law of Grace, and fo to be denominated: (for it is *lis de nomine* that is by him managed). 8. Befides that the whole frame of Caufes in the Work of Redemption, (the Redeemer, his Righteoufnefs, Merits, Sacrifice, Pardoning Act, Interceffion, *&c.*) are fure rather to be called Matters of the Gofpel, than of the Law.

And yet we grant him eafily; 1. That Chrift perfectly fulfilled the Law of Innocency, and was juftified thereby, and that we are juftified by that Righteoufnefs of his, as the meritorious Caufe. 2. That

2. That we being guilty of Sin and Death, according to the tenor of that Law, and that Guilt being remitted by Christ, as aforesaid, we are therefore justified from that Law, (that is, from its Obligation of us to Innocency as the necessary terms of Life, and from its Obligation of us to Death, for want of Innocency): But we are not justified by that Law, either as fulfilled or as satisfied by *us our selves*, either personally or by an Instrument, substitute or proper Representative, that was *Vicarius Obedientiæ aut pœnæ*. 3. And we grant that the Jews were delivered from the positive Jewish Law, which is it that *Paul* calleth, *The Law of Works*. And if he please, in all these respects to call *Justification Legal*, we intend not to quarrel with the name, (though what I called *Legal* in those *Aphorisms*, I chose ever after to call rather, *Justitia pro-legalis*). But we cannot believe him, 1. That it is *only Legal*; 2. Or that that is the *only* (or most) proper denomination.

§. 8. He proceedeth thus, [*And it will be vain, if any argue, That yet none can be saved without Evangelical Works, according to which it is confessed that all men shall be judged: for the distinction is easie (which the Author of the Aphorisms somewhere useth) between the first or Private, and the last or Publick Justification.*—— *In the first sense it is never said, That Works justifie, but contrary, That God justifieth him that worketh not,* Rom. 4. 5. *In the latter we confess that Believers are to be justified according to Works, but yet not Of (or By) Works, nor that that Justification maketh men just before God, but only so pronounceth them.*

Answ. 1. This is such another *Consenting Adversary*

verſary as once before I was put to anſwer; who with open mouth calls himſelf conſequentially what he calleth me; if the ſame *Cauſe*, and not the *Perſon* make the Guilt. Nay let him conſider whether his *grand* and moſt *formidable Weapon* [*So alſo ſaith* Bellarmine, *with other Papiſts*] do not wound himſelf: For *they* commonly ſay, That *the firſt Juſtification* is not of *Works*, or *Works* do not firſt juſtifie us. Have I not now proved that he *erreth and complyeth with the Papiſts?* If not, let him uſe better Arguments himſelf.

2. But why is the firſt *Juſtification* called *Private?* Either he meaneth God's *making us juſt conſtitutively*, or his *judging* us ſo: and that *per ſententiam conceptam* only, or *prolatam* alſo.

1. The common diſtinction in Politicks, *inter judicium Privatum & Publicum*, is fetcht from the *Judg*, who is either *Perſona privata vel publica*: a *private* Man, or an *authorized Judg* judging as ſuch: And ſo the Judgment of Conſcience, Friends, Enemies, Neighbours, mere Arbitrators, *&c.* is *Judicium privatum*; and that of a *Judg in foro*, is *Judicium publicum*, (yea, or in ſecret, before the concerned Parties only in his Cloſet, ſo it be deciſive): If this Learned Doctor ſo underſtand it, then, 1. *Conſtitutive Juſtification* (which is truly firſt) is publick Juſtification, being done by God the Father, and by our Redeemer, who ſure are not herein *private* authorized *Perſons*. 2. And the firſt *ſentential Juſtification*, as merely *Virtual*, and not yet *Actual*, viz. as it's virtually in the Juſtifying Law of Grace as *norma Judicis* is *publick in ſuo genere*, being the *virtus* of a Publick Law of God, or of his Donative Promiſe. 3. And the

firſt

first *Actual Justification*, *per Deum Judicem per sententiam conceptam* (which is God's secret judging the Thing and Person to be as they are) is (secret indeed *in se*, yet revealed by God's publick Word but) publick as to the Judg. 4. And the first *sententia prolata* (the fourth in order) is someway publick as opposite to secresie, (for, 1. it is before the Angels of Heaven; 2. And in part by Executive demonstrations on Earth): But it is certainly by a *publick Judg*, that is, God. 5. And the first *Apologetical Justification* by Christ our *Interceding Advocate*, is publick both *quoad personam*, and as *openly* done in Heaven: And if this worthy Person deny any Justification *per sententiam Judicis*, upon our first Believing, or before the final Judgment, he would wofully fall out with the far greatest number of Protestants, and especially his closest Friends, who use to make *a Sentence of God* as Judg to be the *Genus* to Justification.

But if by [*Private* and *Publick Justification*]; he means [*secret* and *open*]. 1. How can he hope to be understood when he will use Political Terms unexplained, out of the usual sense of Politicians: But no men use to *abuse words* more than they that would keep the Church in flames by *wordy Controversies*, as if they were of the terms of Life and Death. 2. And even in that sense our first Justification is *publick* or open, *quoad Actum Justificancantis*, as being by the Donation of a publick Word of God; Though *quoad effectum in recipiente*, it must needs be secret till the Day of Judgment, no Man knowing anothers Heart, whether he be indeed a sound Believer: And so of the rest as is intimated.

Con-

Concerning what I have said before, some may Object, 1. *That there is no such thing as our Justification notified before the Angels in Heaven.* 2. *That the* Sententia Concepta *is God's Immanent Acts, and therefore Eternal.*

Answ. To the first, I say, 1. It is certain by *Luk.* 15. 10. that the Angels know of the Conversion of a Sinner, and therefore of his Justification and publickly Rejoyce therein. Therefore it is notified to them. 2. But I refer the Reader for this, to what I have said to Mr. *Tombes* in my *Disputation of Justification*, where I do give my thoughts, That this is not the Justification by Faith meant by *Paul*, as Mr. *Tombes* asserteth it to be.

To the Second, I say, Too many have abused Theology, by the misconceiving of the distinction of *Immanent* and *Transient Acts* of God, taking all for *Immanent* which effect nothing *ad extra*. But none are properly *Immanent quoad Objectum*, but such as God himself is the *Object* of, (as *se intelligere, se amare*): An Act may be called indeed immanent in any of these three respects; 1. *Ex parte Agentis*; 2. *Ex parte Objecti*; 3. *Ex parte effectus.* 1. *Ex parte agentis*, all God's Acts are *Immanent*, for they are his Essence. 2. *Ex parte Objecti vel Termini*, God's Judging a Man Just or Unjust, Good or Bad, is transient; because it is denominated from the state of the *Terminus* or Object : And so it may be *various* and *mutable* denominatively, notwithstanding God's *Simplicity* and *Immutability*. And so the *Sententia Concepta* is not *ab Æterno*. 3. As to the *Effect*, all confess God's Acts to be Transient and Temporary. But there are some that *effect* not (as to judg a thing to be what it is). 3. Either

3. Either this Militant Disputer would have his Reader believe that I say, That a *Man is justified by Works*, in that which he called [*making just*, and the *first Justification*], or not : If he would, such *untruth* and *unrighteousness* (contrary to the full drift of many of my Books, and even that which he selected to oppose) is not a congruous way of disputing for *Truth* and *Righteousness :* nor indeed is it tolerably ingenuous or modest. If not, then why doth he all along carry his professed agreement with me, in a militant strain, perswading his Reader, that I favour of Socinianism or Popery, or some dangerous Error, by saying the very same that he saith. O what thanks doth God's Church owe such contentious Disputers for supposed Orthodoxness, that like *noctambuli*, will rise in their sleep, and cry, Fire, Fire, or beat an Allarm on their Drums, and cry out, *The Enemy, The Enemy*, and will not let their Neighbours rest!

I have wearied my Readers with so oft repeating in my Writings (upon such repeated importunities of others) these following Assertions about Works.

1. That we are never justified, first or last, by Works of *Innocency*
2. Nor by the *Works* of the Jewish Law (which *Paul* pleadeth against).
3. Nor by any Works of Merit, in point of Commutative Justice, or of *distributive* Governing Justice, according to either of those Laws (of *Innocency*, or *Jewish*).
4. Nor by any Works or Acts of Man, which are set against or instead of the least part of God's

Acts, Christ's Merits, or any of his part or honour.

5. Nor are we at first justified by any *Evangelical Works of Love, Gratitude or Obedience to Christ,* as *Works* are distinguished from our first *Faith* and *Repentance.*

6. Nor are we justified by *Repentance,* as by an *instrumental* efficient Cause, or as of the same receiving Nature with Faith, except as *Repentance* signifieth our change from *Unbelief* to *Faith,* and so is *Faith* it self.

7. Nor are we justified by *Faith* as by a mere Act, or moral good Work.

8. Nor yet as by a proper efficient Instrument of our Justification.

9. Much less by such *Works* of Charity to Men, as are without true love to God.

10. And least of all, by Popish bad Works, called *Good,* (as Pilgrimages, hurtful Austerities, &c.)

But if any Church-troubling Men will first call all *Acts* of Man's Soul by the name of WORKS, and next will call no Act by the name of *Justifying Faith,* but the *belief of the Promise* (as some) or the *accepting* of *Christ's Righteousness given* or *imputed to us,* as *in se,* our own (as others) or [the *Recumbency on this Righteousness*] (as others) or all these three *Acts* (as others); and if next they will say that this *Faith justifieth* us only as the proper *Instrumental Cause*; and next that to look for Justification by any other Act of Man's Soul, or by this Faith in any other respect, is to trust to that Justification by *Works,* which *Paul* confuteth, and to fall from Grace, I do detest such corrupting and

M abusing

abusing of the Scriptures, and the Church of Christ. And I assert as followeth;

1. That the Faith which we are justified by, doth as essentially contain our belief of the Truth of Christ's Person, Office, Death, Resurrection, Intercession, &c. as of the Promise of Imputation.

2. And also our consent to Christ's Teaching, Government, Intercession, as to Imputation.

3. And our *Acceptance* of Pardon, Spirit, and promised Glory, as well as Imputed Righteousness of Christ.

4. Yea, that it is essentially a Faith in God the Father, and the Holy Ghost.

5. That it hath in it essentially somewhat of Initial Love to God, to Christ, to Recovery, to Glory; that is, of Volition; and so of Desire.

6. That it containeth all that Faith, which is necessarily requisite at Baptism to that Covenant; even a *consenting-practical-belief* in God the *Father, Son*, and *Holy Ghost*: and is our Christianity it self.

7. That we are justified by this *Faith*, as it is [*A moral Act of Man, adapted to its proper Office, made by our Redeemer, the Condition of his Gift of Justification, and so is the moral receptive aptitude of the Subject*, or the *Dispositio materiæ vel subjecti Recipientis*]: Where the Matter of it is [*An adapted moral Act of Man*] (by Grace). The *Ratio formalis* of its Interest in our Justification is [*Conditio præstita*] speaking politically, and [*Aptitudo vel Dispositio moralis Receptiva*] speaking logically; which Dr. *Twiss* still calleth *Causa dispositiva*.

8. That Repentance as it is a change of the Mind from Unbelief to Faith, (in God the Father, Son,

Son, and Holy Ghoſt) is this Faith denominated from its *Terminus à quo* (principally).

9. That we are continually juſtified by this Faith as continued, as well as initially juſtified by its firſt Act.

10. That as this *Faith* includeth a *conſent* to *future Obedience*, (that is, Subjection) ſo the *performance* of that *conſent* in *ſincere Obedience*, is the Condition of our Juſtification as continued (Secondarily) as well as Faith (or conſent it ſelf) primarily: And that thus *James* meaneth, that we are Juſtified by Works.

11. That God judging of all things truly as they are, now judgeth Men juſt or unjuſt, on theſe Terms.

12. And his Law being *Norma judicii*, now *vertually* judgeth us juſt on theſe terms.

13. And that the Law of Grace being that which we are to be judged by, we ſhall at the laſt Judgment alſo be judged (and ſo juſtified) thus far by or according to our ſincere Love, Obedience, or Evangelical Works, as the Condition of the Law or Covenant of free Grace, which juſtifieth and glorifieth freely all that are thus Evangelically qualified, by and for the Merits, perfect Righteouſneſs and Sacrifice of Chriſt, which procured the Covenant or free Gift of Univerſal Conditional Juſtification and Adoption, before and without any Works or Conditions done by Man whatſoever.

Reader, Forgive me this troubleſom oft repeating the ſtate of the Controverſie; I meddle with no other. If this be Juſtification by Works, I am for it. If this Doctor be againſt it, he is againſt much of the Gospel. If he be not, he had better have kept his Bed, than to have call'd us to Arms in his Dream, when we have sadly warred so many Ages already about mere words. For my part, I think that such a short explication of our sense, and rejection of ambiguities, is fitter to end these quarrels, than the long disputations of Confounders.

4. But when be saith, [*Works make not a Man just, and yet we are at last justified according to them*], it is a contradiction, or unsound. For if he mean *Works* in the sence excluded by *Paul*, we are not justified *according to them*, viz. such as make, or are thought to make the *Reward to be not of Grace*, but *of Debt* : But if he take *Works* in the sense intended by *James*, *sincere Obedience* is a *secondary constitutive* part of that *inherent or adherent personal Righteousness, required by the Law of Grace, in subordination to Christ's Meritorious Righteousness* ; And what Christian can deny this ? So far it *maketh* us *Righteous*, (as *Faith* doth *initially*). And what is it to be *justified according to our Works*, but to be judged, so far as they are sincerely done, to be such as have performed the secondary part of the Conditions of free-given Life ?

5. His [*According*] but not [*ex operibus*] at the Last Judgment, is but a Logomachie [*According*] signifieth as much as I assert : But [*ex*] is no unapt Preposition, when it is but the subordinate part of Righteousness and Justification, of which we speak, and signifieth (with me) the same as [*According*].

6. His Tropical Phrase, that *Works pronounce us just*] is another ambiguity : That the Judg
will

will *pronounce us just according to them, as the foresaid second part of the Constitutive Cause*, or *Matter* of our *Subordinate Righteousness*, is certain from *Matth.* 25. and the scope of Scripture: But that they are only *notifying Signs*, and no part of the *Cause* of the day to be tryed, is not true, (which too many assert).

§. 9. He proceedeth, [*If there be an Evangelical Justification at God's Bar, distinct from the legal one, there will then also be in each an absolution of divers sins: For if the Gospel forgive the same sins as the Law, the same thing will be done, and a double Justification will be unprofitable and idle. If from divers sins, then the Law forbids not the same things as the Gospel, &c.*]

Answ. It's pitty such things should need any Answer.

1. It's a false Supposition, That *all Justification* is *Absolution from sin:* To justifie the sincerity of our *Faith* and *Holiness*, is one act or part of our Justification, against all (possible or actual) false Accusation.

2. The Law of Innocency commanded not the Believing Acceptance of Christ's Righteousness and Pardon, and so the Remnants of that Law in the hand of Christ (which is the Precept of perfect Obedience *de futuro*) commandeth it only consequently, supposing the Gospel-Promise and Institution to have gone before, and selected this as the terms of Life; so that as a *Law* in *genere* (existent only *in speciebus*) commandeth Obedience, and the Law of Innocency *in specie* commanded [*personal perfect*

perfect perpetual Obedience, as the Condition of Life]; so the Gospel commandeth *Faith* in our *Redeemer*, as the new Condition of Life: on which supposition, even the Law of lapsed Nature further obligeth us thereto: And as the Commands differ, so do the Prohibitions.

There is a certain sort of sin excepted from pardon, by the pardoning Law, *viz.* Final non-performance of its Conditions: And to judg a Man not guilty of this sin, is part of our Justification, as is aforesaid.

§. 10. He addeth, [*If Legal and Evangelical Justification are specie distinct, then so are the Courts in which we are justified. —— If distinct and subordinate, and so he that is justified by the Law, is justified by the Gospel,* &c.]

Answ. 1. No Man is justified by the Law of Innocency or Works, but Christ: Did I ever say that, [*That Law justifieth us*], who have voluminously wrote against it? If he would have his Reader think so, his unrighteousness is such as civility forbids me to give its proper Epithets to. If not, against what or whom is all this arguing?

2. I call it [Legal] as it is that perfect Righteousness of Christ our Surety, conform to the Law of Innocency; by which he was justified (though not absolved and pardoned): I call it [*pro Legali justitia*], because that Law doth not justifie us for it (but Christ only) but by it given us *ad effecta* by the New-Covenant; we are saved and justified from the Curse of that Law, or from Damnation, as certainly as if we had done it our selves: I call

Faith

Faith our Evangelical Righteousness, on the Reasons too oft mentioned. Now these may be called *Two Justifications*, or (rather) *two parts of one*, in several respects, as pleaseth the Speaker. And all such Word-Souldiers shall have their liberty without my Contradiction.

3. And when will he prove that these two Sorts, or Parts, or Acts, may not be at once transacted at the same Bar? Must there needs be *one Court* to try *whether I am a true Believer*, or an *Infidel*, or *Hypocrite*; and *another* to judg that *being such*, I am to be justified against all Guilt and Curse, by vertue of Christ's Merits and Intercession? Why may not these two parts of *one Man's Cause* be judged at the same Bar? And why must your Pupils be taught so to conceive of so great a business, in it self so plain?

§. 11. He proceedeth, [*The Use of this Evangelical Justification is made to be, that we may be made partakers of the Legal Justification out of us, in Christ: And so our Justification applyeth another Justification, and our Remission of sins another.*

Answ. No Sir; but our *particular subordinate sort of Righteousness*, consisting in the performance of the Conditions of the free Gift, (*viz.* a believing suitable *Acceptance*) is really our *Dispositio receptiva*, being the Condition of our Title to that Pardon and Glory, which for Christ's Righteousness if freely given us. And our *personal Faith and Sincerity* must be justified, and we *in tantum*, before our Right to Christ, Pardon and Life can be justified *in foro*.

2. And

2. And to justifie us as sincere Believers, when others are condemned as Hypocrites, and Unbelievers, and Impenitent, is not Pardon of Sin. These Matters should have been put into your (excellent) Catechism, and not made strange, much less obscured and opposed, when laying by the quarrels about mere words, I am confident you deny none of this.

§. 12. He addeth, [*Then Legal Justification is nothing but a bare word, seeing unapplyed; as to the Matter it is nothing, as it is not called Healing by a Medicine not applyed; nor was it ever heard that one Healing did apply another*].

Answ. Alas, alas, for the poor Church, if this be the Academies best! sorrow must excuse my Complaint! If it be an Argument it must run thus: If *Legal* (or *pro-legal*) *Righteousness* (that is, our part in Christ's Righteousness) be none to us (or none of our Justification) when not-applyed, than it is none also when it is applyed: But, &c.

Answ. It is none till applyed: Christ's Merits, or Legal Righteousness justifie himself, but not us till applyed: (Do you think otherwise, or do you wrangle against your self?) But I deny your Consequence: How prove you that it is *none when applyed therefore ?* Or the Cure is none when the Medicine is applyed?

Perhaps you'l say, That *then* our *Personal Righteousness*, and *subordinate Justification*, is ours before Christ's Righteousness, and so the greater dependeth on, and followeth the less.

Answ. 1.

Answ. 1. Christ's own Righteousness is before ours. 2. His Condition, Pardon to fallen Mankind is before ours. 3. This Gift being Conditional, excepteth the non-performance of the Condition; And the nature of a Condition, is to *suspend the effect of the Donation* till *performed*. 4. Therefore the performance goeth before the said Effect, and our Title. 5. But it is not therefore any *cause* of it, but a *removal* of the *suspension*; nor hath the Donation any other dependance on it. And is not all this beyond denial with Persons not studiously and learnedly misled?

But you say, *It was never heard that one Healing applyed another.*

Answ. And see you not that this is a *lis de nomine*, and of a name of your own introduction for illustration? If we were playing at a Game of Tropes, I could tell you that the *Healing* of Mens *Unbelief* is applicatory for the *healing* of their *Guilt*; And the healing of Men's Ignorance, Pride, and Wrangling about words, and frightning Men into a Conceit that it is about Life and Death, is applicatory as to the healing of the Churches Wounds and Shame. But I rather chuse to ask you, Whether it was never heard that a *particular subordinate personal Righteousness* (even *Faith* and *Repentance*) was made by God the Condition of our Right to Pardon, and Life by Christ's Righteousness? Did you never teach your Sholars this, (in what words you thought best?) And yet even our Faith is a Fruit of Christ's Righteousness; but nevertheless the Condition of other Fruits.

If you say that our *Faith* or *Performance* is not
to

to be called *Righteousness*, I refer you to my Answer to Mr. *Cartwright*; And if the word *Righteousness* be not ofter (ten to one) used in Scripture for somewhat Personal, than for Christ's Righteousness imputed, then think that you have said something.

If you say, *But it justifieth not as a Righteousness, but as an Instrument.* I Answer, 1. I have said elsewhere so much of its Instrumentality, that I am ashamed to repeat it. 2. It *justifieth* not at all, (for that signifieth *efficiency*); but only maketh us capable Recipients. 3. *We are justified by-it* as a *medium*, and that is a Condition performed (as aforesaid) : And when that Condition by a Law is made both a *Duty* and a *Condition* of Life, the performance is by necessary resultancy [a *Righteousness*]. But we are not justified by it, as it is a *Righteousness in genere*; nor as a mere moral Virtue or Obedience to the Law of Nature; but as it is *the performance of the Condition of the Law of Grace*; and so as it is *this particular Righteousness,* and no other.

§. 13. [*In Legal Justification* (saith he) *taken precisely, either there is Remission of sin, or not : If not, What Justification is that ? If yea, then Evangelical Justification is not necessary to the application of it; because the Application is supposed,* &c.]

Answ. 1. What I usually call [Evangelical Righteousness] he supposeth me to call *Justification*; which yet is true, and sound, but such as is before explained.

2. This

2. This is but the same again, and needeth no new answer; The performance of the Condition is strangely here supposed to follow the *Right* or Benefit of the Gift or Covenant: If he would have the Reader think I said so, he may as ingeniously tell, that I deny all Justification: If not, what meaneth he?

CHAP. VII.

Dr. Tullies *Quarrel about Imputation of Christ's Righteousness, considered.*

§. 1. *C*Ap. 8. *pag.* 79. he saith, [*Because no Man out of* Socinus *School, hath by his Dictates more sharply exagitated this Imputation of Righteousness, than the Author of the Aphorisms; and it is in all mens hands, we think meet to bring into a clearer Light, the things objected by him (or more truly his Sophistical Cavils) whence the fitter Prospect may be taken of almost the whole Controversie*].

Answ. That the Reader may see by what Weapons Theological Warriours wound the Churches Peace, and profligate brotherly Love; let him consider how many palpable Untruths are in these few Lines, even in matter of Fact.

1. Let him read Dr. *Gell*; Mr. *Thorndike*, and by his own confession, the Papists (a multitude of them)

them) and tell me true, that [*No Man out of So-cinus School hath*, &c.]. To say nothing of many late Writings near us.

2. If I have, 1. never written one word against [*Imputation of Righteousness*] there or elsewhere; 2. Yea, have oft written for it; 3. And if those very Pages be for it which he accuseth; 4. Yea, if there and elsewhere I write more for it than *Olevian, Ursine, Paraeus, Scultetus, Wendeline, Piscator*, and all the rest of those great Divines, who are for the *Imputation* only of the Passive Righteousness of Christ, when I profess there and often, to concur with Mr. *Bradshaw*, *Grotius*, and others that take in the Active also, yea and the Habitual, yea and Divine respectively, as advancing the Merits of the Humane; If all this be notoriously true, what Epithets will you give to this Academical Doctors notorious Untruth?

3. When that Book of *Aphorisms* was suspended or retracted between twenty and thirty years ago (publickly), because of many crude Passages and unapt Words, and many Books since written by me purposely, fully opening my mind of the same things; all which he passeth wholly by, save a late Epistle; what credit is to be given to that Man's ingenuity, who pretendeth that this being in all mens hands, the answering it will so far clear all the Controversie.

§. 2. Dr. *T.* [*He hence assaulteth the Sentence of the Reformed; because it supposeth, as he saith, that we were in Christ, at least, legally before we believed, or were born. But what proof of the consequence doth he be bring?*] (The reſt are but his Reaſons againſt the Conſequences, and his talk againſt me, *as pouring out Oracles*, &c.)

Anſw. 1. Is this the mode of our preſent Academical Diſputers, To paſs by the ſtating of the Controverſie, yea, to ſilence the ſtate of it, as laid down by the Author, whom he oppoſeth in that very place, (and more fully elſewhere often)? Reader, the Author of the *Aphoriſms*, pag. 45. and forward, diſtinguiſhing as Mr. *Bradſhaw* doth, of the ſeveral ſenſes of Imputation, and how Chriſt's Righteouſneſs is made ours, 1. Beginneth with their Opinion, who hold, [*That Chriſt did ſo obey in our ſtead, as that in God's eſteem, and in point of Law we were in Chriſt dying and ſuffering, and ſo in him we did both perfectly fulfil the Commands of the Law by Obedience, and the Threatnings of it by bearing the Penalty, and thus (ſay they) is Chriſt's Righteouſneſs imputed to us,* viz. *His Paſſive Righteouſneſs for the pardon of our ſins, and deliverance from the Penalty; His Active Righteouſneſs for the making of us Righteous, and giving us title to the Kingdom; And ſome ſay the Habitual Righteouſneſs of his Humane Nature, inſtead of our own Habitual Righteouſneſs; Yea, ſome add the Righteouſneſs of the Divine Nature*].

The ſecond Opinion which he reciteth is this, [*That God the Father accepteth the ſufferings and merits of his Son, as a valuable conſideration, on which he will wholly forgive and acquit the Offenders, and receive them into his favour, and give them the addition of a more excellent happineſs, ſo they will but receive his Son on the terms expreſſed in the Goſpel.*

And

And as distinct from theirs, who would thus have the *Passive Righteousness only imputed*, he professeth himself to hold with *Bradshaw, Grotius*, &c. that the Active also is so imputed, being *Justitia Meriti*, as well as *Personæ*, and endeavoureth to prove it: But not imputed in the first rigid sense, as if God esteemed us to *have been*, and *done*, and *suffered* our *selves in* and *by Christ*, and merited *by him*. Thus he states the Controversie; And doth this Doctor fight for Truth and Peace, by 1. passing by all this; 2. Saying, I am against Imputed Righteousness; 3. And against the Reformed? Were not all the Divines before named Reformed? Was not *Camero, Capellus, Placeus, Amyrald, Dallæus, Blondel*, &c. Reformed? Were not *Wotton, Bradshaw, Gataker*, &c. Reformed? Were not of late Mr. *Gibbons*, Mr. *Truman*, to pass many yet alive, Reformed? Must that Name be shamed, by appropriating it to such as this Doctor only?

2. And now let the Reader judg, with what face he denieth the Consequence, (that it *supposeth us to have been in Christ legally*, &c.) When as I put it into the Opinion opposed, and opposed no other. But I erred in saying, that [*most of our ordinary Divines*] hold it; But he more in fathering it in common on the Reformed.

§. 2. Dr. *T.* [2. *Such Imputation of Righteousness*, he saith, *agreeth not with Reason or Scripture*: But what *Reason* meaneth he? Is it that vain, blind, maimed, unmeasurably procacious and tumid *Reason* of the *Cracovian Philosophers*? —— Next he saith, *faith, Scripture is filent of the Imputed Righteoufness of Chrift; what a faying is this of a Reformed Divine?* fo alfo Bellarmine, &c.

Anfw. Is it not a doleful cafe that *Orthodoxnefs* muft be thus defended? Is this the way of vindicating Truth? 1. Reader, my words were thefe, (juft like *Bradſhaws*) [*It teacheth Imputation of Chrift's Righteoufneſs in fo ſtrict a ſenſe, as will neither ſtand with Reaſon, nor the Doctrine of the Scripture, much leſs with the* P H R A S E *of Scripture, which mentioneth no Imputation of Chrift or his Righteoufnefs*]. 1. Is this a denying of Chrift's Righteoufnefs imputed? Or only of that intollerable *fenfe* of it? 2. Do I fay here that Scripture mentioneth not Imputed Righteoufnefs, or only that ſtrict fenfe of it? 3. Do I not exprefly fay, It is the *Phrafe* that is not to be found in Scripture, and the unfound fenfe, but not the found?

2. And as to the Phrafe, Doth this Doctor, or can any living Man find that *Phrafe* in Scripture, [*Chrift's Righteoufneſs is imputed to us*]? And when he knoweth that it is not there, are not his Exclamations, and his Bug-bears [*Cracovian Reafon*, and *Bellarmine*] his diſhonour, that hath no better Weapons to ufe againſt the Churches Peace? To tell us that the *fenfe* or Doctrine is in Scripture, when the queſtion is of the *Phrafe*, or that Scripture ſpeaketh in his rigid fenfe, and not in ours, is but to lofe time, and abufe the Reader, the firſt being impertinent, and the ſecond the begging of the Queſtion.

§. 3.

§. 3. Dr. *T*. *The Greek word answering to Imputation, is ten times in* Rom. 4. *And what is imputed but Righteousness? we have then some imputed Righteousness.* *The Question is, only what or whose it is,* Christ's *or our own? Not ours, therefore* Christ's: *If ours, either its the Righteousness of Works, or of Faith,* &c.

Answ. 1. But what's all this to the *Phrase?* Could you have found that Phrase [*Christ's Righteousness is imputed*], why did you not recite the words, but *Reason* as for the sense?

2. Is that your way of Disputation, to prove that the Text speaketh of the *Imputation of Christ's Righteousness,* when the Question was only, *In what sense?* What kind of Readers do you expect, that shall take this for rational, candid, and a Plea for Truth?

3. But to a Man that cometh unprejudiced, it is most plain, that *Paul* meaneth by [*imputing it for Righteousness*] that the Person was or is, *accounted, reckoned,* or *judged Righteous,* where *Righteousness* is mentioned as the *formal Relation* of the Believer: so that what-ever be the matter of it (of which next) the *formal Relation* sure is our *own,* and so here said: And if it be from the matter of Christ's Righteousness, yet that must be *our own,* by your Opinion. And it must be *our own, in* and *to* the proper *Effects,* in mine. But sure it is not the same *numerical* formal Relation of [*Righteousness*] that is in Christ's *Person,* and *in* ours: And it's that formal Relation, as in *Abraham,* and not in Christ, that is called *Abraham's* Reputed Righteousness

oufnefs in the Text: I fcarce think you will fay the contrary.

§. 4. Dr. T. [*But Faith is not imputed to us for Righteoufnefs.*

Anfw. Exprefly againft the words of the Holy Ghoft there oft repeated. Is this defending the Scripture, exprefly to deny it? Should not reverence, and our fubfcription to the Scripture fufficiently rather teach us to diftinguifh, and tell in *what fenfe it is imputed*, and in *what not*, than thus to deny, without diftinction, what it doth fo oft affert? Yea, the Text nameth *nothing elfe as fo imputed, but Faith.*

§. 5. *If it be imputed, it is either as some Virtue, or Humane Work, (the* τὸ *Credere) or as it apprehendeth and applyeth Chrift's Righteoufnefs? Not (the firft) —— If Faith be imputed relatively only, as it applyeth to a Sinner the Righteoufnefs of Chrift, it's manifeft that it's the Righteoufnefs of Chrift only that is imputed, and that Faith doth no more to Righteoufnefs, than an empty hand to receive an Alms.*

Anfw. 1. Sure it doth as a voluntarily receiving hand, and not as a mere *empty hand*. And voluntary grateful Reception may be the Condition of a Gift.

2. You and I fhall fhortly find that it will be the Queftion on which we fhall be Juftified or Condemned; not only whether we received Chrift's Righteoufnefs, but whether by Faith we received Chrift in all the Effentials of his Office, and to all the effential faving Ufes: Yea, whether according to the fenfe of the Baptifmal Covenant, we firft believingly

lievingly received, and gave up our fel
Father, Son, and *Holy Ghost,* and af
sincerely that Covenant.

3. But let me defend the Word of
is imputed for Righteousness, even
described; 1. *Remotely, ex materiæ*
its fitness to its formal Office; And
1. Because it is an *Act of Obedience*
rally good, (for a *bad* or *indifferent A*
stifie). 2. More specially as it is
trusting, and *giving* up *our selves* to C
Son, and Holy Ghost, to the prope
demption, or a *suitable Reception*
offered Gift; and so connoteth Ch
(for the Object is essential to the *f*
2. But proximately *Faith* is so *repute*
as it is the *performance* of the *Conditi*
fying Covenant or Donation.

And to be *imputed* for *Righteousn*
That [*It is the part required of us*
Grace, to make us partakers of the Ben
Righteousness, which meriteth Salvat
stead of a legal and perfect Righteousn
(which we have not). Or, [*Where*
of a Righteousness of Innocency, Ch
Righteousness hath merited our Pardon
and given title to them by a New Cove
which maketh this Faith the Conditio
and if we do this, we shall be judged
Righteous; that is, such as have done
cessary to their right in Christ and the
and therefore have such a Right].

This is plain English, and plain T
no more against it, and against the

the Text, and againſt your Brethren and the Churches Concord, by making Men believe that there are grievous Differences, where there are none.

Reader, I was going on to Anſwer the reſt, but my time is ſhort, Death is at the door: Thou ſeeſt what kind of Work I have of it, even to detect a Learned Man's Overſights, and temerarious Accuſations. The wearineſs will be more to thee and me, than the profit: I find little before, but what I have before anſwered here, and oft elſewhere; And therefore I will here take up, only adding one Chapter of Defence of that Conciliation which I attempted in an Epiſtle to Mr. *W. Allens* Book of the Two Covenants, and this Doctor, like an Enemy of Peace, aſſaulteth.

CHAP.

CHAP. VIII.

The Concord of Protestants in the Matter of Justification defended, against Dr. Tullies *Oppositions, who would make Discord under pretence of proving it.*

§. 1. WHile *Truth* is pretended by most, that by *envious striving* introduce *Confusion*, and *every evil Work*, it usually falleth out by God's just Judgment, that such are almost as opposite to *Truth*, as to *Charity* and *Peace*. What more palpable instances can there be, than such as on such accounts have lately assaulted me : Mr. *Danvers*, Mr. *Bagshaw*, &c. and now this Learned Doctor. The very stream of all his Opposition against me about Imputation, is enforced by this oft repeated Forgery, that I deny *all Imputation of Christ's Righteousness* : Yea, he neither by *fear*, *modesty*, or *ingenuity*, was *restrained* from writing, *pag.* 117. [*Omnem ludibrio habet Imputationem*] [*He derideth all Imputation*]. Judg by this what credit contentious Men deserve.

§. 2. The conciliatory Propositions which I laid down in an Epistle to Mr. *W. Allens* Book, I will here transcribe, that the Reader may see what it is that these Militant Doctors war against.

Lest

Lest any who know not how to stop in mediocrity, should be tempted by Socinians or Papists, to think that we countenance any of their Errors, or that our Differences in the point of Justification by Faith or Works, are greater than indeed they are; and lest any weak Opinionative Persons, should clamour unpeaceably against their Brethren, and think to raise a name to themselves for their differing Notions; I shall here give the Reader such evidences of our real Concord, as shall silence that Calumny.

Though some few Lutherans did, upon peevish suspiciousness against *George Major* long ago, assert, That [Good Works are not necessary to Salvation]: And though some few good Men, whose Zeal without Judgment doth better serve their own turn than the Churches, are jealous, lest all the good that is ascribed to Man, be a dishonour to God ; and therefore speak as if God were honoured most by saying the worst words of our selves ; and many have uncomely and irregular Notions about these Matters : And though some that are addicted to sidings, do take it to be their Godly Zeal to censure and reproach the more understanding sort, when they most grosly err themselves : And though too many of the People are carried about through injudiciousness and temptations to false Doctrines and evil Lives ; yet is the Argument of Protestants thus manifested.

1. They all affirm that Christ's Sacrifice, with his Holiness and perfect Obedience, are the meritorious Cause of the forgiving Covenants, and of our Pardon and Justification thereby, and of our Right to Life Eternal, which it giveth us. And that this Price was not paid or given in it self immediately

mediately to us, but to God for us; and so, that our foresaid Benefits are its Effects.

2. They agree that Christ's Person and ours were not really the same; and therefore that the same Righteousness, which is an Accident of one, cannot possibly be an Accident of the other.

3. They all detest the Conceit, that God should aver, and repute a Man to have done that which he never did.

4. They all agree that Christ's Sacrifice and Merits are really so effectual to procure our Pardon, Justification, Adoption, and right to the sealing Gift of the Holy Ghost, and to Glory, upon our Faith and Repentance; that God giveth us all these benefits of the New-Covenant as certainly for the sake of Christ and his Righteousness, as if we had satisfied him, and merited them our selves: and that thus far Christ's Righteousness is ours in its Effects, and imputed to us, in that we are thus used for it, and shall be judged accordingly.

5. They all agree, that we are justified by none, but a practical or working Faith.

6. And that this Faith is the Condition of the Promise, or Gift of Justification and Adoption.

7. And that Repentance is a Condition also, though (as it is not the same with Faith, as Repentance of Unbelief is) on another aptitudinal account; even as a willingness to be cured, and a willingness to take one for my Physician, and to trust him in the use of his Remedies, are on several accounts the Conditions on which that Physician will undertake the Cure, or as willingness to return to subjection and thankful acceptance of a purchased Pardon, and of the Purchasers Love and
future

future Authority, are the Conditions of a Rebel's Pardon.

8. And they all agree, that in the first instant of a Man's Conversion or Believing, he is entred into a state of Justification, before he hath done any outward Works: and that so it is true, that good Works follow the Justified, and go not before his initial Justification: as also in the sense that *Austin* spake it, who took Justification, for that which we call Sanctification or Conversion.

9. And they all agree, that Justifying Faith is such a receiving affiance, as is both in the Intellect and the Will; and therefore as in the Will, participateth of some kind of Love to the justifying Object, as well as to Justification.

10. And that no Man can chuse or use Christ as a Means (so called, in respect to his own intention) to bring him to God the Father, who hath not so much love to God, as to take him for his end in the use of that means.

11. And they agree, that we shall be all judged according to our Works, by the Rule of the Covenant of Grace, though not for our Works, by way of commutative, or legal proper merit. And Judging is the Genus, whose Species is Justifying and Condemning: and to be judged according to our Works, is nothing but to be justified or condemned according to them.

12. They all agree, that no Man can possibly merit of God in point of Commutative Justice, nor yet in point of Distributive or Governing Justice, according to the Law of Nature or Innocency, as *Adam* might have done, nor by the Works of the Mosaical Law.

13. They all agree, that no Works of Mans are to be trusted in, or pleaded, but all excluded, and the Conceit of them abhorred.

1. As they are feigned to be against, or instead of the free Mercy of God.

2. As they are against, or feigned, instead of the Sacrifice, Obedience, Merit, or Intercession of Christ.

3. Or as supposed to be done of our selves, without the Grace of the Holy Ghost.

4. Or as supposed falsly to be perfect.

5. Or as supposed to have any of the afore-disclaimed Merit.

6. Or as materially consisting in Mosaical Observances.

7. Much more in any superstitious Inventions.

8. Or in any Evil mistaken to be Good.

9. Or as any way inconsistent with the Tenor of the freely pardoning Covenant. In all these senses Justification by Works is disclaimed by all Protestants at least.

14. Yet all agree, that we are created to good Works in Christ Jesus, which God hath ordained, that we should walk therein; and that he, that nameth the Name of Christ, must depart from iniquity, or else he hath not the Seal of God; and that he that is born of God sinneth not; that is, predominantly. And that all Christ's Members are Holy, Purified, zealous of Good Works, cleansing themselves from all filthiness of Flesh and Spirit, that they might perfect Holiness in God's fear, doing good to all Men, as loving their Neighbours as themselves; and that if any Man have not the

Sancti-

Sanctifying Spirit of Christ, he is none of his, nor without Holiness can see God.

15. They all judg reverently and charitably of the Ancients, that used the word [Merit of Good Works], because they meant but a moral aptitude for the promised Reward, according to the Law of Grace through Christ.

16. They confess the thing thus described themselves, however they like not the name of Merit, lest it should countenance proud and carnal Conceits.

17. They judg no Man to be Heretical for the bare use of that word, who agreeth with them in the sense.

18. In this sense they agree, that our Gospel-Obedience is such a necessary aptitude to our Glorification, as that Glory (though a free Gift) is yet truly a reward of this Obedience.

19. And they agree, that our final Justification by Sentence at the Day of Judgment doth pass upon the same Causes, Reasons, and Conditions, as our Glorification doth.

20. They all agree, that all faithful Ministers must bend the labour of their Ministry in publick and private, for promoting of Holiness and good Works, and that they must difference by Discipline between the Obedient and the Disobedient. And O ! that the Papists would as zealously promote Holiness and good Works in the World, as the true serious Protestants do, whom they factiously and peevishly accuse as Enemies to them ; and that the Opinion, Disputing, and name of good Works, did not cheat many wicked Persons into self-flattery and Perdition, while they are void of that which

they

they difpute for. Then would not the Mahometans and Heathens be deterred from Chriftianity by the wickednefs of thefe nominal Chriftians, that are near them : nor would the ferious practice of that Chriftianity, which themfelves in general profefs, be hated, fcorned, and perfecuted by fo many, both Proteftants and Papifts; nor would fo many contend that they are of the True Religion, while they are really of no Religion at all any further, than the Hypocrites Picture and Carcafs may be called Religion : Were Men but refolved to be ferious Learners, ferious Lovers, ferious Practifers according to their knowledg, and did not live like mockers of God, and fuch as look toward the Life to come in jeft, or unbelief, God would vouchfafe them better acquaintance with the True Religion than moft Men have.

§. 3. One would think now that this fhould meet with no fharp Oppofition, from any Learned lover of Peace; and that it fhould anfwer for it felf, and need no defence. But this Learned Man for all that, among the reft of his Military Exploits, muft here find fome Matter for a Triumph.

And 1. *Pag.* 18. he affaulteth the third Propof. [*They all deteft the Conceit, that God fhould aver, and repute a Man to have done that which he never did*].

And is not this true? Do any fober Men deny it, and charge God with Error or Untruth? Will not this Man of Truth and Peace, give us leave to be thus far agreed, when we are fo indeed?

But

But faith he, [*Yea, the Orthodox abhor the contrary, if* [*to have done it*] *be taken* in senfu forenfi, *(for in a Physical and Personal, they abhor it not, but deride it): Doth the Aphorist abhor these and suchlike sayings,* [*We are dead, buried, risen from the Dead with Christ ?*]

Answ. 1. Take notice Reader, that it is but the *Words,* and not the *Matter* that he here affaulteth; fo that all here feemeth but *lis de nomine.* He before, *pag.* 84. extolleth *Chrysostom* for thus expounding, [*He made him sin for us*]; *that is, to be condemned as an Offender, and to die as a Blasphemer.* And this fenfe of Imputation we all admit; (But *Chrysostom* in that place oft telleth us, That by [Sin] he meaneth both one counted a wicked Man by his Persecutors, [not by God] and one that suffered that cursed Death, which was due to wicked cursed Men: And which of us deny not Justification by Works as *Chrysostom* doth ? I fubfcribe to his words, [*It is God's Righteousness; seeing it is not of Works (for in them it were necessary that there be found no blot) but of Grace, which blotteth out and extinguisheth all sin: And this begetteth us a double benefit, for it suffereth us not to be lift up in mind, because it is all the Gift of God, and it sheweth the greatness of the benefit*]. This is as apt an Expression of my Judgment of *Works* and *Grace* as I could chufe. But it's given to fome Men to extol that in one Man, which they fervently revile in others. How frequently is *Chrysostom* by many accufed as favouring Free-Will, and Man's Merits, and fmelling of Pelagianifm? And he that is acquainted with *Chrysostom,* muft know, That he includeth all thefe things in Juftification. 1. Remiffion

is living, quickeneth the dead, and as he that is strong giveth strength to the weak; so he that is Righteous, doth suddenly make them Righteous that were lapsed into sin], as he there also speaketh. And he oft tells us, It is *Faith it self*, and not only Christ believed in, that is imputed for Righteousness, or Justifieth: And in *Rom.* 4. *p.* 80. he calleth the Reward, [the *Retribution of Faith*]. And *pag.* 89. he thus conjoyneth [*Faith and Christ's Death*] to the Question, *How Men obnoxious to so much sin are justified,* [*he sheweth that he blotted out all sin, that he might confirm what he said, both from the Faith of* Abraham *by which he was justified, and from our Saviours Death, by which we are delivered from sin*]. But this is on the by.

2. But saith Dr. *T. The Orthodox abhor the contrary in sensu forensi.*

Answ. How easie is it to challenge the Titles of *Orthodox, Wise,* or *good Men* to ones self? And who is not Orthodox, himself being Judg? But it seems with him, no Man must pass for Orthodox that is not in so gross an error of his Mind, (if these words, and not many better that are contrary must be the discovery of it) *viz.* That will not say, that *in sensu forensi, God esteemeth Men to have done that which they never did.* The best you can make of this is, that you cover the same sense, which I plainlier express, with this illfavoured

Phrase

Phrafe of Man's inventing: But if indeed you mean any more than I by your *fenfus forenfis, viz.* that fuch a *fuffering* and *meriting* for us may, in the lax improper way of fome Lawyers fpeaking, be called, [*Our own Doing, Meriting, Suffering,* &c.] I have proved, that the Doctrine denied by me, fubverteth the Gofpel of Chrift.

Reader, I remember what *Grotius* (then Orthodox, thirty years before his Death) in that excellent Letter of Church-Orders, Predeftination, Perfeverance, and Magiftrates, animadverting on *Molinæus,* faith, *How great an injury thofe Divines, who turn the Chriftian Doctrine into unintelligible Notions and Controverfies, do to Chriftian Magiftrates; becaufe it is the duty of Magiftrates to difcern and preferve neceffary found Doctrine, which thefe Men would make them unable to difcern.* The fame I muft fay of their injury to all Chriftians, becaufe all fhould hold faft that which is proved True and Good, which this fort of Men would difable them to difcern. We juftly blame the Papifts for locking up the Scripture, and performing their Worfhip in an unknown Tongue. And alas, what abundance of well-meaning Divines do the fame thing by undigefted Terms and Notions, and unintelligible Diftinctions, not adapted to the Matter, but cuftomarily ufed from fome Perfons reverenced by them that led the way? It is fo in their Tractates, both of Theology and other Sciences; and the great and ufeful Rule, *Verba Rebus aptanda funt,* is laid afide: or rather, Men that underftand not Matter, are like enough to be little skilful in the expreffing of it: And as Mr. *Pemble* faith, A cloudy unintelligible ftile, ufually fignifieth a cloudy dy unintelligent Head, (to that sense): And as Mr. *J. Humfrey* tells Dr. *Fullwood*, (in his unanswerable late Plea for the Conformists against the charge of Schism) *pag.* 29. [*So overly are men ordinarily wont to speak at the first sight, against that which others have long thought upon*]; that some Men think, that the very jingle of a distinction not understood is warrant enough for their reproaching that Doctrine as dangerous and unsound, which hath cost another perhaps twenty times as many hard studies, as the Reproachers ever bestowed on that Subject.

To deliver thee from those Learned Obscurities, read but the Scripture impartially, without their Spectacles and ill-devised Notions, and all the Doctrine of Justification that is necessary, will be plain to thee: And I will venture again to fly so far from flattering those, called Learned Men, who expect it, as to profess that I am perswaded the common sort of honest unlearned Christians, (even Plowmen and Women) do better understand the Doctrine of Justification, than many great Disputers will suffer themselves or others to understand it, by reason of their forestalling ill-made Notions: these unlearned Persons commonly conceive, 1. That Christ in his own Person, as a Mediator, did by his perfect Righteousness and Sufferings, merit for us the free pardon of all our sins, and the Gift of his Spirit and Life Eternal, and hath promised Pardon to all that are Penitent Believers, and Heaven to all that so continue, and sincerely obey him to the end; and that all our after-failings, as well as our former sins, are freely pardoned by the Sacrifice, Merits, and Intercession of Christ, who also giveth

us

us his Grace for the performance of his imposed Conditions, and will judg us, as we have or have not performed them]. Believe but this plain Doctrine, and you have a righter understanding of Justification, than many would let you quietly enjoy, who tell you, [That Faith is not imputed for Righteousness; that it justifieth you only as an Instrumental Cause, and only as it is the reception of Christ's Righteousness, and that no other Act of Faith is justifying, and that God esteemeth us to have been perfectly Holy and Righteous, and fulfilled all the Law, and died for our own sins, in or by Christ, and that he was politically the very Person of every Believing Sinner]; with more such like.

And as to this distinction which this Doctor will make a Test of the Orthodox, (that is, Men of of his Size and Judgment) you need but this plain explication of it.

1. *In Law-sense, a Man is truly and fitly said himself to have done that, which the Law or his Contract alloweth him to do either by himself or another*; (as to do an Office, or pay a Debt by a Substitute or Vicar). For so I do it by my Instrument, and the Law is fulfilled and not broken by me, because I was at liberty which way to do it. In this sense I deny that we ever fulfilled all the Law by Christ; and that so to hold subverts all Religion as a pernicious Heresie.

2. But in a tropical improper sense, he may be said to [*be esteemed of God to have done what Christ did; who shall have the benefits of Pardon, Grace, and Glory thereby merited, in the manner and measure given by the free Mediator, as certainly as if he*
had

had done it himself]. In this improper sense we agree to the *Matter*, but are sorry that improper words should be used as a snare against sound Doctrine, and the Churches Love and Concord. And yet must we not be allowed *Peace* ?

§. 4. But my free Speech here maketh me remember how sharply the Doctor expounded and applyed one word in the retracted Aphorisms: I said (not of the *Men*, but of the *wrong Opinion* opposed by me) [*It fondly supposeth a Medium betwixt one that is just, and one that is no sinner*] *one that hath his sin or guilt taken away, and one that hath his unrighteousness taken away: It's true in bruits and insensibles that are not subjects capable of Justice, there is, &c. There is a Negative Injustice which denominateth the Subject* non-justum, *but not* injustum, *where Righteousness is not due. But where there is the* debitum habendi, *its privative.* The Doctor learnedly translateth first the word [*fondly*] by [*stolide*]; and next he (*fondly*, though not *stolide*) would perswade the Reader, that it is said of the *Men*, though himself translate it [*Doctrina*].

And next he bloweth his Trumpet to the War, with this exclamation, [*Stolide ! O vocis mollitiem, & modestiam! O stolidos Ecclesiæ Reformatæ Clarissimos Heroas ! Aut ignoravit certè, aut scire se dissimulat, (quod affine est calumniæ) quid isti statuant, quos loquitur, stolidi Theologi*].

Answ. 1. How blind are some in their own Cause ? Why did not Conscience at the naming of Calumnie say, [*I am now committing it ?*] It were better write in English, if Latin translations must needs

needs be so false ! we use the word [*fond*] in our Country, in another sense than [*foolish*]; with us it signifieth any byassed Inclination, which beyond reason propendeth to one side: and so we use to say, That *Women are fond of their Children*, or of any thing *over-loved*: But perhaps he can use his Logick, to gather by consequences the Title of the *Person*, from the Title of his *Opinion*, and to gather [*foolishly*] by consequence out of [*fondly*]. To all which I can but answer, That if he had made himself the *Translator* of my Words, and the Judg of my Opinions; if this be his best, he should not be chosen as such by me. But it may be he turned to *Riders Dictionary*, & found there [*fondly, vide foolishly*].

2. The *Stolidi Theologi* then is his own phrase ! And in my Opinion, another Mans Pen might better have called the Men of his own Opinion [*Ecclesiæ Reformatæ clarissimos Heroas*] compared with others! I take *Gataker, Bradshaw, Wotton, Camero*, and his followers; *Ursine, Olevian, Piscator, Paræus, Wendeline*, and multitudes such, to be as famous Heroes as himself: But this also on the by.

§. 5. But I must tell him whether I abhor the Scripture Phrase, [*We are dead, buried, and risen with Christ*].

I answer, No; nor will I abhor to say, That *in sensu forensi, I am one political Person with Christ*, and am *perfectly holy* and *obedient* by and *in him*, and died and redeemed my self by him; when he shall prove them to be Scripture Phrases: But I desire the Reader not to be so *fond*, (pardon the word) as by this bare question to be enticed to believe, that it is any of the meaning of those Texts that use that Phrase which he mentioneth, that

O [*Legally*,

[*Legally*, or *in sensu forensi, every Be*
ed by God to have himself personall
death on the Cross, and to have been
have risen again, and ascended into
yet to be now there in Glory, because
doth all this in our very Legal Per
but 1. consider the Text, 2. ar
3. and the Analogy of Faith, and he
ther sense; *viz.* That *we so live by F
buried, risen and glorified Saviour,
he dwelleth objectively in our Hearts,
so of the Fruits of his Death, Buri
rection, and Glory, as that we follow
Communion, being dead and buried to
Sin, and risen to newness of Life, be
his Power we shall personally, after
burial, rise also unto Glory.* I will
are perfectly *holy and obedient by an*
far as we are now *dead, buried,*
him.

§. 6. And here I will so far look
member, That he (as some other
telleth us, That [*the Law bound u
Obedience, and to punishment for our
fore pardon by our own suffering in Ch
with the reputation, that we were per
and Righteous in Christ.*]

Answ. And to what purpose is
long, where so notorious a contradic
ly not discerned, but obtruded as t
cessary to our Orthodoxness, if not
tion? I ask him,

1. Was not Christ as our Mediato
ly habitually, and actually, withou
Actual Sin?

2. If all this be reputed to be *in se*, our own as *subjected in* and *done* by *our selves political*, or *in sensu forensi*; Are we not then reputed *in foro*, to have no original or actual sin, but to have innocently fulfilled all the Law, from the first hour of our lives to the last? Are we reputed *innocent* in Christ, as to *one* part only of our lives, (if so, which is it?) or as to all?

3. If as to all, is it not a *contradiction* that in Law-sense, we are reputed perfectly Holy and Innocent, and yet sinners.

4. And can he have need of Sacrifice or Pardon, that is reputed never to have sinned (legally)?

5. If he will say that in Law-sense, we have or are *two Persons*, let him expound the word *Persons* only, as of *Qualities* and *Relations*, (nothing to our Case in hand); or else say also, That as we are holy and perfect in one of our own Persons, and *sinful, unrighteous*, or *ungodly* in another; so a Man may be in Heaven in one of his own Persons, and on Earth, yea and in Hell in the other: And if he mean that the same Man is *justified* in his Person in Christ, and condemned in his other Person; consider which of these is the *Physical* Person; for I think its that which is like to suffer.

§. 7. *pag.* 224. He hath another touch at my Epistle, but gently forbeareth contradiction as to *Num.* 8. And he saith so little to the 11*th*, as needeth no answer.

§. 8. *pag.* 127. He assaulteth the first *Num.* of *N.* 13. That *we all agree against any conceit of Works that are against or instead of the free Mercy of God*].

And what hath he against this? Why that which

Church-Controverſies, [O *Antichr*
Bellarmine, &c.] ſhould be of the ſar
take the ſame courſe in greater Matt
perceive it, nor acknowledg their agr
them ! But as Mr. *J. Humfrey* ſaith i
Book of the word [*Schiſm*, *Schiſm*
out againſt them, that will not ſacri
render their Conſciences, or deſert th
[*The great Bear hath been ſo oft le*
ſtreets, that now the Boys lay by all fe
or make ſport at him] ſo ſay I of this S
bear, [*Popery*, *Antichriſtian*, *Bellar*
the Papiſts really ſay as we do, or the
not, is this Doctor more to be blame
them *better than* they are, or for mak
which ever it be, *Truth* ſhould defend
do, I heartily rejoyce, and it ſhall b
labour any more (whatever I did in
of Faith) to prove that they do no
will manage ſuch ungrateful Work.
I take it for a better Character of any
Papiſts and Proteſtants agree in it,
Proteſtants hold it alone. And ſo m
piſts and *Bellarmine*] though I thinl
ter what they teach, than his Book:
me.

§. 9. But he addeth, [*Humane J*
are in reality adverſe to the free Mercy
fore to be accounted of no value to *Righ*

ut whose phrase is *Justifying Works*?
t the *Holy Ghost* say, That a *Man* is
ks, and *not by Faith only?* Jam. 2.
t Christ say, *By thy words thou shalt*

I over and over tell the World, That
ation by Works in no sense, but as
same as [*According to Works*] which
d so both *Name* and *Thing* are con-
o be Scriptural.
efore desired the Reader to turn to
Righteous, *Righteousness*, *Justificati-*
is Concordance. And if there he
ess mentioned as consisting in some
many hundred times, let him next
that they are to *be had in no price*
s.: Or let him read the Texts cited
onfession of Faith.
, Faith, Repentance, Love, Obedi-
whose sincerity is to be judged in or-
e or Death ere long; I will not say
o be vilified as to such a Righteous-
ation, as consisteth in our vindicati-
charge of Impenitency, Infidelity,
ypocrisie, &c. The reading of *Mat.*
ne for this Opinion.
t he noteth our detesting such Works
or instead of Christ's Sacrifice, Righ-
rits, &c. To this we have the old
pists say the like.
proved that the generality of Prote-
eed in all those twenty Particulars,
he material Doctrines about Man's
stification, while this warlike Doctor

O 3 would

would set us all together by the ears still, he is over-ruled to assert that the Papists also are agreed with us. The more the better, I am glad if it be so, and will here end with so welcome a Conclusion, that maketh us all herein to be Friends: only adding, That when he saith that [*such are all Works whatever,* (even Faith it self) *which are called into the very least part of Justification*]; even as a *Condition or subordinate personal Evangelical Righteousness*, such as Christ and *James*, and a hundred Texts of Scripture assert; I answer, I cannot believe him, till I cease believing the Scriptures to be true; which I hope will never be: And am sorry that so worthy a Man can believe so gross an Opinion, upon no better reasons than he giveth: And yet imagine, that had I the opportunity of free conference with him, I could force him to manifest, That he himself differeth from us but in meer words or second Notions, while he hotly proclaimeth a greater discord.

AN ANSVVER
TO
Dr. *TULLIES*
Angry Letter.

By *Rich. Baxter*.

LONDON,
Printed for *Nevil Simmons* and *Jonath. Robinson*, at the Princes-Arms and Golden-Lion, in St. *Pauls* Church-yard, 1675.

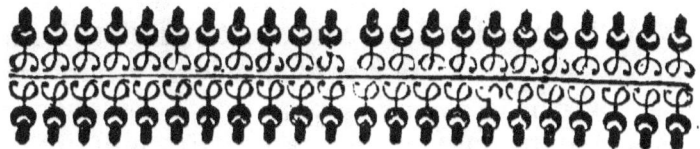

An Answer to Dr. Tullies Angry Letter.

Reverend Sir,

F I had not before *perceived* and *lamented* the great *Sin of Contenders*, the dangerous *snare for ignorant* Christians, and the *great Calamity* of the Church, by making *Verbal Differences* seem *Material*, and variety of some Arbitrary Logical Notions, to seem *tantum non*, a variety of Religions; and by frightning Men out of their Charity, Peace, and Communion, by Bugbear-Names, of this or that *Heresie* or *dangerous Opinion*, which is indeed but a Spectrum or Fantasm of a dreaming or melancholy Brain, your *Justificatio Paulina*, and your *Letter* to me, might be sufficient means of my full Conviction. And if once reading of your Writings do not yet more increase my love of the *Christian simplicity*, and plain old *Divinity*, and the amicable Communion of practical Christians upon those terms, and not medling with Controversies in a militant way, till by long impartial studies they are well understood, I

must

With your self I have no great business; I am not so vain as to think my self able to *understand you*, or to be *understood* by you : and I must not be so bold as to tell you why, much less will I be so injurious to the Reader, as by a *particular examining all your words*, to extort a confession that their *sense is less* or *worse* than I could wish : For *cui bono* ? What would this do but more offend you ? And idle words are as great a fault in writing as in talk : If I have been guilty of too many, I must not so much add to my fault, as a too particular examination of such Books would be. But for the sake of your *Academical Youth*, whom you thought meet to allarm by your Caution, I have answered so much of your Treatise as I thought necessary to help even Novices to answer the rest themselves. For their sakes (though I delight not to offend you) I must say, That if they would not be deceived by such Books as yours, it is not an *Answer* to them that must be their preservative, but an orderly studying of the Doctrines handled ; Let them but learn truly the several senses of the word [*Justification*], and the *several sorts*, and *what they are*, and still constrain *ambiguous words* to confess *their sense*, and they will need no other Answer to such Writings.

§. I. Between twenty and thirty years ago, I did in a private Disputation prove our guilt of the sins of our nearer Parents ; and because many
doubted

doubted of it, I have ott since in other writings mentioned it: About three years ago, having two Books of Mr. *William Allens* in my hand to peruse, in order to a Publication, (a *Perswasive to Unity*, and a *Treatise of the Two Covenants*) ; in a Preface to the latter, I said, [*That most Writers, if not most Christians, do greatly darken the Sacred Doctrine, by overlooking the Interest of Children in the Actions of their nearer Parents, and think that they participate of no guilt, and suffer for no original sin, but* Adam'*s only,* &c.] You fastened on this, and warned seriously the *Juniors*, *not rashly to believe one that brings forth such Paradoxes of his* (or *that*) *Theologie* , which you added to your [*O cæcos ante Theologos quicunque unquam fuistis*]: The charge was expressed by [*aliud invenisse peccatum Originale, multo citerius quam quod ab* Adamo *traductum est*]. Hereupon I thought it enough to publish that old private Disputation, which many before had seen with various Censures: Now you send me in your Letter the strange tidings of the success: You that deterred your *Juniors* by so frighful a warning, seem now not only to *agree with me*, that we *are guilty of our nearer Parents sin*, and contract additional pravity from them as such, (which was my Assertion) but over-do all others, and Truth it self in your Agreement! Now you take it for an injury to be reported to think otherwise herein than I do: yea, and add, [*Which neither I, nor any Body else I know of, denies as to the thing, though in the extent, and other circumstances, all are not agreed, and you may in that enjoy your Opinion for me*]. This is too kind : I am loth to tell you how many

that

that I know, and have read, deny it, left I tempt you to repent of your Agreement.

But doth the World yet need a fuller evidence, that some Men are *de materiâ* agreed with them, whom they raise the Country against by their Accusations and Suspicions?

But surely what passion or spatling soever it hath occasioned from you, I reckon that my labour is not lost: I may tell your *Juniors*, that I have sped extraordinary well, when I have procured the published consent of such a Doctor. Either you were of this mind *before* or *not*: If not, it's well you are brought to confess the Truth, though not to confess a former Error. If yea, then it's well that so loud and wide a seeming disagreement is confessed to be none, that your Juniors may take warning, and not be frightned from Love and Concord by every melancholy Allarm.

Yea, you declare your conformity to the Litany, [*Remember not our Offences, nor the Offences of our Fore fathers*], and many words of indignation you use for my questioning it. All this I like very well as to the Cause; And I matter it not much how it looks at me: If you *agree* more *angrily* than others disagree, the *Cause* hath some advantage by the Agreement. Though me-thinks it argueth somewhat unusual, that seeming Dissenters should close by so vehement a Collision.

But yet you *will not agree* when you *cannot chuse but agree*, and you carry it still as if your Allarm had not been given without cause: Must we *agree*, and not *agree?* What yet is the Matter? Why it is [*a new original sin*]. My ordinary expressions of

it,

it may be fully seen in the Disputation : The phrase you laid hold on in a Preface is cited before, [*That we participate of no guilt, and suffer for no original sin but* Adam's *only*], I denied. And what's the dangerous *Errour* here ? That our *nearer Parents* sin was *Adams*, I may presume that you hold not. That we are *guilty* of such, you *deny not :* That *it is sin*, I find you not denying : sure then all the difference must be in the word [ORIGINAL].

And if so, you that so hardly believe your loud-noised disagreements to be but *verbal*, must patiently give me leave here to try it. Is it any more than the *Name* ORIGINAL that you are so heinously offended at ? Sure it is not : Else in this Letter purposely written about it, you would have told your *Reader what it is.* Suffer me then to summon your Allarm'd Juniors to come and see what a *Spectrum* it is that must affright them ; and what a Poppet-Play or dreaming War it is, that the Church is to be engaged in, as if it were a matter of Life and Death ? *Audite juvenes !* I took the word [ORIGINAL] in this business to have several significations. First, That is called [*ORIGINAL*] *Sin*, which was the *ORIGO* of all other sins in the Humane World : And that was not *Adam's sin*, but *Eves.*

2. That which was the *ORIGO* of sin to all the World, save *Adam* and *Eve*, communicated by the way of Generation : And that was *Adams* and *Eves* conjunct, *viz.* 1. Their first sinful Acts ; 2. Their Guilt ; 3. And their habitual pravity (making it full, though in Nature following the Act). This Sin, Fact, Guilt, and Habit, as Accidents

cidents of the Persons of *Adam* and *Eve*, are not Accidents of our Persons.

3. *Our personal participation*; 1. *In the guilt* of the sin of *Adam* and *Eve*; 2. And of a vicious *privation* and *habit* from them, as soon as we are Persons. Which is called *Original* sin, on three accounts conjunct; 1. Because it is a participation of their *Original Act* that we are guilty of; 2. Because it is in us *ab Origine*, from our *first Being*; 3. And because it is the *Origo* of all our *Actual Sins*.

4. I call that also [ORIGINAL] (or *part of Original Sin*) which hath but the two later only; *viz*. 1. Which is in us *AB ORIGINE*, from our first personal being; 2. Which is the *Root* or *ORIGO* in our selves of all our *Actual Sins*: And thus our *Guilt* and *Vice* derived from our *nearer Parents*, and not from *Adam*, is our *Original Sin*; That is, 1. Both *Guilt* and *Habit* are in us from our *Original*, or first Being; 2. And all our Actual Sin springeth from it as a partial Cause: For I may presume that this Reverend Doctor doth not hold that *Adam*'s sin derived to us is in one *part* of the *Soul*, (which is not partible) and our nearer *Parent*'s in another; but will grant that it is *one vitiosity* that is derived from both, the latter being a Degree added to the former; though the *Reatus* having more than *one fundamentum*, may be called *diverse*. That *Origo & Active & passive dicitur*, I suppose we are agreed. Now I call the *vicious Habits* contracted from our nearer Parents by special reason of *their own sins*, superadded to the degree, which else we should have derived from
Adam,

Adam, a *part* of our *original sinful Pravity*, even a secondary part. And I call our *guilt* of the sins of our *nearer Parents* (not *Adam*'s) which you will, either a *secondary Original Guilt*, or *Sin*, or a secondary *part* of our *Original Guilt*. See then our dangerous disagreement: I call that ORIGINAL, which is in us *ab Origine*, when we are first Persons, and is partly the Root or *Origo* in us of all our following Actual Sin: though it was not the *Original Sin* of *Mankind*, or the first of Sins. The Doctor thinks this an Expression, which all *Juniors* must be warned to take heed of, and to take heed of the Doctrine of him that useth it. The Allarm is against this dangerous word [*ORIGINAL*]. And let a Man awake tell us what is the danger.

But I would bring him yet to agreement even *de nomine*, though it anger him. 1. Let him read the *Artic. 9. of the Church of England*, and seeing there *Original Sin* is said to be that *corruption of Nature whereby we are far gone from Original Righteousness, and are of our own Nature inclined to evil, so that the flesh lusteth against the Spirit. The lust of the flesh called* φρόνημα σαρκὸς, *which some do expound the Wisdom, some Sensuality, some the Affection, some the desire of the Flesh, not subject to the Law of God*]: Seing a degree of all this same Lust is in Men from the special sins of their Fore-fathers, as well as from *Adam*'s; Is not this Degree here called *Original Sin*? (why the Church omitted the *Imputed Guilt* aforesaid, I enquire not).

2. If this will not serve, if he will find me any Text of Scripture, which useth the Phrase, [*ORIGINAL Sin*], I will promise him hereafter to use

use it in no other sense, than the Scripture useth it.

3. If that will not serve, if the Masters of Language will agree, (yea, to pass by our *Lexicons*, if the Doctors of that University will give it us under their hands) that the word [ORIGINAL] is unaptly and dangerously applyed to that sinful *Guilt* and *Pravity* which is in us *ab Origine Nostræ existentiæ*, and is the internal *Radix vel Origo* of all our Actual Sin, in part of Causality, I will use that Epithete so no more.

4. If all this will not serve, if he himself will give me a *fitter Epithete*, I will use it : And now we *over-agree* in Doctrine, a word shall not divide us, unless he will be angry because we are agreed, as *Jonas* was that the *Ninivites* were spared, because it seemed to disgrace his Word.

§. II. *pag.* 4, 5, &c. You invite me to, [*a full entire retractation of my Doctrine of Justification* (you add, *By Works*) and the *secondary Original Sin*].

1. Will you take it well if I retract that which you profess now to hold, and know none that denyeth, then there is no pleasing you : If I must be thought to wrong you for seeming to differ from you, and yet must retract all :. What, yours and all Mens ?

2. Do you mean the *words* or the *sense* of *Justification*(as you call it)*by Works?*For the words,I take you for a subscriber to the 39 *Articles* ; and therefore that you reject not the Epistle of St. *James:* And for the *sense*, I confess it is a motion suitable to the Interest of your *Treatise*, (though not of the Truth) : He that cannot confute the Truth, would

, and I thank you for it: But is it that such as I am in, between two of Accusers? When Mr. *Danvers*, :s on that side, Reproach me daily *us*, and *you* for want of them? How ow to Mankind, to desire to be the :. World, and that all should be *Si-* *acted*, which is against their Minds? all on me for Retractation? Mr. *Ar. Danvers*, for what I have Writts-Baptism: The *Papists* for what I against them: And how many more? it *I have Retracted, One* reproached me other either knoweth not of it, or thers that it is not done.

ag. 6. [*A great out-cry you have made rging you with things you have Retra-* l *pag. 7. What's the reason you have rested us to the particulars of your Re-* *at, when, where? —— You direct one small Book, above Twenty years a-go* All I can pick up of any seeming is that you say, *that Works are necef-* *the continuation of our Justification.* her this is Written by *a Wilful*, or mistaking of my words. The first I ect; it must therefore be the second, not judg you *Unable* to understand 1). And is it any wonder if you have
P   many

many such Mistakes in your disputes
on, when you are so *heedless* abou
Fact? Where did I ever say, that I
Or that I *Retracted* any of the Doct
cation, which I had laid down? C
stinguish between *Suspending*, or *Re*
tracting a *particular Book*, for the
Crude and Incongruous Expressions,
or Recanting *that Doctrine of Ju*
can you not understand words, th
Distinguish? Why talk you of *wh*
and *where*, and conjecture at the *n*
would make the Reader believe, th
some confessed Errors of mine, wh
futed? and that I take it for an Inj
Retracted them? And so you think
Confutation, whatever you do by
and Justice: But you have not so
leaves for either. It was the *Aphori*
that I said was above Twenty years a
When in my Treatise of Infant-Ba
craved Animadversions on it, and p
ter Edition, if I Published it any m
the Reprinting it, till I had time to C
when many called for it, I still deny
when the *Cambridg* Printer Printe
time, he did it by Stealth, pretendin
beyond Sea. In my *Confession* Twer
I gave the Reasons, *Preface, pag.* 35
there are some Incautelous Passages in
not fitted to their Reading, that come t
and seek for a Word to be Matter of
Food for their Censuring opinionative 2
pag. 42. *If any Brother understand no*

my Aphorisms which is here Interpreted, or mistake my sense about the Matter of that Book, which is here more fully opened; I must expect, that they interpret that by this. And if any one have so little to do as to write against that Book (which is not unlikely) if he take the Sense contrary to what I have here and else where since then Published, I shall but neglect him as a Contentious, Vain Wrangler, if not a Calumniator]. I Wrote this sharply, to forwarn the Contentious, not knowing then that above Twenty years after Dr. *Tully* would be the Man. Pag. 43. *[If any will needs take any thing in this Book to be rather a Retractation, than an Explication, of what I have before said, though I should best know my own Meaning; yet do such commend me, while they seem to blame me: I never look to write that which shall have no need of Correction.*—— And Cap. 1 pag. 2. *[Lest I should prove a further Offence to my Brethren, and a Wrong to the Church, I desired those who thought it worth their Labour, to vouchsafe me their Animadversions, which I have spent much of these Three last years in considering, that I might Correct what-ever was discovered to be Erroneous, and give them an account of my Reasons of the rest. I have not only since SUPPRESSED that Book which did offend them, but also laid by those Papers of Universal Redemption, which I had written, let I should be further offensive,* &c.] In my Apologie else-where I have such like Passages, ever telling Men that *[It was the first Book I wrote in my Unexperienced Youth; that I take the Doctrines of it to be sound and needful, save that in divers places they are unskilfully and incautelously worded.* (As the Word [*Covenant*] is oft put for [*Law,*] &c.) And that

I wrote my *Confeſſion*, and *Diſputes* tion, as an Expoſition of it; and tha or *Suſpended*, or *Revoked*, not the the *Book*, till I had Corrected it, an it as too unmeet an Expreſſion o which I had more fully expreſt in oth

And is not this plain Engliſh? D rant a *Wiſe* and *Righteous* Man, to in accuſe him of writing againſt that Juſtification which I *Recanted*, and *What*, and *Where*, and *When?* Yea, that I [*refer you to a ſmall Book*] wl *referring* you to it, I only blame you to that alone, when I had ſaid as befc

When many Divines have publ Edition of their Works imperfectly corrected and enlarged them in a *Beza* his *Annotations*, *Polanus* his Sy many ſuch) all Men take it for an Neighbour twenty years after, to f Edition to confute as the Author' Much more might I, when I pub World, that I *Suſpended the whole B* *theſe twenty* four years hindred the Pi profeſſing that I have in many larger intelligibly and fully opened the ſame

Yea, you fear not *pag.* 23. to ſay you of *about* 60 *Books* of *Retractation* *leaſt which I have Written*]; when word fell from me. If I ſay, That o publiſhed his *Suſpenſion* of a *ſmall Bo Youth*, not for the *Doctrine of it*, bi Expreſſions, and hath ſince in al Years time, written about ſixty Books most of which is somewhat of the same Subject, and in some of them he fuller openeth his Mind; should be dealt with by an Adversary, according to some of his later and larger Explications, and not according to the Mode and Wording of that one Suspended Book alone: Shall such a Man as you say, that I [*tel you of about sixty Books of Retractations*]? Or will it not abate Mens reverence of your disputing Accurateness, to find you so untrusty in the Recitation of a Man's words? The truth is, it is this great Defect of *Heed* and *Accurateness*, by hasty Temerity, which also spoileth your Disputations.

But, *pag.* 7. the Aphorisms must be, [*The most Schollar-like, and Elaborate (though Erroneous) Book in Controversie, you ever Composed*]. Answ. 1. Your Memory is faulty: Why say you in the next, that I *appeal* to my Disputation of Justification and *some others; but you cannot Trudg up and down, to every place I would send you, your Legs are too weak?* Either you had read all the sixty Books which you mention (the Controversal at least) or not: If *not*, How can you tell that the Aphorisms is the most *Elaborate*? If *yea*, Why do you excuse your Trudging, and why would you select a Suspended Book, and touch none that were Written at large on the same Subject? 2. By this (I suppose to make your Nibble to seem a Triumph) you tell your Reader again, how to value your Judgment. Is it like that any Dunce that is diligent, should Write no more *Schollar-like* at Sixty years of Age than at Thirty? And do you think you know better what of mine is *Elaborate*, than I do? Sure that Word might have been spared;

When

When I know that one printed Leaf of Paper hath cost me more Labour than all that Book; and perhaps one Scheme of the Distinctions of Justification, which you deride. If indeed you are a competent Judg of your own Writings, Experience assureth me, that you are not so of mine. And *pag.* 25. you say, You *desire not to be preferred before your Betters, least of all when you are singular*; as here I think you are.

§. III. Pag. 9. You are *offended* for being *put in the Cub, with divers mean and contemptible Malefactors.*]

Answ. O for Justice! 1. Was not *Bellarmin*, or some of the *Papists* and the *Socinians*, as great Malefactors, with whom (as you phrase it) you put me in the Cub? 2. Are *they Malefactors* so far as they *agree with you in Doctrine*, and are *you Innocent?* What is the Difference between *your Treatise*, in the part that toucheth me, and that of Mr. *Eyres*, Mr. *Crandon*, and some others such? Dr. *Owen*, and Dr. *Kendale*, indeed differed from you; the latter seeking (by Bishop *Usher*) an amicable Closure, and the former (if I understand his Book on the *Hebrews*) less differing from me in Doctrine, than once he either did, or seemed to do. (And if any of us all grow no Wiser in thirty years Study, we may be ashamed). But to give you your due Honour, I will name you with your Equals, as far as I can judg, *viz.* *Maccovius*, *Cluto*, *Coccejus*, and *Cloppenburgius*, (I mean but in the Point in Question; it's no Dishonour to you to give some of them Precedencie in other things): It may be also *Spanhemius*, was near you. But (if I may presume to liken my Betters) no Men seem to me to have been so like you, as *Guilielmus Rivet*, (not *Andrew*), Mr. *George Walker*, and Mr. *Roborough*. (I hope this Company is no Dishonour to you). And very unlike you are *Le Blank*, *Camero*, *Davenant*, Dr. *Hammond*, Mr. *Gataker*, Mr. *Anthony Wotton*, and in Complexion *Scotus* and *Ockam*, and such as they: If yet I have not Chosen you pleasing Company, I pray you choo se so your self.

But you say on, [*Had you not (in your Memory many Scores of greatest Eminence and Repute in the Christian World, of the same Judgment with me—— Know you not, I speak the same thing with all the Reformed Churches*, &c.—— *For shame let it be the Church of* England, *with all the rest of the Reformed*, &c.]

Answ. 1. I know not what you hold, even when I read what you write: (I must hope as well as I can, that you know your self): How then should I know who are *of the same Judgment* with you?

2. Yet I am very confident, that all they whom you mention, are of the same in some thing or other; and in particular, that we are *Justified by Faith, and not by the Works of the Law, or any Works in the sence denied by St.* Paul, &c.

3. Do not I, with as great Confidence as you, lay Claim to the same Company and Concord? And if one of us be mistaken, must your bare Word determine which it is? Which of us hath brought the fuller Proofs? I subscribe to the Doctrine of the Church of England, as well as you; and my Condition these thirteen or fourteen years, giveth

P 4   as

as much Evidence, that I am loth to subscribe to what I believe not, as yours doth of you. And you that know which of my Books is the most Elaborate, sure know, that in that Book which I Wrote to explain those Aphorisms (called my *Confession*) I cite the Words of *above an Hundred Protestant Witnesses*, that give as much to *Works* as I do: And that of this Hundred, one is the *Augustine* Confession, one the *Westminster* Synod, one the Synod of *Dort*, one the Church of *England*, each one of which being Collectives, contain many. (And here I tell you of more). And have you brought *more* Witnesses? Or *any* to the contrary? Did you *Confute*, or once *take Notice* of any of these?

4. Do you not here before you are aware, let your Reader know that it was, and still is, in the Dark, that you Alarm the World about our *dangerous Differences*, and run to your Arms undrest, before your Eyes are open? *Qui conveniunt in aliquo tertio*, &c. They that agree with the Church of *England*, in the Doctrine of Justification by Faith, do so far agree between themselves: But Dr. *Tullie*, and R. B. do agree with the Church of *England*, in the Doctrine of Justification by Faith. *Ergo.*—— The Article referreth to the Homilies, where it is more fully Explained.

5. May not I then retort your Argument, and bid you [*For shame let it be no longer* Bellarmine, *and* R. B. *but the Church of* England, *and all the Reformed, and* R. B.]? Disprove the Witnesses twenty years ago, produced by me in this very Cause; or else speak out, and say, [*The Church of* England, *and the rest of the Reformed, hold Justification by Works,*

Works, *just as* Bellarmine *and the Papists do*] which is it which you would fasten on me, who agree with them (as if you had never there read my Answer to Mr. *Crandon*, objecting the same thing).

§. IV. Your Censure, *pag.* 10, 11. of my *Windings*, *Clouds* of *Novel Distinctions*, *Preambles*, *Limitations*, &c. is just such as your Treatise did bid me expect: Till you become guilty of the same Crime, and fall out with *Confusion*, and take not equivocal ambiguous Words unexplained, instead of Univocals, in the stating of your Questions, I shall never the more believe that *Hannibal* is at the Gates, or the City on Fire, for your Allarms.

§. V. *Pag.* 11. Where you tell me, that [*You have no Profit by my Preface:* I shall not deny it, nor wonder at it; you are the fittest Judge: Where you say, that [*I have no Credit*,] You do but tell the World at what Rates you write. *Honor est in honorante.* And have all my Readers already told you their Judgment? Alas! How few? In all *London*, not a Man hath yet given me Notice of his Dislike, or Dissent. And sure your *own Pen* is a good Confuter of you. It is *some Credit*, that such a Man as you, is forced to profess a *full Consent* to the Doctrine, though with passionate Indignation.

You tell me of [*Nothing to the Question*]. But will you not be angry if I should but tell you, how little you did to *state* any Question, and in Reason must be supposed, when you assaulted my
Doctrine,

Doctrine, to take it *as I stated it*; which I have fully shewed you?

You tell me, that *You Charged me only with new Original Sin, underived from* Adam, *unknown, unheard of before, in the Christian World*.

Answ. De re, is not our Guilt of nearer Parent's Sins such which you and all that you know (now at last) confess? *De nomine*, 1. Tell the World if you can, when I called it [*New Original Sin, or underived from* Adam, *or unknown, or unheard of*]. There are more ways than one of Derivation from *Adam*. It is not derived from him by such *Imputation* as his first Sin; but it is derived from him as a *partial Causa Causæ*, by many Gradations. All Sin is some-way from him. Either you mean that *I said, that it was not Derived from* Adam, or you gather it by some Consequence from what I said. If the First, shew the Words, and the Shame shall be mine. If not, you know the old Law, that to false Accusers, it must be done as they would have done to the Accused. But if it be your *Consequence*, prove it, and tell the World, what are the Premises that infer it.

§. VI. *Pag*. 12. You friendly help me to *profit by my self*, however you profess that *you profit not* by me! What I have said to you against [*Hasty Judging*], I have first said to my self, and the more you warn me of it, the more friendly you are: If it be not against such as you but *my self*, it is against my self that I have a Treatise on that Subject; but I begin to think my self in this more *Seeing* than you; for I *see it both in my self and you*, and *you* seem to see it in *me*, and *not in your*

your self. But with all Men, I find, that to see the Spots in our own Face immediately is hard, and to love the Glass which sheweth them, is not easie; especially to some Men that neither are low, nor can endure to be so, till there is no Remedy.

But, Sir, how easie a Way of Disputing have you happily light on, Who instead of Examining the hundred Witnesses which I brought, and my else-where oft proving the Doctrine opposed by me to be *Novel, and Singular*, do in few words talk of your *holding the Doctrine delivered to the Saints*, and of the *many Worthies that concur with you*, and of my *pelting at their Heads, and draging them by the Hoary-heads, as a Spectacle and Byword to all*, (by proving their consent by express Citations) *what Armies, and of what Strength appear against me, whose Names I defie and wound, through yours?*

Answ. And is not he a weak Man that cannot talk thus upon almost any Subject? But who be these Men, and what *be* their Names? Or rather, first, rub your Eyes, and tell us what is the *Controversie? Tully* sometimes talkt at this rate in his Orations, but verily much better in his Philosophy.

And you see no cause to repent, but you *bless God that you can again and again call to all Youth, that as they love the Knowledg of Truth, they take me not for an Oracle in my bold dividing Singularities*].

Answ. That the Name of *Truth* is thus abused, is no News; I would the Name of God were not: And I am sorry, that *you see no Cause to repent*. I am obliged to love you the better, for being

against

against *dividing Singularities* in the general *Notion*; I hope if you *knew* it, you would not be for *them*, as in *singular Existents*. But sure, none at *Oxford* are in danger of taking me for *an Oracle*? This is another needless Work. So *Spanhemius* took that for a Singularity, which *Dallæus* in a large Catalogue, hath proved the Common Judgment of the Church, till Contention of late caused some Dissenters.

Will you cease these empty general Ostentations, and choose out any one Point of real Difference between you and me about Justification, and come to a fair Trial, on whose side the Churches of Christ have been for 1500 years after Christ; yea, bring me but any two or one considerable Person, that was for a thousand years for your Cause against mine, and I will say, that you have done more to confute me by far, than yet you have done; and if *two only* be against me, I will pardon you for calling me Singular.

§. VII. *Pag.* 13, 14, 15. You again do keep up the *Dividing Fear*, are offended that I perswade you, that by *Melancholy Phantasms you set not the Churches together by the Ears, and make People believe that they differ, where they do not:* And you ask, *Who began the Fray?*

Answ. 1. Do you mean that I began with *you?* You do not sure: But is it that I *began with the Churches*, and you were *necessitated to defend* them? Yes, if *Gallus, Ambsdorfius, Schlusselburgius*, and Dr. *Crispe*, and his Followers, be the Church? But, Sir, I provoke you to try it by the just Testimony of Antiquity, *who began to differ from the Churches*.

In

In this Treatise I have given you some Account, and *Vossius* hath given you more, which you can never answer: But if my Doctrine put you upon this Necessity, what hindred you from perceiving it these twenty years and more, till now? O Sir, had you *no other work* to do, but to Vindicate the Church and Truth? I doubt you had.

§. VIII. But *pag.* 15. You are again incredulous, that [*All the Difference betwixt you and me, or others of the same Judgment in the Point of Justification, is meerly Verbal; and that in the Main we are agreed*]. And again you complain of your *weak Legs*.

Answ. 1. I do agree with very many against *their wills in Judgment* (because the *Judgment* may be *constrained*), but with none in *Affection*, as on their part. Did I ever say, that *I differed not from you?* I tell you, I know not what your Judgment is, nor know I *who is* of your Mind? But I have not barely *said*, but oft proved, that (though not the *Antinomians*) the *Protestants* are mostly here agreed in the Main. If you could not have time to read my larger Proof, that short Epistle to Mr. *Allen's* Book of the Covenant, in which I proved it, might have stopt your Mouth from calling for more Proof, till you had better confuted what was given.

But you say, [*Are perfect Contradictions no more than a difference in Words? Faith alone, and not Faith alone? Faith with and without Works? Excuse our Dulness here*].

Answ. 1. Truly, Sir, it is a tedious thing, when a Man hath over and over Answered such

Objections; yea, when the full Answers have been twenty years in Print, to be put still to say over all again, to every Man that will come in and say, that *his* Legs are *too weak* to go see what was answered before: How many score times then, or hundreds, may I be called to repeat.

2. If I must pardon your *Dulness*, you must pardon my *Christianity* (or chuse) who believe that there is no such [*perfect Contradictions*] between Christ's, [*By thy Words thou shalt be Justified*] and *Paul's*, [*Justified by Faith, without the Works of the Law*] or [*not of Works*]; and *James's* [*We are justified by Works, and not by Faith only*]. Must we needs proclaim *War* here, or cry out, *Heresie*, or *Popery?* Are not all these Reconcileable? Yea, and *Pauls* too, *Rom.* 2. *The Doers of the Law shall be justified.*

3. But did I ever deny that it is [*by Faith alone and without Works*]? Where, and when? But may it not be, *by Faith alone* in one sense, and not *by Faith alone* in another sense?

4. But even where you are speaking of it, you cannot be drawn to distinguish of *Verbal* and *Real Differences.* Is it here the *Words*, or *Sense*, which you accuse? The *Words* you dare not deny to be *Gods own* in Scripture, spoken by *Christ*, *Paul*, and *James.* My *Sense* I have opened to you at large, and you take no Notice of it; but as if you abhorred *Explication* and *Distinction*, speak still against the *Scripture Words.*

§. IX. Pag. 16. But you say, [*Let any discerning Reader compare the* 48 §. *of this Preface with the Words in* pag. 5. *of your Appeal to the Light, and*

and 'tis likely he will concur with me, in that *Melancholy Phantasm*, or *Fear*: For *'tis worth the noting, how in that dark Appeal where you distinguish of Popish Points*, i. e. *some-where the Difference is reconcileable, others in effect but in words; we have no Direction upon which Rank we must bestow Justification, nothing of it at all from you, Name or Thing: But why, next to the All-seeing God, you should know best your self*].

Answ. Alas, Sir, that *God* should be in such a manner mentioned! I answered this same Case at large in my Confession, Apologie, Dispute of Justification, &c. Twenty years ago, or near; I have at large Opened it in a Folio (*Cathol. Theol.*) which you saw, yea, in the *very* part which you take Notice of; and now you publish it [*worth the Noting, that I did not also in one sheet of Paper*, Printed the other day against a Calumnie of some Sectarian Hearers, who gave me no Occasion for such a work: Had it not been a Vanity of me, Should I in that sheet again have repeated, how I and the Papists differ about Justification? Were you bound to have read it in that sheet, any more than in many former Volumns? It's no matter for me; But I seriously beseech you, be hereafter more sober and just, than to deal with your Brethren, the Church and Truth, in such a manner as this! But by this Talk I suspect, that you will accuse me more for opening no more of the Difference in this Book. But,

1. It is enough for to open *my own Meaning*, and I am not obliged to open other Mens: And my own I have opened by so many Repetitions, in so many Books, as nothing but such Mens *Importunity and obstructed* Minds, could have Excused.

2. The

better, and not the worse, because all the Christian World consenteth to it. I am not ambitious to have a *Religion to my self*, which a Papist doth not own. Where they differ, I am sorry for it: And it pleaseth me better, to find in any Point that we are agreed, than that we differ. Neither you, nor any such as you, by crying [*O Popish! Antichristian!*] shall tempt me to do by the Papists, as the *Dominicans*, and *Jansenists*, and some *Oratorians*, do by the *Calvinists*: I will not with *Alvarez, Arnoldus, Gibieuf*, &c. make the World believe, that my Adversaries are much further from me than they are, for fear of being censured by Faction, to be one of them. If I would have been of a Church-Faction, and sold my Soul to please a Party, I would have begun before now, and taken a bigger Price for it, than you can offer me if you would.

Pag. 17. You say, [*Pile one Distinction or Evasion on another, as long as you please; as many several Faiths, and Works, and Justifications, as you can name, all this will never make two Poles meet*].

Answ. And do you cry out for *War* in the Darkness of Confusion, as long as you will, you shall never tempt me by it to renounce my Baptism, and List my self under the grand Enemy of *Love and Concord*, nor to Preach up *Hatred* and *Division*

for

handle such Controversies, without *Distinguishing of Faiths, Works, and Justifications*, I will never perswade any Friend of mine to be your Pupil, or Disciple. Then *Simon Magus*'s faith, and the Devils *faith*, and *Peters* faith must all pass for the same, and justifie accordingly. Then indeed, Believing in God the Father, and the Holy Ghost, yea, and Christ, as our Teacher, King and Judg, &c. must pass for the *Works* by which no Man is Justified! If *Distinction* be *unsound*, detect the Error of it: If not, it is no Honour to a disputing Doctor to reproach it.

§. X. But *pag.*17. you set upon your great *undeceiving* Work, to shew the evil of *ill using Words*: [*Words* (you say) *as they are enfranchised into Language, are but the Agents and Factors of things, for which they continually negotiate with our Minds, conveying Errands on all occasions*, &c. (Let them mark, that charge the vanity and bombast of Metaphors on others, one word [*Signa*] should have served our turn instead of all this). [*Whence it follows, that their use and signification is Unalterable, but by the stamp of the like publick usage and imposition from whence at first they received their being*, &c.]

Answ. O *Juniors*, Will not such deceiving Words save you from my Deceits? But, 1. Is there a *Law*, and unalterable Law for the sense of Words? Indeed, the Words of the sacred Text must have no new Sense put upon them. 2. Are you sure that it was *Publick usage*, and *Imposition from* whence they first received their being? How shall we know

that

sense of Words a strange thing to us? 4. But that which concerneth our Case most, is, Whether there be many Words either of *Hebrew* and *Greek* in the Scripture, or of *Latine*, *English*, or any common Language, which have not *many Significations?* Your Reputation forbids you to deny it. And should not those many Significations be distinguished as there is Cause? Are not *Faith, Works, Just, Justice, Justification*, words of divers senses in the Scripture? and do not common Writers and Speakers use them yet more variously? And shall a Disputer take on him, that the *use* or *signification* of each is but *one*, or *two*, or is so *fixed* that there needeth no distinction? 5. Is the change that is made in all Languages in the World, made by the same publick usage and imposition, from which at first they received their being? 6. If (as you say) the *same thing can be represented by different words, only when they are Synonymous*, should we not avoid seeming to represent the same by *Equivocals*, which unexplained are unfit for it?

Pag. 20. You tell me what *sad work* you are doing; and no wonder, Sin and Passions are self-troubling things: And it's well if it be sad to your self alone, and not to such as you tempt into Mistakes, Hatred, and Division. It should be sad to every Christian, to see and hear those whom they
are

are bound to Love, reprefented as *odious*: And you are ftill, *pag.* 19. feigning, that [*Every eye may fee Men dealing Blows and Deaths about, and therefore we are not wife if we think them agreed.*

But *doubtlefs,* many that feem killed by fuch Blows as fome of yours, are ftill alive? And many a one is in Heaven, that by Divines pretending to be Orthodox, were damned on Earth! And many Men are more agreed than they were aware of. I have known a Knavifh Fellow fet two Perfons of quality on Fighting, before they fpake a word to one another, by telling them fecretly and falfly what one faid againft the other. Many differ, even to perfecuting and bloodfhed, by *Will* and *Paffion* and *Practice,* upon a falfly fuppofed great *difference in Judgment.* I will not fo fuddenly repeat what Proof I have given of fome of this in the place you noted, *Cath. Theol. Confer.* 11, 12, & 13. There is more skill required to *narrow* differences, than to *widen* them; and to *reconcile,* than to *divide*; as there is to *quench* a Fire, than to *kindle* it ; to *build*, than to *pull down*; to *heal,* than to *wound.*

I prefume therefore to repeat aloud my contrary Cautions to your Juniors.

Young-Men, after long fad Experience of the finful and miferable Contentions of the Clergie, and confequently of the Chriftian World, that you may efcape the Guilt, I befeech you, whoever contradicteth it, confider and believe thefe following Notices:
1. *That all Words are but arbitrary Signs, and are changed as Men pleafe; and through the Penury of them, and Mans imperfection in the Art of Speaking,*

ing, *there are very few at all, that have not various Significations.*

2. *That this Speaking-Art requireth so much time and study, and all Men are so defective in it, and the variety of Mens skill in it is so very great, that no Men in the World do perfectly agree in their interpretation and use of Words.* The doleful plague of the Confusion of Tongues, doth still hinder our full Communication, and maketh it hard for us to understand Words our selves, or to be understood by others; for *Words* must have a three-fold aptitude of Signification. 1. To *signifie* the *Matter*, 2. And the *Speakers conceptions* of it. 3. And this as adapted to the hearers Mind, to make a true Impression there.

3. That God in Mercy hath not made *Words* so necessary as *Things*, nor necessary but for the sake of the *Things*: If *God, Christ, Grace,* and *Heaven,* be known, believed, and duly accepted, you shall be saved by what Words soever it be brought to pass.

4. Therefore *Real Fundamentals,* or *Necessaries to Salvation,* are more easily defined than *Verbal ones*: For *more* or *fewer* Words, *these* or *other* Words are needful to help *some* Persons, to Faith, and *Love,* and *Holiness,* as their Capacities are different.

5. But as he that truly *believeth in,* and *giveth up* himself to God the Father, Son, and Holy Ghost, according to the sense of the Baptismal Covenant, is a true Christian, to be loved, and shall be saved; so he that understandeth *such Words,* as help him to that true *Faith* and *Consent,* doth know so much of the *Verbal part,* as is of ne-

cessity to his Christianity and Salvation.

6. *And he that is such, holdeth no Heresie or Error inconsistent with it: If he truly love God, it's a contradiction to say, that he holdeth an Error inconsistent with the Love of God.*

7. *Therefore see that you Love all such as Christians, till some proved or notorious inconsistents nullifying his Profession disoblige you.*

8. *Take your selves to be neither of Roman, or any other Church as Universal, which is less than the Universality of all Christians headed by Christ alone.*

9. *Make this Love of all Christians the second part of your Religion, and the Love of God, of Christ, of Holiness and Heaven, the first; and live thus in the serious practice of your Covenant, even of Simple Christianity: For it's this that will be your Peace, in Life and at Death.*

10. *And if Men of various degrees of Learning (or Speaking-skill) and of various degrees of Holiness, Humility, and Love, shall quarrel about* Words, *and forms of* Speech, *and shall hereticate, and revile, and damn each other, while the Essentials are held fast and practised, discern Right from Wrong as well as you can; but take heed that none of them make* Words a snare, *to draw you injuriously to think hatefully of your Brother, or to divide the Churches, or Servants of Christ: And suspect such a Snare because of the great ambiguity of Words, and imperfection of Mans Skill and Honesty in all Matters of debate: And never dispute seriously, without first agreeing of the Sense of every doubtful term with him that you Dispute with*].

Dr. *Tully*'s Allarm, and other Mens militant Courſe, perſwaded me as a Preſervative, to commend this Counſel to you.

§. XI. *Pag.* 19. You next very juſtly commend *Method, ordering,* and *expreſſing* our *Conceptions, of which* (you ſay) *I ſeem to make little account* in *Compariſon*].

Anſw. 1. Had you ſaid, that I had been unhappy in my Endeavours, your Authority might have gone for Proof with many: But you could ſcarce have ſpoken a more incredible word of *me*, than that I ſeem to make little account of Method, I look for no ſharper Cenſure from the Theological Tribe, than that I *Over-do in my Endeavours after Method*. You ſhall not tempt me here unſeaſonably, to anticipate what Evidence I have to produce for my acquittance from this Accuſation.

2. But yet I will ſtill ſay, that it is not ſo neceſſary either to Salvation, or to the Churches Peace, that we all agree in *Methods and Expreſſions*, as that we agree in the hearty reception of Chriſt, and obedience to His Commands? So much Method all muſt know, as to know the *Beginning* and the *End*, from the *Effects* and *Means*, God from the Creature, and as our true conſent to the Baptiſmal Covenant doth require; and I will thankfully uſe all the help which you give me to go further: But I never yet ſaw that Scheme of Theologie, or of any of its Heads, which was any whit large, (and I have ſeen many) which was ſo exact in *Order*, as that it was dangerous in any thing to forſake it. But I cannot think meet to talk much of *Method*, with a Man that talketh as you

do

do of *Distinguishing*, and handleth the Doctrine of Justification no more Methodically than you do.

§. XII. But *pag. 19.* you instance in the difference between Protestants and Papists, about the *Necessity of Good works, which is wide in respect of the placing or ranking of them,* viz. *The one stretching it to the first Justification, the other not, but confining it to its proper rank and province of Inherent Holiness, where it ought to keep*].

Answ. Wonderful! Have you that have so loudly called to me to tell how I differ about Justification, brought your own, and as you say, the Protestants difference to this? Will none of your Readers see now, who cometh nearer them, you or I?

1. Is this distinction our proof of your accurateness in *Method,* and *Order,* and *Expression?* What meaneth a distinction between [*First-Justification,*] and [*Inherent Holiness*]? Do you difference them *Quoad ordinem,* as *First* and *Second?* But here is no *Second* mentioned: Is it in the nature of the things [*Justification,* and *Inherent Holiness*]? What signifieth the [*First*] then? But Sir, how many Readers do you expect who know not, 1. That it is not to the *First Justification* at all, but to that which they call the *Second* or *Increase,* that the Church of *Rome* asserteth the necessity or use of Mans meritorious *Works?* See what I have fully cited out of them for this, *Cath. Theol. Lib.* 2. *Confer.* 13. *pag.* 267. *&c.* saving that some of them are for such *Preparatives* as some call *Merit of Congruity,* and as our English

Q 4 Divines

Divines do conſtantly preach for, and the Synod of *Dort* at large aſſert; though they diſown the *name of Merit*, as many of the *Papiſts* do. They ordinarily ſay with *Auſtine, Bona opera ſequuntur Juſtificatum, non præcedunt Juſtificandum.*

2. But, I hope, the word [*Firſt*] here overſlipt your your Pen, inſtead of [*Second*]: But ſuppoſe it did ſo: What's the difference between *the Papiſts firſt or ſecond Juſtification*, and the *Proteſtants Inherent Holineſs?* None that ever I heard or read of: Who knoweth not that the *Papiſts* take *Juſtification* for *Inherent Holineſs?* And is this the great difference between *Papiſts* and *Proteſtants*, which I am ſo loudly accuſed for not acknowledging? viz. *The Papiſts place Good-Works before Juſtification*, that is, *Inherent Holineſs*; and the *Proteſtants more rightly place them before Inherent Holineſs?* Are you ſerious, or do you prevaricate?

The *Papiſts* and *Proteſtants* hold, that there are ſome *Duties and common Grace*, uſually *preparatory to Converſion* (or *Sanctification*); which ſome *Papiſts (de nomine)* call *Merit* of *Congruity*, and ſome will not. The *Papiſts* and *Proteſtants* ſay, that *Faith* is in order of nature, at leaſt, before that *Habitual Love*, which is called *Holineſs*, and before the *Works thereof*. The *Papiſts* and *Proteſtants* ſay, that *Works of Love* and *Obedience*, follow our Firſt Sanctification, and make up but the *Second part of it*, which conſiſteth in the *Works of Holineſs*. If you ſpeak not of *Works* in the ſame ſenſe in each part of your Aſſignation, the Equivocation would be too groſs, viz. If you ſhould mean [*Papiſts* rank the *neceſſity of preparatory Common Works*, or the *Internal act of Faith, or Love, ſtretching it*

to

to the *First Justification*; and *Protestants* rank other *Works*, viz. *The fruits* of *Faith* and *Love*, with *Inherent Holiness.* All agree, 1. That *Common Works* go before *Sanctification.* 2. That Internal Love, and other Grace, do *constitute* Sanctification in the First part of it. 3. That *Special Works* proceeding from *Inward Grace*, are the effects of the First *Part*, and the constitutive Causes of the Second Part of Sanctification; as the word extendeth also to *Holiness of Life:* And whilst *Papists* take *Justification* for *Sanctification*, in all this there is *De re* no difference. (But your accurate Explications by such terms, as [*Stretching, Confirming, Province*, &c.] are fitter for *Tully*, than for *Aristotle*).

And is this it in the Application that your Zeal will warn Men of, that we must in this take heed of joyning with the *Papists*? Do you mean [*Rank Good-Works with Inherent Holiness*, and not with *the First Sanctification*, and *you then* do *widely differ from the Papists*]? Will not your Reader say, 1. What doth *Inherent Holiness differ from* the First *Sanctification?* 2. *Do you not invite me thus herein to be a Papist*, when they rank them no where but, as you say, the *Protestants* do? 3. Do not you here proclaim, that *Papists* and *Protestants* differ not about the necessity of Good-works to Justification? But yet I that would make no Differences wider than they are, can find some greater than you have mentioned.

Truly Sir, I am grieved and ashamed, to foresee how Learned *Papists* will make merry with such Passages; and say, *See here how we differ from the Protestants! See what it is for*, that the *Protestant*

stant Doctors separate from the Church of Rome? viz. Because we make Good-Works necessary to the First Justification, which unless equivocally spoken, is false; and because the Protestants rank them with Inherent Holiness, as we do]. What greater advantage will they desire against us, than to choose us such Advocates? And to shew the World that even where their keenest Adversaries condemn them, and draw Men from them, they do but justifie them? Who knoweth what a Temptation they may make of such passages to draw any to Popery? It is my assurance, that such *Over-doing*, is *Undoing*; and that mistaken Accusations of the *Papists* greatly advantage them against us, which maketh me the more against such Dealing; besides the *sinfulness*, of pretending that any differences among Christians, are greater than indeed they are.

But may not I think that you take the word [*Justification*] here in the *Protestant Sense*, and not in the *Papists*, when you say that they rank *Good-works-necessity* as stretcht to the First *Justification*? No sure: For, 1. Protestants use not to distingnish of a *First* and *Second* Justification, which Papists do, but of Justification as *Begun, Continued, and Consummate*. 2. If it were so, it were not true: For the First *Justification* in the Protestant Sense, is our *first right* to *Impunity* and *Life Eternal*, freely given to Believers, for the Merits of Christs perfect Righteousness and Satisfaction. And Papists do not make *Good-works* (unless Equivocally so called) necessary to this; but as a Fruit to follow it.

As

As for *Remission of Sin*, I have else-where proved, 1. That most commonly by that word the Papists mean nothing, but that which we call *Mortification*, or Putting away, or destroying the Sin it self, as to the habit and ceasing the Act. 2. That most of them are not resolved, where the *Remission* of the *Punishment* (which Protestants call *Remission of Sin*, or *Forgiveness*) shall be placed: They differ not much as to its *Time*, but whether it be to be called any *part of Justification*: Some say, yea; some make it a *distinct thing*. Most describe *Justification* by it self, as consisting in our *Remission* of, or Deliverance from Sin it self, and the infused habit of Love or Righteousness (all which we call Sanctification), and the *forgiveness of the Penalty* by it self, not medling with the Question, whether the latter be any part of the former; so much are they at a loss in the Notional part among themselves. But they (and we) distinguish of *Forgiveness*, as we distinguish of Penalties: We have a right to Impunity as to everlasting Damnation, upon our first being Justified; but our Right becometh afterward more *full*, and many other Penalties are after to be remitted.

§. XIII. *Pag.* 20. In my 42. *Direct.* for the Cure of Church-divisions, telling the Weak whom they must follow, I concluded, 1. *That the necessary Articles of Faith must be made our own, and not taken meerly on the authority of any; and we must in all such things of absolute necessity keep company with the Universal Church.* 2. *That in Matters of Peace and Concord the greater part must be our Guide.* 3. *That in Matters of humane Obedience,*
our

our Governours must be our Guides. And, 4. *In Matters of high and difficult Speculation, the judgment of one Man of extraordinary Understanding and Clearness, is to be preferred before the Rulers and the major Vote. I instanced in Law, Philosophy, Physick, Languages,* &c. *and in the Controversies of the Object of Predestination, the nature of the Will's Liberty, Divine Concourse, the determining way of Grace, of the definition of Justification, Faith,* &c.] Here I *was intreated before God and my Conscience, to search my self, with what Design or Intent I wrote this,* and to tell you, *Who that One is, that we may know whom to prefer, and to whom, in the Doctrine of Justification,* &c.

Answ. How greatly do you dishonour your self, (and then you will impute it to me) by insisting on such palpably abusive Passages? Had you not been better, have silently past it by? 1. Doth not the World know, that Heathens and Christians, Papists and Protestants, are Agreed on this general Rule? 2. And will you make any believe that *Definition* of *Justification* is none of these *Works* of *Art,* which depend on humane Skill? How then came you to be so much better at it than I? I find not that you ascribe it to any *special Revelation* which you *have.* And if you should ascribe it to *Piety,* and say, *Hoc non est Artis, sed Pietatis opus:* I would go to many a good Woman before you. Nor do you plead general Councils, nor the Authority of the Church. 3. And what sober Scholar will you make believe, that by laying down this common Rule, I signifie some *One singular Person,* as an *Individuum determinatum*

whom'

whom therefore I muſt acquaint you with? Theſe things are below a Grave Divine.

Pag. 21. Where you *called me to ſeriouſneſs* or *diligence* in my *ſearch*, and I told *you* by what, and how many Writings, I have manifeſted my almoſt thirty years *Diligence* in this Controverſie, and that I am now grown paſt more *ſerious* and *diligent* Studies; that I might ſhew you what a trifling way it is, for a Man to wrangle with him that hath written ſo many things, to tell the World what his ſtudies of this Point have been, and never to touch them, but to call him a-*new* to *ſerious* diligence: You now expoſtulate with me, whether you *accuſed* me *for want of diligence?* I talk not of *Accuſing*, but I tell you, that I have done my beſt; and that it were a poor kind of dealing with your ſelf, if you had written againſt many, as you have done againſt me twenty five years ago, and very often, if inſtead of taking any notice of your Labours, I ſhould call you now to diligent Studies.

As for your Leſſon, *pag.* 22. that *tumbling over many Books without meditation, may breed but Crudities,* &c. It is very true, and the calamity of too many of the literate Tribe, who think that they have deſerved Credit and Reverence, when they ſay the words which others, whom they would be joyned with, have ſaid before them: Want of good Digeſtion is a common Diſeaſe of many that never complain of it, nor feel any preſent trouble by it.

Pag. 22, 23. You inſinuate that about *Retractation*, which I before detected: I told you when, and where, I *Suſpended* or *Retracted* the Book,

and

and for what Reasons, and you presently feign a Retractation of the Doctrine, and *of about sixty Books* of Retractions.

It's well that *pag.* 23. you had the justice not to justifie your [*Nec dubito quin imputatam Christi justitiam incluserit*]; But to confess your Injustice, was too much: It is not your *own Retractation* that you are for, it seems.

§. XIV. *Pag.* 23, 24. You talk as if my supposing that both [*Justice*] and [*Imputation*], are capable of Definitions which are not the Things, were a Fallacy, because [*or*] is a disjunctive; *viz.* When I say that the *Definition* of the *one, or* the *other*, is not the *Thing*. Do you grant it of them Disjunctively, and yet maintain the contrary of them Conjunct? Yes, you say, [*Imputed Justice cannot differ from its true definition, unless you will have it to differ really from it self*]. And, *pag.* 34. you say, [*I am ashamed you should thus over and over expose your self — as if supposing* (Definitions) *true, they were not the same* Re, *with the* Definitum. — *Good Sir, talk what you please in private, to such as understand not what you say, and let them give* you *a grand* Σοφᾶς *for your pains; but you may do well to use more Civility to the reason of a Scholar, though he hath not yet worn out his Freshmans Gown*].

Answ. This is no light or jesting Matter: The comfort of Souls dependeth on it. I see some Men expect that *Reverence of their Scholarship* should give them great advantage: But if one argued thus with me for Transubstantiation, I would not turn to him, to escape the Guilt of *Incivility*.

If

If the *Definition*, and the *Definitum*, as in question now, *be the same Thing*, wo to all the Unlearned World, and wo to all Freshmen, that yet have not learnt well to define; and wo to all Divines that differ in their Definitions, except those that are in the right.

I know that a *Word* and a *Mental Conception*, are not *Nothing*: They may be called *Things*, but when we distinguish the *Things* from their *Signs*, *Names*, or *Definitions*, we take not the word [*Things*] so laxly, as to comprehend the said *Signs*, *Names*, &c. When we say, that the *Thing defined* is *necessary*, but to be able *to Define it*, or actually to *Define it*, is not necessary (to Salvation) it is notorious that we take *Definition* (as *Defining*) *actively*, as it is *Actus definientis*; and *Definire sure* is not the same with the *Thing defined*. I have heard before your Letter told me, that *Definitum & definitio idem sunt*: But, I pray you, let us not quibble almost all the World under a sentence of Damnation. As long ago as it is since I read such words, I remember our Masters told us, (I think *Scibler* in his *Topicks* for one) that when they are taken *Pro terminis Logicis definitio & definitum non sunt idem*; but only when they are taken *Pro rebus per eos terminos significatis*; and that there they differ in *Modo significandi essentiam*, the *definitum* signifying the *Essence confusedly*, and the *Definition distinctly*. If you will take the *Res definita*, for that which is strictly nothing but *Rei conceptus inadæquatus seu partialis*, (that is, a *Species*) and that not as the *thing* is *Existent extra intellectum*, but as the conception is an operation of the Mind, so I confess, that he that hath a *true Conception* of

a

a *Species* as *meerly denominated,* or *as defined,* hath *the same conception* of it : And also the *Thing named,* and the *Thing defined,* is the *same thing in it self.* *Homo & Animal rationale,* are the same; that is, it is the *same essence,* which is *denominated Homo,* and *defined Animal rationale.* And it is the same *Conceptus mentis,* which we have (if true) when we *denominate,* and when we *define.* But as *Things* are distinct from the *knowledg and signs* of *Things,* nothing is *Res,* that is not *existent ;* and nothing *existeth* but in *Singulars* (or *Individuals*): And as nothing can be defined but a *Species,* so a *Species,* or any *Universal,* is *nothing* but a *Notion,* or *Ens rationis,* save as it *existeth* in the said *Individuals.* And in the *Individuals,* it is nothing but *their being* as *partially,* or *inadequatly taken,* or a *Conceptus objectivus partialis,* (whether it be of a thing *really,* or only *intellectually* partible, or any thing which our narrow Minds cannot conceive of, *Uno & simplici conceptu activo).* Now if you take the word [*Definition*] for the *Species,* as *existent in Individuals,* it is *really a part* of the thing ; that is, a *Partial objective conceptus,* or somewhat of the *Thing* as *Intelligible :* But this is to take [*Definition*] in *Sensu passivo,* for the Thing defined ; which our Case distinguisheth.

But Sir, I crave your leave, to distinguish *Real objective Beings,* from, 1. The *Knowledg.* 2. and the Names, and other Logical Organs, by which we *know* them, and *express* our knowledg of them : God, Christ, Grace, Glory, Pardon, Justification, Sanctification, the Gospel-Doctrine, Precept, Promises, Faith, Hope, Love, Obedience, Humility, Patience, *&c.* are the *Res definitæ*

in

in our *Case*, not as they are *in esse cognito*, or in the notion or idea of them, but *in esse reali*. To *Define* properly, is either, 1. *Mentally* to conceive of these things; 2. or *Expressively*, to signifie such *Conceptions*, agreeably to the nature of the things *known*, or *Expressively defined*: Which is, if the Definition be perfect, under the notions of a *Genus* and *Differentia*. The Definition as in *Words*, is but a *Logical Organ*, (as *Names* are also *Notifying signs*): *Mental defining*, is but the said *distinct knowledg* of the thing defined, and is neither really the *Thing it self*, nor usually of necessity to the Thing: Which two, I shall prove distinctly as to the sense of our Case.

1. The Definition of Justification, is either our *Distinct knowledg*, or *Expression* of it: Justification is not our *Distinct knowledg*, or *Expression* of it: Therefore the Definition of Justification, and Justification, are not the same.

Justification *In sensu activo*, is not an Act of God, and *In-sensu passivo*, is the Relative state of Man thereby effected: But the Definition of Justification is neither.

The Definition of Justification, is a work of Art; but Justification is a Work of Grace.

A wicked damnable Man, or a damned Devil, may *define* Justification, and so have the *Definition* of it; but not Justification it self.

The Definition of Justification, Faith, Love, &c. is *Quid Logicum*; but *Justification*, Faith, Love, &c. are things *Physical* and *Moral*.

A Man is Justified (or hath Christs Righteousness imputed to him) in his sleep, and when he thinketh not of it; but he hath not the Active *definition* of Justification in his sleep, *&c.*

Other things be not the same Really with their Definition, therefore neither is *Justification*, *Faith*, &c.

The Sun is not really the same thing with a Definition of the Sun; nor Light, Heat, Motion, *&c.* A Brute can see, taste, feel, smell, that cannot define them. If you have a Bishoprick, because you *define* a Bishoprick, or have a Lordship, a Kingdom, Health, *&c.* because you can define them, your Axiome hath stood you in good stead.

The Definition is but *Explicatio rei*: But *Rei explicatio non est ipsa res.*

Individuals (say most) are not *Definable*: But nothing is truly *Res*, but Individuals. *Vniversals* as they are *in the Mind*, are *existent Individual Acts, Cogitations, Notions*: As they are *out of the Mind*, they are *nothing* but *Individuorum quid intelligibile.*

The Definition of Learning, of a Doctor, *&c.* may be got in a day: If Learning and Doctorship may be so, what useless things are Universities and Books?

Perswade a hungry Scholar, that he hath Meat and Drink; or the Ambitious, that he hath Preferment; or the Covetous, or Poor, that he hath Money, because he hath in his Mind, or Mouth, the *Definition* of it; and quibble him into satisfaction by telling him, that *Definitio & definitum sunt idem re.* We *know* and *express* things *narrowly* by *Names*, and *largely* and *distinctly* by *Definitions*: The *Definition* here, is *Explicatio nominis*, (as *Animal*.

mal rationale, of the *name Homo*); and both *Name* and *Definition*, as they are *Verba mentis vel oris*, or *Verborum significatio*, are surely divers from the things *named* and *defined*, known and expressed; unless by the *Thing* you mean only the *Knowledg*, or *Notion* of the Thing.

Therefore though *Cui competit definitio eidem quoq; competit definitum, & contra, & quod convenit definitioni convenit definito:* Yet say not that *Imputed Righteousness in Re*, is the same with the *Definition*, as it is the *Definers* act.

By this time you have helpt Men to understand by an Instance, why St. *Paul* so much warneth Christians to take heed lest any deceive them by vain Philosophy, even by Sophistry, and abused arbitrary Notions.

Remember, Sir, that our Case is of grand Importance; As it is stated in my *Direct.* 42. which you assaulted; it is [*Whether if the Question were of the Object of Predestination, of the nature of the Will's liberty, Divine concourse, and determining way of Grace, of the Definition of Justification, Faith,* &c. *a few well studied Divines are not here to be preferred before Authority, and the major Vote.* Such are my words. I assert, 1. That the *Defining of Justification, Faith,* &c. is a work of Art. 2. And I have many and many times told the World (which you seem to strike at) that Christians do not differ so much in their *Real conceptions* of the *Matter*, as they do in their *Definitions*. 1. Because *Definitions* are made up of *Ambiguous words*, whose Explication they are not agreed in; and almost all Words are ambiguous till explained; and ambiguous Words are not fit to define, or
be

be defined, till explained. And, 2. Because both selecting fit terms, and explaining them, and ordering them, are works of Art, in which Men are unequal; and there is as great variety of Intellectual Conceptions, as of Faces. 3. And I have often said, That a *Knowledg intuitive*, or a *Simple apprehension* of a thing as *Sensate*, or an *Internal experience*, or *Reflect act*, and a general notion of some things, may prove the truth of Grace, and save Souls, and make us capable of Christian Love and Communion, as being true saving Knowledg. 4. And consequently I have often said, that many a thousand Christians have *Faith*, *Hope*, *Desire*, *Love*, *Humility*, *Obedience*, *Justification*, *Adoption*, *Union with Christ*, who can *define* none of these: Unless you will speak equivocally of *Definition* it self, and say as good *Melancthon*, and as *Gutberleth*, and some other Romists, that *Notitia intuitiva est definitio*, who yet say but what I am saying, when they add, [*Vel saltem instar definitionis*]. If all are without *Faith*, *Love*, *Justification*, *Adoption*, who cannot give a true Definition of them, how few will be saved? How much more then doth *Learning* to Mens salvation, than Grace? And *Aristotle* then is not so far below *Paul*, or the Spirit of Christ, as we (justly) believe.

The Case is so weighty and palpable, that you have nothing to say; but as you did about the Guilt of our nearer Parents sins, to yield all the Cause, and with a passionate clamour to tell Men that I mistake you, or wrest your words; of which I shall appeal to every sober Reader, that will peruse the words of mine which you assault, and yours

as

as they are an Answer to mine.

In a word, you go about by the abuse of a trivial *Axiome* of *Definitions*, 1. To sentence most Christians to Hell, and cast them into Desperation, as wanting the Grace which they cannot define. 2. And to destroy Christian Love and Concord, and tear the Church into as many Shreds, as there be diversities of Definitions used by them. 3. And you would tempt us to think much hardlier of your self, than we must or will do; as if your *Faith*, *Justification*, &c. were unsound, because your Definitions are so.

I know that *Unius rei una tantum est Definitio*, speaking, 1. Not of the *Terms*, but the *Sense*. 2. And supposing that *Definition* to be perfectly true; that is, the *truth* of *Intellection* and *Expression* consisting in their congruity to the *Thing*; while the *thing* is *one* and the *same*, the *conception* and *expression* which is perfectly true, must be so too. But, 1. Our *understandings* are all imperfect, and we know *nothing* perfectly but *Secundum quædam*; and *Zanchez* saith truly, that *Nihil scitur*; if we call that only *Knowledg* which is *perfect*: And consequently no *Mental Definition* is perfect. 2. And *Imperfections* have many degrees. 3. And our *Terms*, which make up that which you know I called a *Definition* in my *Dir.* 42. (as it is in words) are as aforesaid, *various*, *mutable*, and variously understood and used.

§. XV. Pag. 24. Again you are at it, [*Whom do you mean by that one rare Person, whose single Judgment is to be preferred in the point of Justification, and to whom*].

Answ.

Anſw. 1. No one that knoweth not the difference between an *Invididuum vagum & determinatum.* 2. No one that is of ſo hard Metal, as in deſpite of the plaineſt words, to inſinuate to the World, that theſe words [*A few well-ſtudied Judicious Divines*] do ſignifie only one; and that theſe words [*One Man of extraordinary underſtanding and clearneſs*], (*is to be preferred before the Rulers and major Vote, in difficult ſpeculations*) do ſignifie *one individuum determinatum* in the World, and that the Speaker is bound to name the Man. No one that thinketh that *Pemble,* who in his *Vind. Grat.* hath almoſt the very ſame words, ſaid well, and that I who repeat them, am as criminal as you pretend: No one who either knoweth not, that almoſt all the World (even Papiſts) agree in this Rule, or that thinketh his judgment fit herein to bear them all down: No one who, when his abuſes are brought into the open Sun-ſhine, will rather accuſe the Light than repent.

But, *pag.* 25. After ſome words to jeer away Conviction, you tell me, [*We muſt have ſome better account of you,* quem quibus, *than what you have given us yet. I ſhall take leave to preſent our indifferent Readers with a more ingenuous and truer ſtate of the Queſtion, far more ſuitable both to my plain meaning and the clear purport of your Direction.* Let the Caſe be this: *There is One who of late hath raiſed much duſt among us, about the grand Article of Juſtification; Whether it be by Faith without Works, or by Faith and Works too? All our old Renowned Divines on this ſide and beyond the Seas are unanimouſly agreed, that Juſtification is by Faith alone,* i. e. *without Works. This one Perſon hath*

hath often published his Judgment to the contrary ——. *so that a poor Academical Doctor may very rationally enquire of you, Who in this case is to be preferred? That one, or those many?*

Answ. There was a Disputant who would undertake to conquer any Adversary: When he was asked, *How?* He said he would pour out upon him so many and so gross untruths, as should leave him nothing to answer congruously, but a *Mentiris*; and then all the World would judg him uncivil, and condemn him for giving such an unreverent answer. But you shall not so prevail with me, but I will call your Reader to answer these Questions:

1. Whether it be any truer, that [*This is the clear purport of my Direction*] than it is that I say, *There is but one Star* in the Firmament, because I say that *one Star is more Luminous than many Candles?*

2. Whether if a diseased Reader will put such a Sense upon my words, his Forgery be a true *stating* of the Question between him and me, without my consent?

3. Whether an intimation that this ONE is either *Unicus*, or *Primus*, or *Singular*, in the definition of Justification, or the interest of Works, be any truer, than that he is the only ejected Minister in *England*, While the writings of *Bucer, Ludov. Crocius, Joh. Bergius, Conrad. Bergius, Calixtus, Placeus, le Blank, Dave Gatak. Wott. Prest. Ball,* and multitudes such are visible still among us?

4. Whether he deals *truly*, *wisely*, or *friendly* with the holy Scripures, and the Protestants, who would perswade the Ignorant, that this is the true state of the Controversie, [*Whether it be by Faith without Works, or by Faith and Works too, that we*

are

are justified] While the Scripture speaketh *both*, and all Protestants hold both in several senses? And whether this easie stating of Controversies, without more Explication or Distinction, be worthy an Academical Disputant?

5. Whether it be true or notoriously false, that [*All our Renowned Divines on this side, and beyond the Seas, are agreed*], of that in this Question of the interest of Works, which this one contradicteth?

6. Whether this Doctors naked Affirmation hereof be better proof, than that *one* Mans citation of the words of above an Hundred (yea many Hundred) as giving as much to Works as he doth, is of the contrary?

7. Whether it be an ingenuous way beseeming Academics, to talk at this rate, and assert such a stating of the Question and such consent, without one word of notice or mention of the Books, in which I state the Question, and bring all this evidence of consent?

8. If such a Doctor will needs enquire, whether the secret thoughts of the Writer meant *not himself*, when he pretendeth but to accuse the Rule there given, and should enquire but of the meaning of the words, whether it favour more of *Rationality*, or a presumptuous usurping the Prerogative of God?

§. XVI. *Pag.* 27. Though your approach be wrathful, you are constrained to come *nearer* yet, and you *cannot* deny my Rule of Direct. in other Points, but only those of [*High and difficult speculation*]: And do you deny it there? You
will

will deal with it but as the application of that Rule to the *Definition of Justification*? (And shall we lose your favour, by forcing you to lay by your Opposition as to all the rest?) But here you say you [*exceedingly differ from me*]; Or else you would be ashamed of so much Combating in the dark: *Exceeding* oft signifieth some extream.

Your Reasons are, 1. *You hold not the Doctrine of Justification to be properly of Speculative concern, but wholly Practical:* Where yet you confess, that in all *Practical knowledg, there be some antecedent contemplations of the Nature, Properties, End, Object,* and that to *know the certain number of Paces home-ward, is a Speculative nicety*].

Answ. And can you find no fairer a shift for disagreement? I would such as you made not the Doctrine of Justification too little *Practical?* I am far from thinking that it is not Practical: But is not a *Logical definition* the opening the *Nature, Properties, End, Object,* or some of these which you call Contemplations? Make not plain things dark, Sir: The use of Art is not to shut the Windows, and confound Mens Minds. I take all *Theologie* to be together, *Scientia-affectiva-practica*; for our *Intellect, Will,* and *Practice,* must be possest or ruled by it: But it is first *Scientia,* and we must *know* before we can *will* and *practise*. And though all right knowledg tend to Practice, yet forgive me for telling you, that I think that many holy Persons in Scripture and Primitive times, loved and practised more than you or I, who knew not how to form an exact Logical Definition. And that he that knoweth the things of the Spirit spiritually, by Scripture Notions, may practise them

as

as fully, as he that knoweth and speaketh them in the Notions of *Aristotle*; or else the School-Men excel the Apostles. Though ambling be an easie Pace, which Horses are taught by Gives and Fetters, it followeth not that a Horse cannot travel as far in his natural pace. When you have said all, *Logical defining* shall be a work of Art, and the *Church should* not *be torn*, and *Souls shall not be damned,* for want of it. He that *Loveth, Believeth, Hopeth, Obeyeth,* and by *doing* them hath a reflecting perception what they are, and hath but such a knowledg of the Gospel as may be had without a proper Definition, shall be saved.

2. Pag. 28, 29. you say, [*Nor is the Doctrine of Justification so high and difficult, but that the meanest Christian may understand it sufficiently to Salvation, so far as words can make it intelligible*].

Answ. Your own blows seem not to hurt you. I thank you for granting so much *hope* to the *meanest Christians.* But what's this to your Case? 1. Do the meanest Christians know how to *define* Justification, and all the Grace which they have? 2. Are they acquainted with all the [*Words that should make it intelligible?*]

Pag. 29. you add, [*You have done little service to your weaker Christians to perswade them otherwise (as well as to the great blessed Charter of Salvation) and to lead them out of the plain road into Woods and Mazes, to that one Man of extraordinary Judgment and Clearness; no body must know what his Name is, or where he dwells, and so to whirle them about till you have made them giddy*——].

Answ. How easie is it to talk at this rate for any Cause in the World? Is this Disputing or Reasonsoning? Cannot I as easily say thus against you? But the question is of *Things visible:* I willingly appeal to any intelligent impartial Divine, who will read what you and I have written of Justification, which of us it is that hath done more to bring Men *out of Woods and Mazes,* into the *plainest Road?* Let them, that have leisure for no more, read but my *Preface to my Disput. of Justif.* and mark which side wrongeth *weak Christians,* and the *Charter of Salvation.*

§. XVII. Pag. 29. you add, [*Sir, I understand something at these years, without your Tutorage, of the duty both of Pastors and People: But I know not what you mean to make the way to Heaven (revealed sufficiently to all,* &c.*) to be a matter of high abstruse Speculation, as if none but great Scholars, and Men of extraordinary Judgment, could by the right use of Scriptures, and other ordinary common means, be able to find it out, till they have met with that Elias,* &c.]

Answ. Still I see we shall agree whether you will or not: O, Sir, it is just the contrary that I wrote for: And I need but repeat your words to answer you. I am not disparaging your understanding, otherwise than you may so call the vindicating of needful truth: Nor did I ever presume to offer you my Tutorage: You speak all this with too much tenderness. But that which I have written almost all my Books of Controversie against, is this *making the Way to Heaven more difficult* and bewildring, than the Scriptures make it. Therefore it is that I have perswaded Men to lay less stress on arbitrary humane Notions: But the question

ſtion is now, whether it be your (
that is guilty of this? Are *Logical*
neceſſary Way to Heaven? Doth th(
ciently reveal ſuch *Definitions* to al
nary Believers by the *uſe of the S*
how to *define?* Do not Logicians
fining one of the ſureſt ſigns of *cle*(
knowledg? Why ſhould you and
about Matters of Fact? I know b
of Conformity, that your Judgm(
to be *narrower* than *mine* about the
minate Individuals: I ſuppoſe you
many to the *Lords Supper* as Believ(
and *abſolve* as many, and *pronounce*
at *Buryal.* Let you and I call but (
next Families together, and deſire
Woman of them, to give you a De
ſtification, (out of the hearing of t
they all *give you a true definition,* an(
I will write a Retractation. I k(
but by your now telling me, of you
of the duties of *Paſtors* and *People,*
that you *have been a Paſtour,* (elſe-
ſo, that you have had perſonal co
moſt (if not *all*) of your Flock.
found them all ſuch *able concordant* 1
ſtification, you have had a more lear(
I had. I doubt your *Learned Scho*(
do it, till they met with ſome ſuch
ſtotle, as you! Yea, let us take only ſ
Lives we commonly judg truly Goc
And if all *theſe* give you *one* and a (
of Juſtification, then do you tell t(
ning is no ſuch difficult work, but o

ſtians may and do attain it, and I that make it difficult, make the way to Heaven difficult, for Defining is the way to Heaven: But if not one of many Score or Hundred (till you teach them anew) do give you a *true* and the *same* Definition; I will go on and ſtill ſay, that *They wrong Souls, the Goſpel, and the Church, who pretend ſuch neceſſity and facility of defining, and will cenſure, reproach,* or damn all that agree not with them in a Definition, when they have as *real* though leſs *diſtinct* a knowledg of the thing.

I doubt not but you know how much difference there is among Learned Men about *Definitions* themſelves in general: Whether they belong to Metaphyſicks, Logicks, or Phyſicks? Whether *Definitio Phyſica* (as *Man* is defined *per Animam, Corpus & Unionem*) be a *proper Definition?* Whether a true *Logical* and *Phyſical* definition ſhould not be the ſame? Whether *Definitio objectiva* be properly called *Definitio,* or only *Formalis?* Whether *Accidents* may be properly defined? *An Genus definiri poſſit? An pars Logica definiri poſſit? An individua poſſint definiri?* (*Inquit* Hurtado, *Negari non poteſt Individuis definitio ſubſtantialis; & quidem eſſentialis Phyſice; eſt enim de eſſentia hujus hominis hæc anima cum hoc Corpore; Imo & eſſentialis Metaphyſice—— ſi individua recte poſſent penetrari, illorum definitio eſſet omnium perfectiſſima*) *An ea quæ differunt definitione diſtinguantur realiter?* With a multitude ſuch. And is the *Art of Defining* ſo *eaſie,* as that *ordinary Chriſtians ſalvation* muſt lie upon it, when ſo many things about Defining are among the ſubtileſt Doctors undetermined?

And

(54)

And as Ignorant as I am, while you suppose me unable to define *Justification*, I would wish yo (not for my sake, but *theirs*) that you will not sentence all as unjustified to Damnation, that are no more skilful in defining than I, and that you wil not reject all such from the Sacrament and Com munion of the Church.

§. XVIII. Yet again, *pag.* 30. you tell me, [cannot well swallow down in the lump, what yo would have me and others to do, when you direct us t prefer that one Man before the Rulers and majorit of Votes, till you acquaint us who that Gentlema is, and what sort of Rulers and Majorities yo mean].

Answ. What you cannot swallow you must leave: I will not cram or drench you. I could wish for your own sake, that you had not thus often told the World of such a Malady, as that must needs be which hindreth your swallow: When. 1. You your self receive the same Rule in other Instances, and make all this stir against it only, as to the *Definition of Justification*, even the *Logical definition*, which is *Actus definientis*, called *Definitio formalis*, and not the *Definitio objectiva*, as the *Ipsum definitum* is by some improperly called. 2. And when the words in that Instance are not [ONE MAN] but [*a few Men*] which your Eyes may still see; and when in the *General direction* where *one Man* is mentioned, there is no such word as [*that one Man*], or the least intimation of an *Individuum determinatum*; You greatly wrong your Honour by such dealing; As you do by adding,

1. For

1. [*For the single Person (that Monarch in Divinity) to whom we are upon differences to make our Appeals,* &c.]

Answ. If you hold on thus to talk as in your sleep, and will not shut your Chamber-door, but commission the Press to report your words to the World, how can your best Friends secure your reputation? Is not all this talk of *single Person*, and *Monarch in Divinity*, and *Appeals*, the effects of a Dream, or somewhat worse? These *Fictions* will serve no honest ends. But you next come indeed to the true *difficulty of the Case*, and ask:

[*I beseech you Sir, how shall your ignorant or weaker Christian be able to judg of fitness?* —— *He had need to have a very competent measure of Abilities himself, who is to give his verdict of anothers,* &c.]

This is very true and rational: But it concerneth *you* as *much* as *me* to *answer* it, unless you will renounce the Rule. And seeing you grant it in other Instances, if you please to answer your own question as to those other, you have answered it as to this: And if you will not learn of your self, I am not so vain as to think, that you will learn of me.

In case of *Subtilties* which depend upon *Wit*, and *Art*, and *Industry*, in that proportion which few, even faithful Men attain, I remember but one of these ways that can be taken; Either wholly to *suspend* our *Judgments*, and not to meddle with them, till we can reach them our selves; Or to take them *fide humana*, or as *probabilities* on the Credit of some Men, rather than others: As to the first, I am for as much *suspension* of Judgment,

pear in *ascertaining evidence*. Therefore here the Question is, Whose judgment I shall take as *most probable*? (Were the case only, how far we should *Preach* our Judgment to others, there *Rulers* must more determine; or if it were, How to manage our Judgment so as to keep *Unity* and *Concord*, the *Church*, or *major Vote* must over-rule us). But it being the *meer Judgment* or *Opinion* that is in question, either we must adhere to the Judgment, 1. Of *Rulers* as *such*, 2. Or the *major Vote as such*, 3. Or to those that are *most Excellent* in that *part of Knowledg*: Why should I waste time to give you the Reasons against the two first, which are commonly received? When even the *Papists*, who go as far as any I know living in ascribing to *One Man*, and to *major Votes*, yet all agree, that *a few subtile Doctors*, yea *one* in the things in which he excelleth, is to be preferred before *Pope* or *Council*: And therefore the *Scotists* prefer one *Scotus*, *Lycheius*, *Memisse*, *Rada*, &c. before a *Pope* or Multitude, and so do the *Nominals*, one *Ockam*, *Gregory*, *Gabriel*, *Hurtado*, &c. and so the other Sects.

The thing then being such as neither you, nor any Man can deny, the difficulty which you urge, doth press you and all Men: And it is indeed one *grand calamity* of *Mankind*, and not the least hinderance of Knowledg in the World; that he that *hath it not*, *knoweth not* what another hath, but by

dark

dark Conjectures. 4. And therefore Parents and Pupils know not who is their best Tutor: The hearers that are to chuse a Teacher, hardly know whom to chuse; for, as you say truly, he must know much that must judg of a knowing Man.

God hath in all *Arts and Sciences* given some few Men an excellency of *Wit and Reach* above the generality of their Profession, and they have a more clear and solid Judgment: If *all Men* could but know *who these be*, the World would in one Age be more recovered from Ignorance than it hath been in ten. But the *power* of the *Proud*, and the *confidence* of the *Ignorant*, and the *number of all these*, and the *Slanders* and *Scorn*, and peevish Wranglings of the *common Pride* and *Ignorance* against those *few* that *know* what *they know not*, is the Devils great means to frustrate their endeavours, and keep the World from having knowledg. This is *certain* and *weighty* Truth, and such as you should make no Malignant applications of, nor strive against. Mankind must needs acknowledg it. Your urgent questioning here, [*Do you not mean your self?*] doth but expose you to pity, by opening that which you might have concealed.

And to your Question I say, could I enable all Ignorant Men to know who are the best Teachers, I should be the grand Benefactor of the World: But both the *blessing of excellent Teachers*, and also of *acquaintance* with them and *their worth*, is given by God, partly as it pleaseth Him, freely, even to the unworthy, and partly as a Reward to those that have been faithful in a little, and obeyed lower helps; (for there is a *Worthiness* to be found in some Houses, where the Preacher cometh with the

S voice

voice of *Peace*, and *unworthiness*, w[hich depri]veth Men of such Mercies.) Both [...]
Grace, and also *Rewarding-Grace*, [...]
themselves.

But yet I add, 1. That *Light* [is a pene]strating thing; and will not easily b[e hid from] those that are the Children of Light, [who are] true to former helps and conviction[s, wil]ling to sell all for the Pearl, and fe[tch buy]ers by the price of *Knowledg*, but [...] fers by the price of *Knowledg*, but [...] whatever Labour or Suffering it [cost:] who search for it impartially and [...] forfeit it not by Sloth, or a flesh[ly and] worldly Mind; these, I say, are prep[ared for] the Light; when others fall under t[he judg]ment of being deceived by the *Wra[th,]* *Clamours* and *Threatnings* of PE[RSEVE]RANCE. And thus one *Augusti[ne,]* in his time, and though such as [Pelag]*ius*, &c. knew him, *Pelagius* and [...] wrangled against him: And *Lut[her,]* *Bucer, Phagius, Zuinglius, Calvin, M[...]* were such in their times; and some [ceased] to be so, and more did not: If [all had] gone by the judgment of Rulers[, and the] Vote of Teachers, what had beco[me of Re]formation? If you can better dire[ct us to] discern Gods Gifts and Graces in H[is Servants,] it, and do not cavil against it.

As for your [*One single Protestan[t Article]* *of Justification*], and your [*I wi[sh you]* *meaning*] Pag. 31. they deserve no [answer,] nor I all the anger, pag. 31, 32, 33.

is not *Objective Definitions*, (as some *call* them) but [*Logical, Artificial Definitions,*] supposed to be Mens needful *Acts*, which you say are *Re*, the same with the *Definitum*. 2. And that yet you must have it [*supposed that these Definitions are true*]. And I suppose that few Good Christians comparatively know a *true one*, no, nor what a Definition, (or the *Genus* and *Differentia* which constitute it) is.

You say, [*I absolutely deny what you so rashly avow, that the Definition of Justification is controverted by the greatest Divines: This is one of your liberal Dictates: The Reformed Divines are all, I think, before you, agreed about the nature of Justification, its Causes,* &c. *and consequently cannot differ about the Definition*].

Answ. 1. But what if *all Divines* were so agreed? So are not *all honest Men and Women* that must have Communion with us: Therefore make not *Definitions* more *necessary* than they are, nor as necessary as the Thing.

2. You must be constrained for the defending of these words, to come off by saying, that you meant, That though they agree not in the *Words*, or *Logical terms of the Definition*; but one saith, *This* is the *Genus*, and *this* is the *Differentia*, and another that it is not *this but that*; one saith *this*, and another *that* is the *Formal*, or *Material Cause*, &c. yet *de re*, they mean the same thing; were they so happy as to agree in their *Logical* defining terms and notions: And if you will do in this, as you have done in your other Quarrel, come off by saying as I say, and shewing Men the power

of Truth, though you do it with never so much anger, *that you must agree*, I shall be satisfied, that the Reader is delivered from your snare, and that Truth prevaileth, what ever you think or say of me.

3. But because I must now answer *what you say*, and not *what I foresee you will or must say*, I must add, that this passage seemeth to suppose that your Reader liveth in the dark, and hath read very *little* of Justification. 1. Do all those great Divines, who deny the *Imputation of Christs active Righteousness*, and take it to be but *Justitia Personæ, non Meriti*, and that we are Justified by the *Passive only*, agree with their Adversaries, who have written against them, about the *Definition and Causes of Justification?* Will any Man believe you, who hath read *Olevian, Ursine, Paræus, Scultetus, Piscator, Carolus Molinæus, Wendeline, Beckman, Alstedius, Camero*, with his followers in *France, Forbes*, with abundance more, who are for the Imputation of the Passive Righteousness only? Were Mr. *Anth. Wotton*, and Mr. *Balmford*, and his other Adversaries, of the same Opinion in this? Was Mr. *Bradshaw* so sottish as to write his Reconciling Treatise of Justification in *Latine* and *English*, to reduce Men of differing minds to Concord, while he knew that there was no difference, so much as in the Definition? Was he mistaken in reciting the great differences about their Senses of *Imputation of Christs Righteousness*, if there were none at all? Did Mr. *Gataker* agree with *Lucius and Piscator*, when he wrote against both (as the extreams)? Did Mr. *Wotton*, and *John Goodwin*, agree with Mr. *G. Walker*, and Mr. *Roborough?* Doth Mr. *Lawson*,

in

in his *Theopolitics* agree with you, and such others? Doth not Mr. *Cartwright* here differ from those that hold the Imputation of the Active Righteousness?

What abundance of *Protestants* do place Justification only in *Forgiveness of Sins*? And yet as many (I know not which is the greater side) do make that *Forgiveness* but one part, and *Imputation of Righteousness* another. And how many make *Forgiveness no part* of Justification, but a Concomitant? And many instead of [*Imputation of Righteousness*] put [*Accepting us as Righteous, for the sake, or merit of Christs Righteousness imputed*] viz. as the *Meritorious Cause*). And *Paræus* tells us, that they are of four Opinions, who are for *Christs Righteousness imputed*; some for the *Passive* only; some for the *Passive* and *Active*; some for the *Passive*, *Active*, and *Habitual*; some for these three and the *Divine*. And who knoweth not that some here so distinguish Causes and Effects, as that our *Original Sin* (or *Habitual* say some) is pardoned for Christ's *Original* (and *Habitual*) Holiness: Our *Omissions* for *Christs Active Obedience*, and our *Comissions* for His *Passive*? Or as more say that Christs *Passive Righteousness* as Satisfaction, saveth us from Hell or Punishment, and His *Active* as meritorious, procureth *Life* as the reward? When many others, rejecting that Division, say; That both freedom from Punishment, and right to Glory are the conjunct effects of His Habitual, Active, and Passive Righteousness, as an entire Cause (in its kind); as *Guil. Forbes*, *Grotius*, *Bradshaw*, and others truly say: Besides that many conclude with *Gataker*, that these are indeed but one thing and effect,

effect, (to be *Glorified*, and *not to b[e]
Punished*); seeing not to be Glorifie[d]
damni, and that the remitting of the
damni & sensus, and so of all Sin of
Commission, is our whole Justificatio[n]

And I need not *tell* any Man that [the]
Writers, that they ordinarily distin[guish in Ju]-
stification, and give not the same De[finition of one]
sort as of *another*, nor of the *Name* [or Thing]
in another.

Many confess (whom you may [add to]
Forbes, and *Vinc. le Blanck*) that th[e word Ju]-
stifie] is divers times taken in Scri[pture (as the]
Papists do.) as including *Sanctifica*[tion. So]
saith *Beza* against *Illyricus*, pag. 21[.]
G. *Forbes*, [*Si Justificationem gener*[aliter, sic]
ut interdum usurpatur ab Apostolo, S[anctificatio]
erit ejus effectus, sed pars aut species]: [And by]
him (*mihi*) pag. 179. *Quamvis Ju*[stificatio ali]-
quando interdum generaliter accipiatur [pro ipso]
Justitiæ dono quam a patre in Ch[risto accipimus,]
&c.

And how little are we agreed wh[ether Recon]-
liation be a *part* of *Justification* or [of]
Adoption either? Saith *Illyricus* [*H[æc non]
posse dici Justificationem esse Causa*[m Benefi]-
ciorum sequentium: Nam justificatio e[st recon]-
ciliatio cum Deo, quæ nos facit ex host[ibus amicos*]
To which *Beza ibid.* saith, (disting[uishing Re]-
conciliation) *Neutro modo idem est* [cum]
Justificatio.— Si Remissio peccatorum [sit ejus]
nis Definitio, quod negare non ausis, &[c.]

Of the three sorts or parts of Ch[rist's Righteous]-
ness imputed to make up three parts o[f our]

tion, see him *de Predest. pag. 405. Col. 2.* which *Perkins* and some others also follow.

Olevian (as all others that grosly mistake not herein) did hold, that *God did not judg us to have fulfilled all the Law in Christ*; and that our righteousness consisteth only in the Remission of Sin, and right to Life as freely given us for anothers Merits: But *Beza* insisteth still on the contrary, and in his Epistle to *Olevian*, (*pag.*248.*Epist.*35.) saith, *Quid vanius est quam Justum arbitrari, qui Legem non impleverit? Atqui lex non tantum prohibet fieri quod vetat,—— verum præcipit quod jubet.—— Ergo qui pro non peccatore censetur in Christo, mortem quidem effugerit; sed quo jure vitam præterea petet, nisi omnem justitiam Legis in eodem Christo impleverit?* (This is the Doctrine which *Wotton* and *Gataker* (in divers Books largely) and *Bradshaw*, after many others do Confute). Yet saith he, *Neque vero id obstat, quominus nostra Justificatio Remissione peccatorum apte & recte definiatur*], Which is a contradiction. Yet was he for Love and Gentleness in these differences; *ibid.*

Yet *Qu. & Resp. Christ. pag.* 670. He leaveth out Christs Original Habitual Righteousness, [*Non illa essentialis quæ Deitatis est, nec illa Habitualis, ut ita loquar, Puritas Carnis Christi.—— Quæ cumm non distingueret Osiander fædissime est hallucinatus.*

And *ibid.* 670. he giveth us this description of Justification.

Qu. *Quid Justificationem vocat* Paulus *hoc loca?* R. *Illud quo Justi simus*, id est, *eousque perfecti, integri,* αμεμπτοι ϰ αμωμοι, *ut plenissime, non tantum aboleatur quicquid in nobis totis in est turpitudinis, qua Deus summe purus offendi ullo modo possit,*

possit, verum etiam in nos comperiatur quicquid in hac humana natura usque adeo potest eum delectare, ut illud vita æterna pro bona sua voluntate coronet].

Yet (as in his *Annot.* in *Rom.* 8. 30. *& alibi*) he confesseth that *Justification* in Scripture, sometime is taken for *Sanctification*, (or as including it) so he taketh our *Sanctification* to contain the Imputation of Christs Sanctity to us. (Qu. & Resp. pag. 671.) 1. *Dico nostras Personas, imputata ipsius perfecta sanctitate & integritate, plene sanctas & integras, ac proinde Patri acceptas, non in nobis sed in Christo censemur.* 2. And next the Spirits Sanctification; and thus Christ is made *Sanctification* to us.

Dr. *Twisse*, and Mr. *Pemble*, *Vind. Grat.* distinguish of Justification as an Immanent Act in God from Eternity, and as it is the notice of the former in our Consciences: But doubtless the commonest Definitions of Justification agree with neither of these: And *Pemble of Justification* otherwise defineth it (as Mr. *Jessop* saith Dr. *Twisse* did).

Lud. Crocius Syntag. pag. 1219. thus defineth it, [*Justificatio Evangelica est actus Divinæ gratiæ, qua Deus adoptat peccatorem per approbationem obedientiæ Legis in sponsore atque intercessore Christo, & per Remissionem peccatorum ac Justitiæ imputationem in eo qui per fidem Christo est insitus*]. And saith, pag. 1223. [*Fides sola justificat quatenus notat Obedientiam, quandam expectantem promissionem ut donum gratuitum — & apponitur illi Obedientiæ quæ non expectat promissionem ut donum omnino gratuitum sed ut mercedem propositam sub Conditione operis alicuius præter acceptationem & gratitudinem debitam, quæ sua Natura in omni donatione quamvis gratuita*

requiri

requiri solet. Et *ejusmodi Obedientia peculiariter opus ab Apostolo, & Latinis proprie Meritum dicitur; & qui sub hac conditione obediunt Operantes vocantur,* Rom. 4. 4. & 11. 6. This is the truth which I assert.

Conrad. Bergius Prax. Cathol. dis. 7. pag. 983. tells us that the Breme Cat chism thus openeth the Matter: [Qu. *Quomodo Justificatur Homo coram Deo?* R. *Accipit Homo Remissionem peccatorum & Justificatur, hoc est, Gratus fit coram Deo in vera Conversione, persolam fidem, per Christum, sine proprio Merito & dignitate.*

Cocceius disp. de via salut. de Just. pag. 189. *Originalis Christi Justitia correspondet nostro Originali peccato,* &c. *vid. cæt. plura vid. de fœder.*

Macovius Colleg. de Justif. distinguisheth Justification into *Active* and *Passive,* and faith, *Justificatio Activa significat absolutionem Dei, quæ Hominem reum a reatu absolvit:* And he would prove this to be before Faith, and citeth for it (abusively) *Paræus* and *Tossanus,* and thinketh that we were absolved from Guilt from Chrifts undertaking our Debt, *Thes.* 12. thus arguing, [*Cujus debita apud Creditorem aliquis recepit exsolvenda, & Creditor istius sponsionem ita acceptat, ut in ea acquiescat, ille jam ex parte Creditoris liber est a debitis: Atque Electorum omnium in singulari debita apud Deum Patrem Christus, ex quo factus est Mediator, recepit exolvenda, & Deus Pater illam sponsionem acceptavit,* &c. Passive Justification, which he supposeth to be our application of Chrifts Righteousness to our selves daily as oft as we offend. *Th.* 5. (And part 4. *disp.* 22. he maintaineth, that *There are no Dis-*

I pass by.

Spanhemius Disput. de Justif. saith, that [The *Form* of *Passive Justification* consisteth in the *apprehension* and *sense* of Remission of Sin and Imputation of Christs Righteousness in capable Subjects] grosly: Whereas Active Justification (*Justificantis*) ever immediately causeth *Passive* (*Justificationem justificati*) which is nothing but the effect of the Active, (or as most call it, *Actio ut in patiente*): And if this were the *Apprehension* and *Sense* (as aforesaid) of *Pardon* and *imputed Righteousness*, then a Man in his sleep were unjustified, and so of Infants, &c. For he that is not Passively justified, is not at all justified.

I told you else-where, that the *Synops. Leidens. de Justif.* pag. 413. *Th.* 23. saith, That Christs Righteousness is both the *Meritorious*, *Material*, and *Formal Cause* of our Justification.

What *Fayus*, and *Davenant*, and others say of the *Formal Cause*, viz. Christs Righteousness imputed, I there shewed: And how *Paræus*, *Joh. Crocius*, and many others, deny Christs Righteousness to be the Formal Cause.

Wendeline defineth Justification thus (*Theol. Lib.* 1. c. 25. p. 603.) *Justificatio est actio Dei gratuita, qua peccatores Electi, maledictioni legis obnoxii, propter justitiam seu satisfactionem Christi fide applicatam & a Deo imputatam, coram tribunali Divino, remissis peccatis, a maledictione Legis absolvuntur & justi censentur.* And pag. 615, 616. He maintaineth that [*Obedientia activa, si proprie & accurate loquamur, non est materia nostræ Justificationis, nec imputatur nobis, ita ut nostra censeatur,*

& *nobis propter eam peccata remittantur, & debitum, legis pro nobis solvatur; quemadmodum Passiva per imputationem censetur nostra,* &c. *Et post* [*Si dicus Christum factum esse hominem pro nobis, hoc est, nostro bono, conceditur: Si pro nobis, hoc est, nostro loco, negatur: Quod enim Christus nostro loco fecit, & factus est, id nos non tenemur facere & fieri,* &c.

Rob. Abbot approveth of *Thompsons* Definition of Evangelical Justification, (pag. 153.) that it is, *Qua pœnitenti & Credenti remittuntur peccata, & jus vitæ æternæ conce*▰*tur per & propter Christi obedientiam illi impu*t*atam:* (Which is found, taking *Imputatam* soundly, as he doth).

Joh. Crocius, Disp. 1. p. 5. thus defineth it, [*Actio Dei qua ex gratia propter satisfactionem Christi peccatoribus in Christum totius Mundi redemptorem unicum, vere credentibus gratis sine operibus aut meritis propriis omnia peccata remittit, & justitiam Christi imputat ad sui nominis gloriam & illorum salutem æternam.* And he maketh only [*Chrifts full satisfaction for Sin*, to be the *Impulsive-External, Meritorious,* and *Material Cause,* as being that which is imputed to us; and the *Form* of Justification to be the *Remission of Sin, Original* and *Actual,* or the *Imputation of Chrifts Righteousness* (which he maketh to be all one) or *the Imputation of Faith for Righteousness*].

Saith Bishop *Downame* of Justif. p. 305. [To be *Formally Righteous by Chrifts Righteousness imputed, never any of us, for ought I know, affirmed.* The like saith Dr. *Prideaux,* when yet very many Protestants affirm it.

Should I here set together forty or sixty Definitions of Protestants verbatim, and shew you how
much

much they differ, it would be unpleasant, and tedious, and unnecessary.

And as to those same Divines that Dr. *Tully* nameth as agreed, Dr. *Davenants* and Dr. *Fields* words I have cited at large in my *Confes.* saying the same in substance as I do; as also Mr. *Scudders*, and an hundred more, as is before said.

And let any sober Reader decide this Controversie between us, upon these two further Considerations.

1. Peruse all the *Corpus Confessionum*, and see whether all the Reformed Churches give us a Definition of Justification, and agree in that Definition: Yea, whether the Church of *England* in its Catechism, or its Articles, have any proper Definition: Or if you will call their words a *Definition*, I am sure it's none but what I do consent to. And if a *Logical Definition* were by the Church of *England* and other Churches held *necessary* to Salvation, it would be in their Catechisms (if not in the Creed): Or if it were held necessary to Church-Concord, and Peace, and Love, it would be in their Articles of Religion, which they subscribe.

2. How can all Protestants agree of the *Logical Definition* of Justification, when 1. They agree not of the sense of the word [*Justifie,*] and of the *species* of that Justification which *Paul* and *James* speak of? Some make Justification to include Pardon and Sanctification, (see their words in G. *Forbes,* and *Le Blank*); many say otherwise. Most say that *Paul* speaketh most usually of Justification in *sensu forensi*, but whether it include [*Making just*] as some say, or only [*Judging just*] as others, or *Nolle punire*, be the act as Dr. *Twisse*, they agree not. And some hold that in *James* Justification is

that

that which is *coram hominibus*, when said to be by *Works*; but others (*truly*) say, it is that *coram Deo*.

2. They are not agreed in their very *Logical Rules*, and Notions, to which their Definitions are reduced; no not so much as of the number and nature of Causes, nor of *Definitions* (as is aforesaid): And as I will not undertake to prove that all the Apostles, Evangelists and Primitive Pastours, knew how to define *Efficient*, *Material*, *Formal* and *Final Causes* in *general*, so I am sure that *all* good Christians do not.

3. And when *Justification* is defined by Divines, is either the *Actus Justificantis*, and this being in the predicament of Action, what wonder if they disagree about the *Material* and *Formal Causes* of it?

Nay, it being an Act of God, there are few Divines that tell us what that Act is: *Deus operatur per essentiam*: And *Ex parte agentis*, his Acts are his *Essence*, and all but one. And who will thus dispute of the Definition and Causes of them, Efficient, Material, Formal, Final? when I presumed to declare, that this Act of Justifying is not an immanent Act in God, nor without a Medium, but Gods Act by the Instrumentality of his *Gospel-Covenant* or *Promise*, many read it as a new thing; and if that hold true that the First Justification by Faith, is that which Gods Gospel-Donation is the Instrument of, as the *Titulus seu Fundamentum Juris*, being but a *Virtual* and not an Actual Sentence, then the Definition of it, as to the Causes, must differ much from the most common Definitions.

But

But most Protestants say that *Justification* is *Sententia Judicis*. (And no doubt but there are three several *sorts*, or Acts called Justification, 1. Constitutive by the *Donative Covenant*, 2. Sentential, 3. Executive.) And here they are greatly at a loss, for the decision of the Case, *what Act of God this Sententia Jucis is*. What it will be after death, we do not much disagree: But what it is immediately upon our believing. It must be an *Act* as in *patiente*, or the Divine essence denominated from such an *effect*. And what Judgment and Sentence God hath upon our believing, few open, and fewer agree. Mr. *Tombes* saith it is a *Sentence* in *Heaven notifying* it to the Angels: But that is not all, or the chief: some run back to an Immanent Act; most leave it undetermined: And sure the *Name* of *Sentence* in general, signifieth no true Conception of it at all, in him that knoweth not what that *Sentence* is, seeing Universals are *Nothing* (out of us) but as they exist in individuals. Mr. *Lawson* hath said that wihch would reconcile Protestants, and some Papists, as to the Name, *viz.* that Gods *Execution* is his *Sentence*; He *Judgeth* by *Executing*: And so as the chief punishment is the *Privation of the Spirit*, so the Justifying Act, is the *executive donation* of the Spirit. Thus are we disagreed about *Active Justification* (which I have oft endeavoured Conciliatorily fuller to open.)

And as to *Passive Justification* (or as it is *Status Justificati*) which is indeed that which it concerneth us in this Controversie to open, I have told you how grosly some describe it here before. And all agree not what *Predicament* it is in: some take it to be in that of *Action*; *ut recipitur in passo*; and some in that of Quality and Relation Conjunct: But most
place

place it in Relation; And will you wonder if all Chriſtian Women, yea or Divines, cannot define that Relation aright. And if they agree not in the notions of the *Efficient, Material, Formal and Final Cauſes,* of that which muſt be *defined* (as it is capable) by its *ſubjectum, fundamentum* and *terminus.*

I would not wiſh that the Salvation of any Friend of mine (or any one) ſhould be laid on the true Logical Definition of Juſtification, Active or Paſſive, *Conſtitutive, Sentential* or *Executive.*

And now the Judicious will ſee, whether the Church and Souls of Men be well uſed by this pretence, that all Proteſtants are agreed in the *Nature, Cauſes* and Definition of Juſtification; and that to depart from that *one* Definition (where is it?) is ſo dangerous as the Doctor pretendeth, becauſe the *Definition* and the *Definitum* are the ſame.

§ XX. P. 34. You ſay [*You tremble not in the audience of God and Man to ſuggeſt again that hard-fronted Calumny,* viz. *that I prefer a Majority of Ignorants before a Learned man in his own profeſſion.*

Anſw. I laid it down as a Rule, that *They are not to be preferred*: You aſſault that Rule with bitter accuſations, as if it were unſound. (or elſe to this day I underſtand you not.) Is it then [*a hard-fronted Calumny*] to defend it, and to tell you what is contained in the denying of it. *The audience of God* muſt be ſo dreadful to (you and) me, that (without calling you to conſider whether the Calumny be not notoriouſly yours) I heartily deſire any judicious perſon to help me to ſee, that I am here guilty, if it be ſo. But you add,

"*You*

"[You know not what the Event of all this may be: For suppose now, being drag'd in my Scarlet, (a habit more suitable for him that Triumphs) at the Wheel of your Chariot in the view of all men, I should happen to be degraded and turned out of my literate Society; would it not trouble you? no doubt: but then it might happen to be too late.

Answ. 1. It would trouble me: because (though I know you not) our fame here saith that you are an *honest*, and *very modest man*, and those that are Nicknamed *Calvinists* prefer you before most others of your rank. But alas, what is Man, and what may Temptation do?

2. did you think that your *Scarlet* or *Mastership* did allow you to write copiously, as you did, against your Neighbour who never medled with you, and made it a crime in him, whom you accuse, to defend himself, and a righteous cause? I see in this age we deal on hard unequal terms with some Men that can but get into Scarlet.

3. You would make your Reader believe by these words that you are really Melancholly, and fear where no fear is. A Reverend Doctor, whose Book hath the Patronage of one of the greatest Eps. *of England* writeth against one of no *Academical degree*, who hath these 13. years and more been judged unworthy to preach to the most ignorant Congregation in the Land, and by the (Contrived) distinction of *Nonconformists* from *Conformists*, goeth under the *scorn* and *hatred* of *such*, as you pretend to be in danger of, and hath himself no security for his liberty in the open Air; that this Learned man in his honour, should conceit that an Answer from this hated person might endanger his degradation and
turning

his place, is so strange a fancie, as will
ders wonder.
:ther you are Melancholly or no I
t if you are not *unrighteous*, I know
hteousness is. Will you bear with the
tory?
Ioors were sentenced to ruin in *Spain*,
iples of *Valdesso* (a Scholar) fell into
of the Bp. of *Toledo*: A Neighbour
ig that the Bps. favour might bestead
ether accidentally or contrivedly I
: upon this happy course: The Scho-
g together in a solemn Convention,
s taking Tobacco, and the Dr. seeing
v first a Glass of Beer in his face, and
re; The Scholar wiped his face, and
Doctor next threw an *Ink-bottle in his*
still *Fire, Fire*; The Scholar being
:rceived that he was like to be taken
d ruined, and he went out and care-
s face: the Doctor charged him open-
g him (yea and injuriously calum-
)y the fact: For saith he, there was
: for what I did: There is no smoak
ire: that which fired you might next
House, and that the next House, and
lown all the City: and your action
f I had done causelesly what I did,
wrong: The Scholar answered him;
:, that it was unlawful to wash me, but
more Tobacco that I may no more
ut if in this frosty weather the *thick-*
th should be called *smoak*. may I not
if you again cast your Ink upon it?

T   No,

(74)

No, saith the Doctor, It is not you, man that must be judg whether you not, in a publick danger: Must the City you say that it is not Fire? The S may I not refer the case to the stande my face if they say, It was no Fire? Dr. that is but to call in your As help, and to add *Rebellion* and *Schis* bedience: I perceive what principl Why then, saith the Scholar, if I r *Moor*, my face and I are at your mer

But pardon this digression, and let to the judgment of any righteous Judge, whether you deal not with m injustice, so be it the Case be truly st

The person whom you assaulted is tempted (with success) the subversi mianism and the clearing of truth; t of which was the Cause of their othe having let fall, (for want of use in incongruous words (as *Covenant* f and that somewhat often, and som gainst the Book, he craved their anir promised to suspend the Book till it w and purposely wrote a far greater Vol cation of what was dark, and defen wrongfully accused, and many other V defence: No man answereth any of tl twenty years, or thereabout, (though print against any that would write a phorisms, without regard to the said you publish your Confutation of part rifms, and that with most notorious u ing me to deny all *Imputation of Christ.*

when I had there profeſt the Contrary, and taking no notice of any after-explication or defence, and parallelling me with *Bellarmine*, if not with Hereticks or Infidels (for I ſuppoſe you take the denyers of *all Imputation* to be little better.) This Book you publiſh without the leaſt provocation with other quarrels, dedicating it to that R. Rd. B. who firſt ſilenced me; (as if I muſt go write over again all the Explications and Defences I had before written, becauſe you (that are bound to accuſe me) are not bound to read them:) and this you do againſt one that at that time had been about 13 years ſilenced, ejected, and deprived of all Miniſterial maintenance; and of almoſt all his own perſonal Eſtate, deſiring no greater preferment than leave to have preached for nothing, where is notorious neceſſity, could I have obtained it, ſometimes laid in the common Jail among Malefactors, for preaching in my own houſe, and *dwelling within five miles of it*: after fined at forty pound a Sermon for preaching for nothing; looking when my *Books* and *Bed* are taken from me by diſtreſs, though I live in conſtant pain and langour, the Conſtable but yeſterday coming to have diſtrained for ſixty pound for two Sermons; hunted and hurryed about to Juſtices at the will of any ignorant—— Agent of—— that will be an Informer, and even fain to keep my doors daily lockt, if it may be to ſave my Books a while: Yet the exciting of wroth by *publick Calumny* againſt one ſo low already, and under the perſecuting wrath of *your friends*, was no fault, no injuſtice in you at all! (nor indeed did I much feel it.)

But for me who am thus publickly by *viſible Calumny* traduced, truly to tell you where you miſtake, and how you wrong Gods Church and Truth more than me, and if alſo I offer peaceably to waſh my own face, this is *hard fronted Calumny, dragging* a Doctor in *Scarlet at the Wheels of my Chariot, which might occaſion his degrading and turning out, &c.*

This over-tenderneſs of your honour as to other mens words, (and too little care of the means of it, as to your own) hath a cauſe that it concerneth you to find out. Had you the tenth part as many Books written againſt you, as are againſt me (by Quakers, Seekers, Infidels, Antinomians, Millenaries, Anabaptiſts, Separatiſts, Semi-ſeparatiſts, Papiſts, Pſeudo-Tilenus, Dioceſans, Conformiſts, and many Enemies of Peace, (to whom it was not I, but your ſelf that joyned you) it would have hardened you into ſome more patience. If you will needs be militant you muſt expect replies: And he that will injuriouſly ſpeak to the World what he ſhould not ſpeak, muſt look to hear what he would not hear. But you add;

Sir, the Name and Quality of a D O C T O R and Maſter of a Literate Society, might have been treated more civilly by you.

Anſw. 1. I am ready to ask you forgiveneſs for any word that any impartial man (yea or your Reverend Brethren of that Academy themſelves, whom I will allow to be *ſomewhat partial* for you) ſhall notifie to me to be uncivil or any way injurious. 2. But to be free with you, neither Doctorſhip, Maſterſhip nor Scarlet will Priviledg you to fight againſt *Truth, Right,* and *Peace,* and to vent groſs miſtakes, and by *groſs untruths in matter of fact,* ſuch as is your [*Omnem ludibrio habet imputationem*] to abuſe your poor Brethren, and keep the long-
con-

consuming flames still burning, by false representing those as Popish, and I know not what, who speak not as unaptly as your self, and all this without contradiction. Were you a Bp. my *Body* and *Estate* might be in your power, but *Truth*, *Justice* and the *Love of Christians*, and the *Churches peace*, should not be cowardly betrayed by me on pretense of reverence to your Name and Quality. I am heartily desirous that for O R D E R-sake the *Name* and *Honour* of my Superiours may be very reverently used. But if they will think that *Errour*, *Injustice*, and *Confusion* must take sanctuary under bare *Ecclesiastical* or *Academical Names* and robes, they will find themselves mistaken: Truth and Honesty will conquer when they pass through Smithfield flames: Prisons confine them not; Death kills them not; No siege will force an honest Conscience by famine to give up. He that *cannot endure* the sight of his own excrements must not dish them up to another mans Table, lest they be sent him back again. And more freedom is allowed against *Peace-Breakers* in *Frays* and *Wars*, than towards men that are in a quieter sort of Controversie.

§ XX. P. 36. 37. You say [*For your various Definitions of Justification, Constitutive, Sentential, Executive, in Foro Dei, in foro Conscientiæ, &c.——— What need this heap of distinctions here, when you know the question betwixt us is of no other Justification, but the Constitutive in foro Dei, that which maketh us righteous in the Court of Heaven? I have nothing to do with you yet in any else, as your own Conscience will tell you when you please: If you have not more Justice and civility for your intelligent Readers, I wish you would*

would shew more Compassion to your Ignorant Homagers, and not thus abuse them with your palpable Evasions.

Answ. Doth the question, *Whether the several sorts of Justification will bear one and the same Definition,* deserve all this anger (and the much greater that followeth)?

1. Seeing I am turned to my Reader, I will crave his impartial judgment: I never *received* and *agreed on* a state of the question with this Doctor: He writeth against my books: In those Books I over and over and over distinguish of Justification, *Constitutive, Sentential,* and *Executive* (besides those subordinate sorts, by *Witness, Evidence, Apology,* &c.) I oft open their differences: He writeth against me, as *denying* all *Imputation* of *Christs Righteousness,* and holding *Popish Justification by works,* and never tells me whether he take the word [*Justification*] in the same sense that I do, or in which of those that I had opened: And now he passionately appealeth to my Conscience that *I knew his sence*: What he saith [*my Conscience will tell me*] it is not true: It will tell me no such thing: but the clean contrary, that even after all his *Disputes* and *Anger,* and these *words,* I profess I know not what he meaneth by [*Justification.*]

2. What [*Constitutive in foro Dei, that which maketh us Righteous in the Court of Heaven*] meaneth with him, I cannot conjecture. He denyeth not my Distinctions, but saith, *what need they:* I ever distinguished *Making Righteous, Judging Righteous. Executively useing as Righteous:* The first is in *our selves*; The second is by Divines said to be *in foro Dei,* an act of Judgment; the third is *upon us* after both:

both: now he seemeth to confound the *two first*, and yet denyeth not their difference; and faith, he meaneth [*Constitutive in foro* :] He that is. *made Righteous* is such *in se*; and as such is *Justifiable in foro* :] We are *Made Righteous by God* as free *Donor* and *Imputer*, antecedently to judgment: We are *in foro sentenced Righteous by God as Judg*: so that this by *sentence* presupposeth the former: God never *Judgeth us Righteous* and Justifieth us against *Accusation*, till he have first *Made us Righteous* and *Justified us from* adherent Guilt by *Pardon and Donation.* Which of these meaneth he? I ask not my *Ignorant homagers* who know no more than I, but *his Intelligent Reader.* He taketh on him to go the Commonest way of Protestants: And the Commonest way is to acknowledg that a *Constitutive Justification*, or making *the man Just*, (antecedent to the *Actus forensis*) must need go first: but that it is the *second* which *Paul* usually meaneth, which is the *actus forensis*, the *sentence of the Judg in foro*, contrary to *Condemnation:* And doth the Doctor think that to *make Righteous* and to *sentence as Righteous* are all one? and that we are *made Righteous in foro* otherwise than to be *just* in *our selves*, and so *Justifiable in foro*, before the *Sentence*? or do Protestants take the *Sentence* to be *Constituting or Making us Righteous*? All this is such talk as had I read it in Mr. *Bunnyan* of the Covenants, or any of my *Ignorant Homagers*, I should have said, the Author *is a stranger to the Controversie, into which he hath rashly plunged himself:* but I have more reverence to so learned a man, and therefore blame my dull understanding.

3. But what if I had known (as I do not yet) what sort of Justification he meaneth? Doth he not know

know that I was then debating the Case with him, whether the *Logical Definitions* of *Justification, Faith,* &c. are not a work of Art, in which a *few well-studied judicious Divines* (these were my words) *are to be preferred before Authority, or Majority of Votes.* And Reader, what Reason bound me to confine this Case, to *one only sort* of *Justification*? And why, (I say, *why*) must I confine it to a *sort* which Dr. *Tully meaneth,* when my *Rule and Book* was written *before his,* and when to this day I know not what he meaneth? Though he at once chide at my Distinguishing, and tell me that *All Protestants agree* in the *Nature, Causes,* and *Definition,* (and if all agreed, I might know by *other Mens words* what *he* meaneth) yet to all before-said, I will add but one contrary Instance of many.

Cluto, in his very *Methodical* but unsound *Idea Theol.* (signalized in *Voetii Biblioth.*) defineth Justification so, as I suppose, best pleaseth the Doctor, *viz.* [*Est Actio Dei Judicialis, qua redemptos propter passiones justitiæ Divinæ satifactorias a Christo sustentatas, redemptisque imputatas, a peccatis puros, & consequenter a pœnis liberos, itemque propter Obedientiam a Christo Legi Divinæ præstitam redemptisque imputatam, justitia præditos, & consequenter vita æterna dignos, ex misericordia pronunciat*]. In the opening of which he telleth us, *pag.* 243. (against multitudes of the greatest Protestants Definitions.) [*Male alteram Justificationis partem, ipsam Justitiæ Imputationem statui, cum Justificatio non sit ipsa Imputatio, sed Pronunciatio quæ Imputatione, tanquam fundamento jacto, nititur.*

And

And he knew no sense of Justification, but [*Vel ipsam sententiæ Justificatoriæ in mente Divina prolationem, sive Constitutionem, vel ejus in Cordibus redemptorum manifestantem Revelationem*: And saith, *Priori modo factum est autem omnem fidem, cum Deus omnes, quibus passiones & justitiam Christi imputabat, innocentes & justos reputaret, cum ejus inimici, adeoque sine fide essent,* (so that here is a Justification of Infidels, as innocent for Christs Righteousness imputed to them): *Quare etiam ut jam facta fide apprehendenda est*. The second which follows Faith, is Faith, *ingenerating a firm perswasion of it*. Is not here sad defining, when *neither of these* are the Scripture-*Justification* by *Christ* and *Faith* ?

And so §. 32. the *time* of Justification by Faith he maketh to be the time when we receive the *feeling* of the former: And the time of the former is presently after the *Fall*; of all at once: And hence gathereth that [*Ex eo quod Justificatio dicitur fieri propter passiones & obedientiam Christi, quibus ad perfectionem nihil deest, nobis imputatas* (before Faith or Birth) *consequitur innocentiam & justitiam in Redemptis quam primum perfectas & ab omni macula puras esse*——] and so that neither the pronunciation in *mente Divina*, or imputation *ullis gradibus ad perfectionem exsurgat*.

But what is this pronunciation in *mente Divina* ? He well and truly noteth, §. 29. that [*Omnes actiones Divinæ, si ex eo æstimentur quod re ipsa in Deo sunt, idem sunt cum ipso Deo, ideoque dependentiam a Causa externa non admittant: Si tamen considerentur quoad rationem formalem hujus vel illius denominationis ipsis impositæ in relatione ad Creaturas consistentem, ipsis causæ impulsivæ assignare possunt*

sunt, &c. This distinction well openeth, how God may be said to *justifie in His own Mind:* But what is that effect, *Unde essentia vel mens Divina ita denominatur justificans?* Here he is at a loss, neither truly telling us what is *Justication Constitutive, Sentential,* nor *Executive* (but in the little part of [*Feeling*] *Gods secret Act)* yet this dark Definer truly saith [*Ex sensu Scripturæ verissime affirmetur hominem per fidem solam justificari, quia ex nostra parte nihil ad Justificationem conferendum Deus requirit, quam ut Justificationem in Christo fundatam credamus, & fide non producamus, sed recipiamus.*

If yet you would see whether all Protestants agree in the Definition of Justification, read the multitude of Definitions of it in several senses; in Learnrd *Alstedius* his *Definit. Theol.* c. 24. §. 2. pag. 97. &c. [*Justificatio hominis coram Deo est qua homo in foro Divino absolvitur, seu justus esse evincitur contra quemvis actorem, Deo ipso judice, & pro eo sententiam ferente*]. But what is this *Forum?* *Forum Divinum est ubi Deus ipse judicis partes agit, & fert sententiam secundum leges a se latas?* But where is that *Est internum vel externum? Forum divinum internum est in ipsa hominis Conscientia, in qua Deus Thronum justitiæ erigit in hac vita ibi agendo partes actoris & judicis: Forum Conscientiæ.* (But it is not *this* that is meant by the *Justification by Faith*). *Forum divinum externum est, in qua Deus post hanc vitam extra hominem exercet judicium,* 1. *Particulare,* 2. *Universale.* This is true and well: But are we no where Justified by Faith but in *Conscience,* till after Death? This is by not considering, 1. The *Jus ad impunitatem & vitam donatum*

natum per fœdus Evangelicum upon our Believing, which supposing *Faith* and *Repentance* is our *Constitutive Justification*, (*virtually* only *sentential*). 2. And the Judgment of God begun in this Life, pronounced specially by *Execution*. Abundance of useful Definitions subordinate you may further there see in *Alstedius*, and some wrong, and the chief omitted.

The vehement passages of the Doctors Conclusion I pass over; his deep sense of *unsufferable Provocations*, I must leave to himself; his warning of the *dreadful Tribunal* which I am near, it greatly concerns me to regard: And Reader, I shall think yet that his Contest (though troublesome to me that was falsly assaulted, and more to him whose detected Miscarriages are so painful to him) hath yet been *Profitable* beyond the Charges of it to *him or me*, if I have but convinced thee, that 1. *Sound mental Conceptions of so much as is necessary to our own Justification, much differ from proper Logical Definitions: And that,* 2. *Many millions are Justified that cannot define it:* 3. *And that Logical Definitions are Works of Art more than of Grace, which require so much Acuteness and Skill, that even worthy and excellent Teachers may be, and are disagreed about them, especially through the great ambiguity of Words; which all understand not in the same sence, and few are sufficiently suspicious of, and diligent to explain.* 4. *And* therefore that our Christian *Love, Peace,* and *Concord, should not* be laid *upon such Artificial* things. 5. And that *really* the Generality of *Protestants* are agreed mostly in the *Matter,* when they quarrel sharply about many Artificial Notions and Terms in the point of Justification.

tion. (And yet after all this, I shall as earnestly as this Doctor, desire and labour for *accurateness in Distinguishing, Defining* and *Method*, though I will not have such things to be Engins of Church-Division.)

And lastly, Because he so *oft* and earnestly presseth me with his *Quem quibus, who is the Man*, I *profess* I dreamed not of *any particular Man*: But I will again tell you whom my Judgment magnifies in this Controversie above all others, and who truly tell you how far *Papists and Protestants agree*, viz. *Vinc. le Blank*, and *Guil. Forbes*, (I meddle not with his *other Subjects*), *Placeus* (in Thes. Salmur.) *Davenant*, Dr. *Field*, Mr. *Scudder* (his daily Walk, fit for all families) Mr. *Wotton*, Mr. *Bradshaw*, and Mr. *Gataker*, Dr. *Preston*, Dr. *Hammond*, (*Pract. Cat.*) and Mr. *Lawson* (in the main) Abundance of the French and Breme Divines are also very clear. And though I must not provoke him again by naming some *late English* men, to reproach them by calling them *my disciples*, I will venture to tell the plain man that loveth not *our wrangling tediousness*, that Mr. *Trumans Great Propit.* and Mr. *Gibbons serm. of Justif.* may serve him well without any more.

And while this worthy Doctor and I do both concord with such as *Davenant* and *Field* as to *Justification by Faith or Works*, judg whether we differ between our selves as far as he would perswade the World, who agree *in tertio*? And whether as he hath angrily profest his concord in the two other Controversies which he raised (*our Guilt of nearer Parents sin, and our preferring the judgment of the wisest*, &c.) it be not likely that he will do so also

in

in this, when he hath leifure to read and know what it is that I fay and hold, and when we both underſtand our felves and one another. And whether it be a work worthy of *Good* and *Learned* men, to allarm Chriſtians againſt one another for the fake of arbitrary words and notions (which one partly ufeth lefs aptly and skilfully than the other) in matters wherein they really agree.

2 **Tim.** 2. 14. *Charging them before the Lord that they ſtrive not about words, to no profit, but to the ſubverting of the Hearers (yet) ſtudy to ſhew thy ſelf approved unto God, a workman that need not be aſhamed, rightly dividing the word of Truth.*

Two

Two Sparks more quenched, which fled after the rest from the Forge of Dr. Tho. Tully.

§. 1.

Did I not find that some Mens *Ignorance* and *factious Jealousie* is great enough to make them combustible Recipients of such Wildfire as those *Strictures* are; and did not *Charity* oblige me to do what I have here done, to save the assaulted Charity of such Persons, more than to save any Reputation of my own, I should repent that I had written one Line in answer to such *Writings* as I have here had to do with: I have been so wearied with the haunts of the like Spirit, in Mr. *Grandon,* Mr. *Bagshaw,* Mr. *Danvers,* and others, that it is a work I have

have not patience to be much longer in, unlefs it were more neceffary.

Two fheets more tell us that the Doctor is yet angry; And little that's better that I can find. In the firft, he faith again, that [*I am bufie in fmoothing my way where none can ftumble in, a thing never queftioned by him, nor by any Man elfe, he thinks, who owns the Authority of the fecond Commandment*]. And have I not then good Company and Encouragement not to change my Mind?

But, 1. He feigneth a Cafe ftated between him and me, who never had to do with him before, but as with others in my Writings, where I ftate my Cafe my felf. 2. He never fo much as toucheth either of my Difputations of *Original Sin*, in which I ftate *my Cafe* and *defend* it. 3. And he falfly feigneth the Cafe ftated, in words (and he fuppofeth in a fenfe) that I never had do do with: Saying, [*I charge you with a new fecondary Original Sin, whofe Pedegree is not from* Adam: *I engage not a fyllable further*]. And pag. 8. [*You have afferted that this Novel Original Sin is not derived from our Original Father; no line of Communication between them; a fin befides that which is derived from* Adam, *as you plainly and poſſitively affirm*]. I never ſaid that it had no *Pedegree*, no line of *Communication*, no kind of derivation from *Adam*. 4. Yea, if he would not touch the Diſputation where I ſtate my Caſe, he ſhould have noted it as ſtated in the very Preface which he writeth againſt; and yet there alſo he totally overlooketh it, though opened in divers Propoſitions. 5. And the words in an Epiſtle to another Mans Book, which he faſteneth ſtill on were theſe; [*Over-looking the Intereſt of Children in the Actions of their nearer Parents, and think that they participate of no Guilt, and ſuffer for no Original Sin, but* Adams *only*]. And after, [*They had more Original Sin than what they had from* Adam]. 6. He tells me, that [*I ſeem not to underſtand my own Queſtion, nor to know well how to ſet about my Work*]; and he will teach me how to manage the *Buſineſs* that *I have undertaken*, and ſo he tells me *how* I MUST ſtate the Queſtion hereafter, (ſee his words). Reader, ſome Reaſons may put a better Title on this Learned Doctors actions; but if ever I write at this rate, I heartily deſire thee to caſt it away as utter DISHONESTY and IMPUDENCE.

It

It troubleth me to trouble thee with Repetitions. I hold, 1. That *Adams* Sin is imputed (as I opened) to his Posterity. 2. That the degree of Pravity which *Cains* nature received from *Adam*, was the dispositive enclining Cause of all his Actual Sin: 3. But not a necessitating Cause of *all those* Acts; for he might possibly have done less evil and more good than he did. 4. Therefore not the *Total principal Cause*; for *Cains free-will* was *part* of that. 5. *Cains actual sin increased* the *pravity* of his *nature.* 6. And *Cains Posterity* were (as I opened it) *guilty* of *Cains actual sin*; and their *Natures* were the more *depraved* by his *additional pravity*, than they would have been by *Adams sin alone* (unless Grace *preserved* or *healed* any of them).

The Doctor in this Paper, would make his Reader believe that he is [*for no meer Logomachies*] and that the difference is not in *words only*, but *the thing*. And do you think that he differeth from me in any of these Propositions, or how this *sin is derived from* Adam? Yet this now must be the Controversie *de re*.

Do you think (for I must go by *thinking*) that he holdeth any other *Derivation* than this? Or did I ever deny any of this?

V But

But it is vain to state the Case to him: He will over-look it, and tell me what I *should have* held, that he may not be thought to make all this Noise for nothing.

He saith *pag* 8. ⸢*If it derive in a direct line from the first Transgression, and have its whole Root fastened there, what then? why then some words which he sets together are not the best sense that can be spoken.* It is then but *words,* and yet it is the *thing:* What he may mean by [a *direct Line*], and what by [*whole Root fastened*] I know not; but I have told the World oft enough *what I mean* ; and what *he meaneth,* I have little to do with.

But if he think, 1. That *Adams Person* did commit the sin of *Cain,* and of all that ever were since committed; and that *Judas his act,* was *Adams personal act.* 2. Or that *Adams sin* was a *total* or *necessitating* Cause of all the evil since committed; so do not I, (nor doth he, I doubt not). And now I am cast by him on the strait, either to accuse him of *differing de re,* and so of *Doctrinal errour,* or else that he knoweth not when the difference is *de re,* and when *de nomine,* but is so used to confusion, that *Names and Things* do come promiscuously into the Queſtion with him: And which of theſe to chuſe, I know not.

The Reader may ſee that I mentioned [*Actual Sin, and Guilt*]: And I think few will doubt, but *Adams* [*Actual ſin*, and *Cains*,] were divers; and that therefore, the *Guilt* that *Cains* Children had of *Adams* ſin and of *Cains* was not the ſame: But that *Cauſa cauſæ* is *Cauſa cauſati*, and ſo that all following Sin was *partly* (but partly) *cauſed* by *Adam's*, we ſhall ſoon agree.

He addeth that I muſt make good that *new. Original Sin* (for he can make uſe of the word *New*, and therefore *made* it) *doth mutare naturam, as the Old doth*. *Anſ.* And how far it *changeth it*, I told him, and he taketh no notice of it: The *firſt ſin* changed Nature from *Innocent* into *Nocent*; the *Second* changeth it from *Nocent* into more *Nocent*: Doth he deny this? Or why muſt I prove any more? Or doth nothing but Confuſion pleaſe him?

3. He ſaith, I muſt prove that the *Derivation of Progenitors ſins is conſtant and neceſſary, not uncertain and contingent*. *Anſ.* Of this alſo I fully ſaid what I held, and he diſſembleth it all, as if I had never done it: And why muſt I prove more?
By

By what Law can he impose on me what to hold?

But really doth he deny that the *Reatus culpæ*, yea and *ad Pœnam*, the Guilt of nearer Parents sins is *necessarily* and *certainly* the *Childs*, though Grace may *pardon* it? If he do not, why doth he call on me to prove it? If he do confess the *Guilt*, and deny it *necessary*, when will he tell us what is the *Contingent uncertain Cause*? For we take a *Relation* (such as *Guilt* is) *necessarily* to *result a posito fundamento*.

§. 2. He next cavilleth at my Citations, about which I only say, either the Reader will peruse the *cited words*, and *my words, which shew* to what *end I cited them* (to prove our *Guilt* of our *nearer Parents* sins) or he will not. If he *will not*, I cannot expect that he *will read* a further *Vindication*: If *he will*, he *needeth not*.

§. 3. His second *Spark* is *Animadversions* on a sheet of mine, before mentioned, which are such as I am not willing to meddle with, seeing I cannot either *handle* them, or *name* them as the nature of them doth require, without offending him: And if what is here said (of *Imputation* and *Repre-*

presentation) be not enough, I will add no more, nor write over and over still the same things, because a Man that will take no notice of the many Volumns which answer all his Objections long ago, will call for more, and will write his Animadversions upon a single Sheet that was written on another particular occasion, and pretend to his discoveries of my Deceits from the *Silence* of that *Sheet*, and from my naming the *Antinomians*.

I only say, 1. If this Mans way of Disputing were the *common way*, I would abhor *Disputing*, and be ashamed of the *Name*.

2. I do friendly desire the Author of the *Friendly Debate*, Mr. *Sherlock*, and all others that would fasten such Doctrines on the *Non-Conformists*, as a Character of the *Party*, to observe that this Doctor sufficiently confuteth their partiality; and that their Academical Church-Doctors, are as *Confused*, as *Vehement* maintainers of such expressions as they account most unfavoury, as any even of the *Independants* cited by them: Yea, that this Doctor would make us question whether there be now any *Antinomians* among us, and so whether all the Conformists that have charged the Conformists, yea,

yea or the *Sectaries*, with having among them Men of such unsound Principles, have not wronged them, it being indeed the Doctrine of the Church of *England* which they maintain, whom I and others call *Antinomians* and *Libertines*: And I hope at least the sober and sound *Non-Conformists* are Orthodox, when the vehementest *Sectaries* that calumniated my Sermon at *Pinners Hall*, are vindicated by such a Doctor of the Church.

3. I yet conclude, that if this *One Mans Writings* do not convince the Reader, of the *Sin and Danger* of Allarming Christians against one another, as Adversaries to great and necessary Doctrines, on the account of meer *Words* not *understood*, for want of accurateness and skill in the expressive Art, *I take him to be utterly unexcusable.*

Pemble Vind. Grat. p. 25. *It were somewhat if it were in Learning as it is in bearing of a Burthen; where many weak Men may bear that which One or few cannot: But in the search of* Knowledg, *it fares as in discrying a thing afar off; where* one quick-sight will see further than a thousand clear Eyes.

A POSTSCRIPT,
ABOUT
Mr. DANVERS's
Laſt BOOK.

WHen this Book was coming out of the Preſs, I received another Book of Mr. Danvers againſt Infants Baptiſm, in which he mentioneth Dr. *Tullies* proving what a *Papiſt* I am, in his *Juſtif. Paul.* (with Dr. *Pierces* former Charges) and lamenting that no more yet but *one Dr. Tully* hath *come forth to Encounter me*, Epiſt. and Pag. 224. The peruſal of that Book (with Mr. *Tombs ſhort Reflections*) directeth me to ſay but this inſtead of any further Confutation.

That it is (as the former) ſo full of falſe Allegations ſet off with the greateſt Audacity (even a few Lines of my own about our meeting at Saint *James*'s left with the Clerk, groſly falſified) and former falſifications partly juſtified, and partly paſt over, and his moſt paſſionate Charges grou̇nd-
F   ed

A Postscript about

ed upon Mistakes, and managed by Misreports, sometime of *Words*, sometime of the *Sense*, and sometime of *Matters* of *Fact*; in short, it is such a bundle of *Mistake, Fierceness* and *Confidence*, that I take it for too *useless* and *unpleasant* a Work to give the World a particular Detection of these Evils. If I had so little to do with my Time as to write it, I suppose that few would find leisure to read it: And I desire no more of the willing Reader, then seriously to peruse my Book (*More Reasons for Infants Church-membership*) with his, and to examine the Authors about whose Words or Sense we differ. Or if any would be Informed at a cheaper rate, he may read Mr. *Barrets* Fifty *Queries* in two sheets. And if Mr. *Tombes* revile me, for not transcribing or answering more of his *Great Book*, when I tell the Reader that I *suppose him to have the Book before him*, and am not bound to transcribe such a Volume already in Print, and that I answer as much as I think needs an Answer, leaving the rest as I found it to the Judgment of each Reader, he may himself take this for a *Reply*; but I must judg of it as it is.

I find but one thing in the Book that needeth any other Answer, than to peruse what is already Written: And that is about Baptizing Naked: My Book was written 1649. *A little before, common uncontrolled Fame was*, that not *far from us* in *one place many of them* were *Baptized naked*, reproving the Cloathing way as Antiscriptural: I never heard Man deny this Report: I conversed with divers of Mr. *Tombes*'s Church, who denied it not: As never any denied it *to me*, so I never *read* one that did deny it to my knowledg: He now tells me Mr.
Fisher,

ggar, and Mr. *Tombes* did: Let any
Tombes Answer to me, yea and that
now cited, and see whether there
enial: Mr. *Fisher* or *Haggar* I never
Books I had seen, but never read
my remembrance of Mr. *Fishers*,
bered it with those that were writ-
bject, as well I might: I knew his
his Friends, and I saw the Great
he turned *Quaker*, but I thought it
d Mr. *Tombes* and others that wrote
it I read not him, nor all Mr. *Hag-*
l, I had not taken them for compe-
f a fact *far from them*, and that
r: Could they say, that *no one ever*
truth is that three years after, mista-
s, as if I had affirmed it to be *their*
e (as you may read in them) which
nor thought, they vehemently deny
ch *heedless reading* occasioneth many
rs Accusations). I never said that
enied it; for I have not read *all that*
en, nor spoken with all the World:
er *denied it to me*, nor did I *ever read*
l it. And in a matter of Fact, if that
redible, which is of things *Late* and
t *Contradicted* by *any one* of the *most*
ous themselves, no not by Mr. *Tombes*
ust surcease humane Converse: Yet
e undertake that the same was true,
Persons, or such as other Writers
ve said it off. I *saw not* any one Bap-
Tombes or any other in *River* or else-
ping at Age: If you *do no such thing*,

F 2   I

A Postscript about

I am sorry that I believed it, and will recant it. Had I *not seen* a *Quaker* go naked through *Worcester* at the Assizes, and read the *Ranters* Letters full of Oathes, I could have proved neither of them. And yet I know not where so long after to find my Witnesses: I abhor Slanders, and receiving ill Reports unwarrantably: I well know that this is not their ordinary Practice: The *Quakers* do not those things now, which many did at the rising of the Sect; and if I could, I would believe they never did them.

2. This Book of Mr. *Danvers*, with the rest of the same kind, increase my hatred of the *Disputing Contentious* way of writing, and my trouble that the Cause of the *Church* and *Truth* hath so oft put on me a necessity to write in a Disputing way, against the Writings of so many Assailants.

3. It increaseth my Grief for the Case of Mankind, yea of well-meaning godly Christians, who are unable to judg of many Controversies agitated, otherwise than by some Glimpses of poor Probability, and the esteem which they have of the Persons which do manage them, and indeed take their Opinions upon trust from those whom they most reverence and value; and yet can so hardly know whom to follow, whilst the grossest Mistakes are set off with as great confidence and holy pretence, as the greatest Truths. O how much should Christians be pitied, that must go through so great Temptations!

4. It increaseth my Resolution, had I longer to live, to converse with Men that I would *profit*, or *profit* by, either as a *Learner* hearing what they have to say, without importunate Contradiction, or as a *Teacher* if they desire to Learn of me: A *School*

way

way may do something to increase Knowledg; but *drenching Men*, and *striving* with them, doth but set them on a fiercer striving against the Truth: And when they that have need of seven and seven years Schooling more, under some clear well studied Teacher, are made Teachers themselves, and then turned loose into the World (as *Sampsons* Foxes) to militate *for* and *with* their *Ignorance*, what must the Church suffer by such Contenders?

5. It increaseth my dislike of that Sectarian dividing hurtful Zeal, which is described *James* 3. and abateth *my* wonder at the rage of Persecutors: For I see that the same Spirit maketh the same kind of Men, even when they most cry out against Persecutors, and separate furthest from them.

6. It resolveth me more to enquire less after the Answers to Mens *Books* than I have done: And I shall hereafter think never the worse of a Mans writings, for hearing that they are answered: For I see it is not only easie for a *Talking Man* to *talk on*, and *to say something for* or *against any thing*, but it is *hard* for them to *do otherwise*, even to hold their *Tongues*, or *Pens*, or *Peace*: And when I change this Mind, I must give the greatest *belief* to *Women* that will talk most, or to them that *live longest*, and so are like to have the last word, or to them that can train up militant Heirs and Successors to defend them when they are dead, and so propagate the Contention. If a sober Consideration of the first and second writing, (yea of *positive Principles*) will not inform me, I shall have little hope to be much the wiser for all the rest.

7. I am fully satisfied that even good Men are here so far from Perfection, that they must bear
with

with odious faults and injuries in one another, and be habituated to a ready and easie forbearing and forgiving one another. I will not so much as describe or denominate Mr. *Danvers* Citations of Dr. *Pierce*, to prove my Popery and Crimes, nor his passages about the Wars, and about my Changes, Self-contradictions, and Repentances, lest I do that which favoureth not of Forgiveness: O what need have we all of Divine Forgiveness!

8. I shall yet less believe what any Mans *Opinion* (yea or Practice) is by his *Adversaries Sayings, Collections, Citations*, or most vehement Asseverations, than ever I have done, though the Reporters pretend to never so much Truth, and pious Zeal.

9. I shall less trust a *confounding ignorant* Reader or Writer, that hath not an accurate *defining* and *distinguishing* Understanding, and hath not a *mature, exercised, discerning* Knowledg than ever I have done; and especially if he be engaged in a *Sect* (which alas, how few parts of the Christian World escape!) For I here (and in many others) see, that you have no way to seem Orthodox with such, but to run quite into the contrary Extream: And if I write against both Extreams, I am taken by such Men as this, but to be *for both and against both*, and to *contradict my self*. When I write against the Persecutors, I am one of the Sectaries, and when I write against the Sectaries, I am of the Persecutors side: If I belie not the Prelatists, I am a Conformist: If I belie not the *Anabaptists, Independants*, &c. I am one of them: If I belie not the Papists, I am a Papist; if I belie not the *Arminians, I* am an *Arminian*; if I belie not the *Cal-*
vinists

vinists, I am with *Pseudo-Tilenus* and his Brother, *purus putus* Puritanus, and one *Qui totum Puritanismum totus spirat* (which *Joseph Allen* too kindly interpreteth): If *I* be for *lawful Episcopacy*, and *lawful Liturgies* and *Circumstances* of *Worship*, I am a *temporizing Conformist:* If *I* be for *no more*, I am an intollerable Non-Conformist (at this time forced to part with House, and Goods, and Library, and all save my Clothes, and to possess nothing, and yet my Death (by six months Imprisonment in the Common Goal) is sought after and continually expected. If *I* be as very *a Fool*, and as *little understand my self*, and as much *contradict my self*, as all these Confounders and Men of Violence would have the World believe, it is much to *my cost*, being hated by them all while I seek but for the common peace.

10. But I have also further learned hence to *take up my content in Gods Approbation*, and (having done my duty, and pitying their own and the Peoples snares) to make but small account of all the Reproaches of all sorts of Sectaries; what they will say against me living or dead, I leave to themselves and God, and shall not to please a Censorious Sect, or any Men whatever, be false to my Conscience and the Truth: If the Cause I defend be not of God, I desire it may fall: If it be, I leave it to God how far He will prosper it, and what Men shall think or say of me: And I will pray for Peace to him that will not hate and revile me for so doing. Farewell.

Septemb. 4.
1675.